The Hobbits

# MY SAN FRANCISCO

# BOOKS BY GERTRUDE ATHERTON

## CALIFORNIA

My San Francisco: A Wayward Biography
Golden Gate Country
California: An Intimate History

## HISTORICAL NOVELS

The Conqueror
Rezánov
The Immortal Marriage
The Jealous Gods
Dido: Queen of Hearts
Golden Peacock

## THE SAN FRANCISCO SERIES

A Daughter of the Vine (The Sixties)
Sleeping Fires (The Sixties)
The Californians (The Eighties)
American Wives and English Husbands (The Eighties)
A Whirl Asunder (The Nineties)
Ancestors (Twentieth Century)
Sisters-in-Law (Twentieth Century)
The Avalanche (Twentieth Century)
The Horn of Life (The Twenties)
The House of Lee (The Thirties)

## IN OTHER PARTS OF THE WORLD

Tower of Ivory (Munich and England)
Julia France and Her Times (B.W.I. and England)
Perch of the Devil (Montana)
The White Morning (World War I)
Rulers of Kings (Austria, Hungary and the Adirondacks)
Black Oxen (New York)
The Crystal Cup (New York)
The Traveling Thirds (Spain)
Mrs. Balfame (New York)
The Gorgeous Isle (Nevis, B.W.I.)
Senator North (Washington, D.C.)
Patience Sparhawk and Her Times (California and New York)
The Aristocrats (Adirondacks)
The Doomswoman (Old California)
The Sophisticates

## SHORT STORIES

The Splendid Idle Forties (Old California)
The Bell in the Fog
The Foghorn

## AUTOBIOGRAPHY

Adventures of a Novelist

## MISCELLANEOUS

The Living Present
Can Women Be Gentlemen?
A Few of Hamilton's Letters

THE SAN FRANCISCO FERRY BUILDING

# MY SAN FRANCISCO

## A WAYWARD BIOGRAPHY

*By*

## GERTRUDE ATHERTON

THE BOBBS-MERRILL COMPANY

INDIANAPOLIS     *Publishers*     NEW YORK

*First Edition*

To

MURIEL ATHERTON RUSSELL

# ACKNOWLEDGMENTS

ACKNOWLEDGMENTS with many thanks are made to the following: Zilfa Estcourt, San Francisco *Chronicle;* Joseph Henry Jackson, San Francisco *Chronicle;* Barbara Price, San Francisco *News;* Elliott McAllister, Vice-President of the Bank of California; Virginia Conroy, formerly with the Anglo-California Bank; Monroe A. Bloom, Anglo-California Bank; Wilhelmina Hoagland, Wells, Fargo Bank; Marguerite A. Downing, San Francisco Bank; Marion Mills Brown, Pacific Coast Women's Press Association; Judith Yagodka, California Labor School; Esther Lawler, Century Club; Violet E. White, California Club of California; Katherine Hanrahan, Queen's Bench; Robert C. Elliott, San Francisco *News;* Mrs. Marcus Cauffman Sloss; Mrs. John Ward Mailliard; Mrs. Oliver Remick Grant; Philip Lilienthal; John J. Newbegin; Julian Dana; Oscar Lewis; Carroll D. Hall; Jerome Landfield; San Francisco *Life;* the Oxford University Press for permission to quote from Gilbert Murray's translations of the *Medea* of Euripides and *Oedipus Coloneus* of Sophocles; the D. Appleton-Century Company, Inc.; and the Liveright Publishing Corporation.

# PREFACE

WHEN my editor, Mr. John L. B. Williams, asked me to write a book about San Francisco I replied with an emphatic *No!* Charles Caldwell Dobie had left little to be told about Chinatown and the various foreign "colonies" in his admirable stories. Herbert Asbury had written the last word on the Barbary Coast; Evelyn Wells on the "Champagne Days" of the Nineties. I'd just completed *Golden Gate Country*. No more of all that.

He replied suavely that he had no desire for a history of a subject that had been dealt with many times. What he had in mind was a more or less intimate book about many phases of San Francisco as she is today, which as yet may have been overlooked by other writers, but with which I must be familiar. Please think it over. I did so, and finally realized that there was a great deal as yet unwritten about this most omniform of cities.

Somewhere in everyone's brain is a large group of cells each containing an impression, a memory, an experience long forgotten or imperfectly realized. Tap! Tap! Tap! Intensive thinking had given my brain a jolt and they were demanding to spring forth—many aspects of the city of my birth where I had spent the greater part of my life—aspects and phases which for some reason others had ignored, or, for lack of opportunity, knew no more of than they did of Timbuktu, some of them of vital importance both in her past and to her future.

Enthusiasm for the task welled. It would be a wayward biography all right, but I concluded to begin with a general description of the city for the benefit of those who had never seen her, and to write a preliminary chapter in the form of a short story to demonstrate how close California came to having a history of another sort and a lamentable one.

After that was accomplished I wrote as the subjects occurred to me. There is little continuity, and in some cases it may read like a memoir, for I had had personal contact with certain of those aspects and phases.

I shall probably be reprimanded for devoting so much space to "Our Literati" and making but a passing reference here and there to San Francisco's equally important artists, sculptors, architects and musicians. Well—after I had finished with my own kind, and a chapter on certain outstanding women to prove a point, I felt that I had written all the biographical sketches either I or my readers could stand. Someday I shall bring my *California: An Intimate History* up to date and give them many words.

A word as to the "Bay Area," a region dominated by San Francisco. It has more than one interpretation. Some maintain that it includes all the towns on the northern and southern arms of the Bay, but as that long sweep contains enough notables to fill another book, I decided to confine myself to the immediate area: towns that may be seen, with the aid of a binocular if one is nearsighted, from the tip of Telegraph Hill: Oakland (the second largest city in the north), Berkeley, Piedmont, Alameda, Albany, Richmond (the headquarters of Henry Kaiser). And, opposite the Marina, Sausalito and Mill Valley. This for the enlightenment of those who have never traveled so far as San Francisco nor read any of the thousand, more or less, books that have told the story of California.

G. A.

# CONTENTS

# LIST OF ILLUSTRATIONS

# MY SAN FRANCISCO

# CHAPTER ONE

## *If*

WHY IS IT that San Francisco (no doubt with an unpronounceable name) is not an outpost of the U.S.S.R. today, her magnificent Bay with its area of 450 square miles merely a port for merchant ships sailing empty through those narrow straits we call the Golden Gate to load and leave with the bounties of California's fertile soil? Why, indeed, is not the whole Pacific Coast swarming with muzhiks and their overlords, big, blond and prolific?

Why is it that after the United States had conquered the rest of New Spain the fabulous sweep of land she had long coveted would have been beyond her grasp unless she declared war on Russia? A war with Russia might have been long and bitter, since Britain, who herself had coveted California and was not unwilling to punish her lost colonies on the Atlantic shore, would have lent her aid to Russia after Napoleon Bonaparte had been disposed of. Who knows? The whole face of North America might tell another story, and a lugubrious one at that.

The answer to these *ifs*—and *if* is the most pregnant word in the vocabulary of Life—is so simple as to be almost absurd. In the year 1806 a great Russian nobleman fell in love with the beautiful daughter of the most powerful man in California and all was well for the U. S. A.

When His Excellency, Nicolai Petrovich Rezánov, one of the ten barons of Russia, Privy Councilor and High Chamberlain to His Imperial Majesty Alexander I, first ambassador to the court of

15

Japan, chief partner in the great Shelikov-Golikov Fur Company of Russian America, circumnavigator of the globe, sailed in the bark *Juno* (bought from a Boston skipper) through what was then awkwardly known as the Mouth of the Gulf of the Farallones, on that fateful morning of 1806, he was in no romantic mood. Suffering from malnutrition himself, and further depleted by a recent attack of malarial fever, he was even more concerned for his workmen at Sitka, ravaged with scurvy, their teeth loose or missing, after too long a diet of dried fish, sea dogs, fat of whales. They could no longer eat the tough flesh of those animals whose furry hides were making a fortune for the company in St. Petersburg and Moscow. He had bought the tempting cargo of the *Juno* and embarked for California with the purpose of trading it for farinaceous foods, vegetables and fruits. He also had another purpose, as yet confided to no one. There was little he did not know of that beautiful and fertile department of New Spain and it was his definite intention to annex it to Russia. All in good time. A few agricultural emigrants at first, who would pay handsomely for superfluous acres of those immense ranchos; then, ever-increasing numbers, including many of his own class, 10,000 at least. Spain was weak and Russia too strong to defy.

During his brief visit to the Presidio of San Francisco, which lay on the right of the "Mouth," he had glorious visions of the great sweep of valley before the Mission Dolores, that rugged mass of hills and ravines down on the southeastern shore of the Bay where one of its long arms turned abruptly to the right, those graceful islands in the central waters—all, all, to be magnificent with palaces large and small; towers, battlements, spires, gilded domes, cupolas spherical or helmet-shaped; cathedrals, museums, institutions, government buildings; the architecture, as in Russia, Byzantine, Romanesque, baroque, or the classical columns beloved of Catherine the Great. And every island should be a fortress with guns pointing toward those narrow straits that separated the Pacific Ocean from the grand sweep of inland waters whose like in his travels as circumnavigator he had never seen.

And himself plenipotentiary, overlord. California was 3,000 leagues from Russia and these thousands of fertile acres, that city more imposing than Moscow or St. Petersburg, would virtually be his own.

But alas!

Doña Concha Argüello y Moreaga, daughter of Don José Argüello, Comandante of the Presidio of San Francisco, *La Favorita* of all California, was the most beautiful girl he had ever seen, and he had visited all the capitals of Europe. She had the white skin of her Castilian ancestors, her immense black eyes were trimmed with lashes so long they swept her cheeks, her delicate profile was faintly Roman, and her mouth, although childish, betrayed infinite possibilities. Her tall swaying figure above tiny arched feet was the essence of youth budding into maturity. In her masses of black hair she wore either a Castilian rose or a tall Spanish comb. Although only fifteen she was an accomplished coquette; she managed her numerous adorers with infinite skill, prided herself on her knowledge of men—and believed that babies were left under a rosebush by the Blessed Virgin.

More potent than her beauty, she had a subtle magnetic charm, a unique personality that further bedazzled her suitors, even while it filled them with vague misgivings. She was tired of them all, of their melting eyes, their fervid and flowery protestations, their nightly warbling beneath her grating. She longed for some personage from the City of Mexico to visit this rim of the world and rescue her; take her to Europe, above all to Madrid, give her a place in the great world of which she had read. But only old men came from the capital of New Spain, and it so happened that this distinguished Russian was the first man of the great world she had ever met.

But with Rezánov and Concha it was not that classic adventure, love at first sight, immortal as their romance was to be. He was too hungry. Until he sat down to dinner in the house of the Comandante he had not enjoyed a square meal for three years. Moreover, his mind was preoccupied with the mission upon whose success or failure hundreds of lives and his own future depended. Nevertheless, he made up his mind instantly to marry this daughter of the most important man in California; such an alliance would smooth the way to his ultimate goal.

And *La Favorita?* She too made up her mind, and with no maidenly hesitation—nor doubts. She would marry this *grand seigneur* from the north, and she too was inspired by ambition, not love. She saw herself, the wife of a great noble, at the court of Alexander, Czar of all the Russias, perhaps at that of the almost mythical Napoleon Bonaparte, whose like had not appeared on earth since Julius Caesar. And perhaps even at the court of Spain, the land of her noble ancestors!

Rezánov was forty or more. Although a commanding figure he was by no means a romantic one with his emaciated face, his cold blue eyes (which, however, could light and flash), his severe green uniform, so different from the silks and lace ruffles of her *caballeros,* whose long hair was confined by a ribbon, while this man's pale locks were short and not even powdered, as was the custom in Europe—Concha, unlike other girls of her race, had read many books. But he was of imposing height and physique; he had an air of elegant repose, and was far more interesting to talk to than any man in the length and breadth of California.

Although Rezánov was treated with warm hospitality by the Californians, who liked and admired him, his mission would have failed but for Concha. A recent law had been passed by the Viceroy of New Spain abolishing trade with all foreigners. The Boston skippers came no more with cloth, silks, satins, laces, fans, dainty slippers, to say nothing of more practical wares, and although the hold of the *Juno* was abundantly supplied, the Governor was obdurate. The girls, the women, even the *caballeros,* besought him in vain. The padres of the Mission Dolores, ecstatic over Rezánov's presents of cloth of gold for the church, and heavy brown cloth to replace their threadbare habits, when their eloquence produced no effect, wrote to the Viceroy, setting forth the pressing needs of both Presidio and Mission, subtly insinuating that it might be wise to win the friendship of that formidable settlement in the north, whose need was so great. But letters took long to travel from California to the City of Mexico.

It was Concha who advised him to tempt the padres and win their allegiance, and when hope was ebbing it was she who conceived the brilliant idea of selling the cargo to the Governor, and, as Spanish money was forbidden to leave the country, returning the gold immediately in payment for a cargo of corn, vegetables and dried fruits. No law would be violated, no conscience racked.

And meanwhile? Great hampers of food were sent to the *Juno* every morning. Rezánov dined with the Comandante or one of the officers daily. His strength was restored, his appearance vastly improved. There were picnics (*meriendas*) on the islands, which, during long walks with Concha, he investigated thoroughly. They crossed the Bay in the *Juno* and climbed Mount Tamalpais, from whose crest he had a fine view of the surrounding country with its forests of redwoods, pines, and oak trees, its ranchos with their herds of cattle and abundant harvests. On the eastern side of the Bay was the lofty range of the Contra Costa Mountains, and beyond, he was told, were more fertile valleys, bounded, thirty miles away, by the Sierra Nevada Mountains, a still mightier range. A principality! A kingdom! An empire!

The young people on those excursions were chaperoned by amiable young matrons, and he had many long conversations with Concha. At first it was her intelligence that interested him, although had she been plain she might have interested him less. Moreover, she had a bewildering variety of moods; she was companionable and sympathetic; those great black eyes, that could sparkle with coquetry or flash with anger, grew dim with tears when he dwelt upon the plight of his miserable *promychleniki*.

But when he became aware that he was falling in love—he who had loved so many women in his youth, but for years had been too occupied with great affairs to regard them as aught but a sex created for the pleasure and convenience of man—he was incredulous. He, a man of forty-two, a long-disillusioned man-of-the-world, to fall in love with a girl of fifteen, however beautiful and alluring, to thrill at her touch, at the magnet in her blood, the music of her deep warm voice! His head swam as he watched her dance *la jota* or *el son* in the *sala* at night, when she looked like a floating wraith from another sphere. The *caballeros* applauded and shouted, flung gold and silver, their jeweled chains at her feet (to be returned discreetly by her brother Santiago next day), but he sat silent and enthralled, every nerve quivering.

The time came when he deluded himself no longer. Concha Argüello was the love of his life, and he was consumed not only with the passion of youth but with that of a man for his mate.

But should he ever be able to see her alone?

One morning after a sleepless night he sprang out of bed before dawn, plunged for a moment into the Bay, dressed himself hurriedly, and started for a long walk. He was in a towering bad humor, but his insomnia had not been caused by love alone; the weeks were passing and the hold of the *Juno* was still empty, for Concha had not yet revealed her cunning plan. Nor was there a hint from those cursed Spaniards that they would grant his request. Failure grinned and jabbered at him. His men would starve; his future was black. As he strode through the sand dunes he hated them all. As for love, he anathematized himself for a fool. If he were to win Concha, and she had given him no sign of anything but sweet friendliness, would that compensate for the death of ambition, of power, of the brilliant future he had planned? And what could he offer her? He, a ruined man?

He left the sand dunes and entered that mass of hills and ravines down by the eastern shore. But he gave not a glance to those slopes and crests which his fancy had set with palaces and cathedrals, shining domes and lofty spires, all glittering in the crystal air and sun flood. Vain dreamer that he was!

He climbed to the top of the promontory where the Bay turned to the south, his body tired, but his brain still seething, and stood glaring at the sun rising over Monte Diablo, the loftiest peak of the Contra Costa Range. Suddenly he whirled about. A familiar voice floated up from the ravine below: *"Señor, señor."* He looked down. Concha was forcing a mustang up the side of the ravine. Half-believing, he stumbled down the uneven slope. She reined in and told him hurriedly that, unable to sleep, she had been out in the garden and had seen him striding along the shore. No one else was awake. She had saddled her horse and followed to tell him of the solution of his difficulties she had conceived during a sleepless night. And then all barriers crashed down and there followed a love scene that has no place in a biography.

The opposition by parents, priests and Governor to the marriage of a Catholic maid with a heretic was even more determined than to a mere matter of trade. But Concha and Rezánov were equally determined, and after long hours of discussion and protestations, often violent, the would-be masters of the couple's fate conceived a subtle plan. They would buy the cargo of Rezánov with their own money, promise a constant exchange of goods in the same fashion and consent to the marriage—if he would leave at once and personally obtain the consent of the Holy Father in Rome, and of the King of Spain in Madrid; a journey that would take two years, at least. Meanwhile Concha would forget him and marry a *caballero*.

Rezánov, although appalled, was forced to consent. Two years! His only consolation was that he was permitted to see Concha alone occasionally, and he knew that her love was as deathless as his own. It was a lovely morning in May when he sailed with a bursting hold, and looked his last on Concha as she stood alone on a cliff, the breeze lifting her unbound hair and swirling it, a black cloud, about her tense form.

And so California moved smoothly on to her appointed destiny. Had Rezánov and Concha been permitted to marry at once, they would have lingered at Sitka for a time, then proceeded by slow stages over the vast wastes of Siberia in comfortable sleds, resting at the different outposts. At St. Petersburg he would have presented his bride at court, witnessed her triumphs with adoring pride, confided his plans (although not their ultimates) to the Czar, who would eagerly have welcomed the prospect of that fertile addition to his empire. Emigration would have begun at once. In due course they would have returned to California and he would have outwitted the Spaniards and accomplished his purpose.

Or if Concha had already been married when he arrived in California, or had been paying a long visit to Monterey or Santa Barbara, and his good friend Luis Argüello had conceived this plan to sell and buy, he would still have traveled by slow stages across those terrible wastes, mindful of his damaged constitution, have taken a luxurious rest in his palace in St. Petersburg, and then proceeded to carry out his plans.

In Sitka he had a brief attack of malaria. Persuading himself that he had fully recovered, at the end of ten days he sailed on the *Juno* to Okhotsk, where a caravan with forty horses for relays awaited him.

The first stage of the journey from Okhotsk to Yakutsk, some 650 miles, would have been a rigorous journey for a young man in robust health. The road led over the Stanovoi Mountains in a southwesterly direction to the Maya River, along the latter's wavering course to Aldan, then south beside the Lena. He galloped far ahead of his caravan, splashing through bogs and streams, fording rivers without ferries, sleeping at night in forests whose bitter cold penetrated his abundant furs. On the eighth day the rains began; they descended in torrents and without intermission.

In a rapid swollen torrent his horse lost its footing and fell. He was soaked to the skin and they did not reach a hut where a fire could be made until nine hours later. It was then that the germs of malaria stirred more vigorously than in Sitka. He rode on in a burning fever. On the following day his servant Jon and one of the Cossack guards caught him as he fell from his horse, unconscious. He was doctored from the medicine chest, and Jon used the lancet while Rezánov slept. The fever ebbed and Rezánov insisted upon continuing the journey although he felt heavy with intolerable lassitude. When he reached Yakutsk he went to bed

in the house of the agent of his company, and this time his fever
and convalescence lasted for eight weeks. Despite the stern warn-
ings of the doctor and the supplications of his friends, he started
off again, although this time by sledge. The journey of 1,550
miles to Irkutsk, in the open air and with no effort on his part,
so invigorated him that he mounted his horse and galloped again,
although forced at times to return to the sledge. Then came a
long stretch of country so frozen that sledges were left behind, and
Rezánov was forced to travel in a telega, a conveyance little larger
than an armchair and even lighter. It was drawn by two horses
that galloped up-and-downhill with no change of gait and over
a road so rough that the little vehicle seemed to be propelled by
a succession of earthquakes. At Irkutsk, once more consumed by
fever, he lay in the home of the Governor where he had the best
of nursing and medical care, and if he had remained in that luxurious city for six months he would undoubtedly have lived for
many years longer. But he resumed his terrible journey, for he
was a man of indomitable will and little patience. On March 8,
1807, he succumbed in Krasnoyarsk, and Concha Argüello became the first nun in California.

# CHAPTER TWO

# *Hills and Valleys*

SAN FRANCISCO may not be as gorgeous—and bizarre—as Rezánov's vision but it is impressive with its twenty-nine hills and wide sweep of valley. True, its once harmonious sky line is now distorted by the Coit Tower on Telegraph Hill and several other skyscrapers on the crests, but its business and shopping district on the flat between the water front and the gradual rise of the hills, rebuilt since the fire of 1906, and bounded by North Beach and Market Street, is solid and handsome—for the most part. There are blocks here and there that would disgrace a mining town, but are quickly forgotten as one turns aside and strolls through Chinatown or Little Italy.

Market Street, the wide thoroughfare that divides the hills from the valley, is some four miles long and runs from the Embarcadero—the broad street facing the right arm of the Bay—to Twin Peaks, the high point of the San Bruno Range.

In that valley where the bear, the wildcat, the coyote and the elk once roamed, are miles of streets with no pretensions to beauty or elegance (nor to respectability in certain quarters), but lively with business and important in their way. Market Street, wide enough to hold four car tracks, and terrifying to cross, has many fine buildings—hotels, restaurants, shops, moving-picture houses—but would be vastly improved if lined with trees. So would the narrow streets on the hills, the wider streets out in the Western Addition. But alas, the roots of trees have a mean habit

25

of burrowing under the pavements and shoving them upward.
All but the plane tree, and surely a great city decorated with but
one specimen of the floral kingdom would present a somewhat
monotonous aspect. However, there is no reason why Market
Street and Van Ness Avenue, another wide street separating the
older city from the Western Addition, should not be redeemed,
and no doubt the Art Commission will get around to it in time.
What matter a few taxes more or less for constant repairs?

There was a time, now many years ago, when San Francisco
halted far east of Van Ness Avenue, and with the exception of
the Presidio and the settlement around the old Mission Dolores,
there was nothing to be seen but miles of sand dunes, and the
afternoon winds lifted their shifting surface and swept it through
the streets of the city. Sometimes one could not see the opposite side of the street through the blinding dust and there were so
many afflicted eyes that oculists came from other parts of the
country and retired with comfortable fortunes. The dust also
affected the throat and nasal membranes. "This is the city of
catarrh, and the streets are the streets of ex-pec-to-ra-tion," chanted
a polite New Yorker when visiting our proud city.

But those dunes have long since been leveled and in their place
are the Western Addition, the fashionable residence quarter beginning at Van Ness Avenue; the districts Richmond and Sun-
set, on either side of the Golden Gate Park, little towns with
shopping streets, clubs, playgrounds and schoolhouses; and those
restricted residential quarters called subdivisions, with much elegance and variety of architecture, blossoming with flowers, thickly
planted with trees—at a prudent distance from the sidewalks.
They have pretty names: St. Francis Wood, Ingleside Terrace,
Westwood Park, Sea Cliff, the latter commanding a view of the
Golden Gate and bordering the sea. Two other districts are Mona

Loa, beside the Panhandle, a narrow extension of Golden Gate Park, and the Marina on the northern edge of the city, once an expanse of shallow water, but "filled in" to accommodate the Panama-Pacific Exposition of 1915. There are no gardens here but many homes, impressive or modest, and two fine shopping streets.

The highest of San Francisco's hills have historic names: Telegraph Hill, Russian Hill, Nob Hill, Twin Peaks, Lone Mountain, Calvary and, in its youth, Rincon Hill. The last has been leveled; the headstones and monuments on Lone Mountain with their crumbling coffins have been moved down the peninsula, and its top sliced off to accommodate the San Francisco College for Women (order of the Sacred Heart). But the other five have defied time and the mutations of a wayward city.

Telegraph Hill, from whose crest Rezánov looked his last upon what he fondly believed was his future domain, and which rises abruptly where the Bay sends an arm to the south, has undergone several changes in character. In the 1850's it was the resort of criminals until the Vigilance Committee drove them out. During the Gold Rush Peruvians and Chileans camped there. Then the Irish claimed it as their own until they were gradually but firmly replaced by Italians, who have clung to it ever since. After the fire of 1906 they were the first of the poorer class to rebuild. Hundreds of men who had never caressed a twenty-dollar bill, when the insurance companies (some of them) met their obligations, were so excited at finding themselves possessed of anywhere from $1,000 to $5,000 in hard cash that they indulged in every kind of extravagance the conditions permitted and soon got rid of their sudden wealth. But not the Italians. Their small homes, restaurants, markets, shops, were erected and occupied in an amazingly short time. In this year of 1946 they possess ninety-five per-

cent of the Hill; the mansions and apartment houses for the
wealthy take one percent; the other four percent is held by artists
to whom the superb view of water, islands, mountains and richly
wooded valleys is ever an inspiration.

The hill derives its name from the fact that in the extreme
youth of San Francisco a semaphore on its top informed the inhabitants that a ship was sailing through the Golden Gate, and
ships brought mail and, perchance, more settlers for the little
town. In a few moments after the semaphore extended its arm
the hill would be black with men to welcome the visitor with
shouts and waving of stovepipe hats and large bandanna handkerchiefs, answered less vociferously by the weary travelers crowding
the decks and staring hopefully at the Promised Land. When the
ship docked the citizens ran down to the post office, business forgotten as they stood in line for an hour or more.

Today there is a small park on the crest of the hill, where tourists may enjoy the view—and that eyesore, the Coit Tower, which
looks more like a lighthouse or an incinerator, but has an interesting story behind it.

Lily Hitchcock, the daughter of an eminent physician and a
member of the "Best Society," was the talk of the town in the
1860's—and even before and after: as a schoolgirl she raced
through the streets every time the fire bells rang. Beaux—and
she had more proposals than any girl in San Francisco—dinner
parties, balls interested her far less and she would desert a partner
on the dancing floor, or the hostess of any function, and bid her
waiting coachman gallop her to the scene of disaster. The Knick-
erbocker Fire Company, Number 5, made her an honorary member
and she attended their banquets and balls dressed in their colors,
red and black. They cheered, toasted and adored her.

I remember her vaguely, a handsome dashing creature in a dark blue dress, when, trotting beside my mother, I passed her on Montgomery Street, the center of the shopping district. My family knew hers, but the only other memory I have of them is my sitting on Dr. Hitchcock's knee in his office and being fed ice cream from a tiny freezer, no doubt a bribe or a reward. But a day rarely passed that I did not hear her discussed, for her pranks were many and the women of that era had little to do but gossip.

She eloped with Howard Coit, but the union was brief and, growing tired of California, she deserted it for Europe, sometimes for months, again for years; and the years grew longer and longer. It was not until she was eighty that she returned to San Francisco with the avowed intention of "settling down." Few of her generation were alive, but she was welcomed by their families and entertained them in her suite in the Palace Hotel.

I met her then for the first and only time at Montalvo, Senator Phelan's lovely country place near Saratoga. She was stout and brown, but her bright animated face was still arresting and she looked far younger than fourscore. I pride myself on my tact (when I am rude it is not inadvertently), but this time it failed me. A host of vivid memories raced across my mind; I was thrilled to the core as I walked with my host across the terrace to be presented to the guest of honor, and I exclaimed impulsively, "Oh, Mrs. Coit, I *am* so glad you have come back, for, you know, you are a part of the history of San Francisco." "Yes," she shot back with the utmost good humor, "ancient history!" I wanted to retire behind a door and kick myself, but she took me firmly by the arm and led me off for a walk in the garden and talked of old times, "the happiest of my life," of my mother who was one of the beauties of her day, of my grandfather, Stephen Franklin, whom she remembered as "the handsomest and most courtly old gentleman in San Francisco." She had also read my books and professed to admire them, which of course increased my admiration for her.

When she died she left $100,000 to the city of her birth, to be expended in a manner that would add to its beauty and bear her name.

But alas!

I was a member of the Art Commission when the different models and drawings were submitted to it for approval. None was adequate in my opinion nor in that of Mrs. Musante—the only other woman on the Commission—but the model of a tower by the eminent architect Arthur Brown met with the final approval of the men. Mrs. Musante and I protested in vain; men always stand by other men against women, and after days of wrangling the males of the Commission went into a huddle and emerged with the dictum that they were for the Coit Tower, and that was that. They were very polite about it, and there was nothing for two lone females to do but sulk.

So there it stands, insulting the landscape. Lily Hitchcock deserved a better memorial.

I wish I could state that Russian Hill, Telegraph's neighbor, had been named in memory of Rezánov, but it was not. Long ago a Russian ship whose sailors were afflicted with scurvy came into the harbor. Several of them died while camping on North Beach, and instead of taking the bodies to a cemetery or, more fittingly, consigning them to the deep, graves were dug on that noble outpost, but why or exactly where no one can tell. Nor can anyone say when it was christened.

In its wild state Russian Hill was covered with trees and shrubs and some remain, although it is a hill of many mansions, several of them old, for they escaped the fire of 1906. The first to dis-

COIT TOWER AND TELEGRAPH HILL

**MISSION DOLORES**

cover it were artists and writers, enchanted by the views, and indifferent to the almost perpendicular sides. Among those who have made it famous, although many deserted it later, were Ambrose Bierce, Joaquin Miller, Ina Coolbrith, Stewart Edward White, George Sterling, Frederick O'Brien, Peter B. Kyne, Will and Wallace Irwin, Gelett Burgess, John Dewey, Mary Austin, Charles Caldwell Dobie, James Hopper, Frank, Charles and Kathleen Norris, Inez Haynes Irwin, Douglas Tilden, Haig Patigian and Maynard Dixon.

Its architecture is varied. There are two old octagonal houses, many studios, Tudor villas, neo-French châteaux, dwellings of plywood and glass brick with sun decks and corner windows, and, of late, several apartment houses. There are also many gardens.

Nob Hill, farther inland, was the first exclusive residence quarter to succeed Rincon Hill and South Park, far away in the valley. In its earlier phase the residential district lay north of California Street, and on Taylor Street were the houses of the families Haggin, Tevis, Pelham Ames, Bourne, Butterworth, Beaver, William T. Coleman and others whose names I have forgotten. All were built for entertaining as well as for solid comfort. The Tobin house stood alone on the southeast corner of California and Taylor Streets, and when I climbed the almost upright block below with my chum, Zaidee Bourne, to spend an afternoon with her after school we always stared at the stained-glass windows of a private chapel. There was no entertaining in that mansion until the children grew up, for Mrs. Tobin was an invalid. She was also so devout a Catholic that the awesome word "saintly" was coupled with her name; hence the chapel. To two youngsters of fourteen it was a house of mystery, and we lowered our shrill voices as we passed it.

The Haggins, although they had the largest house on the Hill, did little entertaining and that of the most formal kind. Mrs. Haggin was a tall, dark, austere woman who found it difficult to unbend, and Mr. Haggin took little interest in anything but business and horses. He was also a strict father and would allow no young men to call at the house. His eldest daughter, Rita, with few friends and little diversion, pined away and died young. The second managed to marry Caroll McAfee, and the youngest and brightest, Edith, who was sent east to school, met the man of her choice at a friend's house and married him without benefit of the parental blessing. Mr. Haggin, somewhat softened by the years and the death of his eldest daughter, forgave her and she inherited her share of his large fortune and lived in New York in state. She was a tiny thing, with the dark coloring of her Turkish blood, and although far from pretty had an elfish, fascinating little face and was full of intelligence and charm. There were two sons: Louis, who married the beautiful red-haired Blanche Butterworth, and Ben Ali, whose son of the same name won distinction in New York as an artist.

The appearance of Nob Hill changed in the 1870's when the Bonanza Kings and the railroad magnates, with two exceptions, built huge and hideous houses—on California Street east and west of Taylor Street. One exception was the stately and impressive Flood mansion built of brownstone imported from New York (possibly the architect came with it). It was surrounded by a low fence that looked as if made of solid gold from the Mother Lode but no doubt was mere brass. The Colton house, modeled on the wing of an Italian palace, was an exquisite bit of architecture. But the others! The Crocker house—long, huge, white and nothing more. The Mark Hopkins house looked as if several architects had been employed, and they had fought one another to a finish. The Stanford mansion resembled an enormous packing case painted white.

These nabobs soon began to entertain on the grand scale; an impoverished and charming lady of the old regime took them in hand and made a small fortune steering them through the sacred portals of the old set. She was a friend of my grandfather and induced him to attend the first of these balls. When he came home he told us the story.

"Everybody" attended that ball—or nearly everybody. "Never! Never!" exclaimed a haughty few to the sponsor. "How can you even suggest such a thing to *us?* Those—those *persons!*" But the majority accepted those embossed invitations, either out of curiosity or because they were becoming a trifle bored with their exclusive selves. The floor of the great ballroom was properly canvassed; the band, needless to state, was the finest in San Francisco.

The matrons wore gowns of subdued elegance, gowns made either at City of Paris or The White House, the two leading dry goods stores of the city, each with a dressmaking department, and were gracious to their nervous hostess—who wore cloth of gold and a diamond necklace a yard long. The girls looked like a flower garden. The men, in swallowtail and white tie, held brief conversations with their prowling host. Supper was served at twelve o'clock, the tables heavily laden with chicken salads, oysters in every form from stews to patties and on the half shell, squabs, cold ham, turkeys weighing at least twenty-four pounds each, plum cake, spongecake, ladycake, poundcake—all of immense proportions—candies, nuts, dates and raisins. And every guest might refresh himself with several quarts of champagne if capacity permitted.

Then came the climax. As the grandfather's clock in the hall loudly proclaimed the hour of one, the host stood up and shouted,

"I wish you would all come back to the ballroom. I have something to say to you." And he trotted out, followed by his wife, whose complacent expression suddenly veered to one of alarm. The guests followed as rapidly as their semitorpid condition would permit, wondering what was coming next.

At the head of the ballroom stood the host and hostess. When the last train had swished into silence he began his oration.

"Ladies and gentlemen," he shouted, "I just want to tell you that this is the proudest night of my life. Just thinking that I am entertaining here in my own house the grand aristocracy of the grandest little old city on earth, bar none, sends hot chills running up and down my spine. And ladies and gentlemen, let me tell you why I am so proud. I was a long time making my pile. There was a time when I was poor as Job's turkey; luck didn't come my way overnight. Our home was a shack and many a night me and my wife lay there with big milk pans on our top side to catch the rain that leaked through the roof. Oh, I can tell you—you who have been rich or well off all your lives, had it good and soft—you can never make a guess at how I feel tonight, one of the richest men in the world, giving the biggest ball ever given in 'Frisco—" here the entire audience shuddered—"and five years ago, mebbe a good deal less, not one of youse had ever heard my name, and your butler would have kicked me out if I'd tried to get past your front door. And I done—did it all myself. There I was with my good wife—and now here I am—the proudest man that ever lived. Now," he finished abruptly, "I'm sleepy. I'm going to bed. But you just stay here all night if you like. And there's plenty more champagne for all. *Good* night."

He waved his hand genially and made his exit. His wife, whose countenance had undergone a variety of expressions, alarm, appeal, horror, purple mortification, ran after him and was seen no more.

The sponsor gave the signal, the band began to play a polka, the stunned company relaxed, smiled cynically or sympathetically; and although the elders, all but a few chaperons, soon departed, the young people danced until dawn. Truth compels me to add that quite a number of the young bloods who had patronized the bar too frequently rolled down the steep hill between California and Pine Streets.

David S. Colton had two handsome daughters, one of whom married Crittendon Thornton, a scion of one of those Southern families that formed San Francisco's first social group on Rincon Hill, in South Park and a few contiguous streets. Carrie Colton, the youngest, was very beautiful, with her large "starry" gray eyes and hair we called silvery gold but is now known as platinum blonde. She married thrice. While both girls were young Mrs. Colton entertained with taste and splendor, but misfortune overtook her husband, and the house was bought by Collis P. Huntington, one of the Big Four who built the first transcontinental railroad. Whether or not the Huntingtons ever entertained in that magnificent ballroom I do not remember, if I ever knew, but they spent the greater part of their time in New York. Their adopted daughter, Clara, married Prince Hatzfeldt and spent the rest of her life in Europe. Her dowry was $22,500,000.

William S. O'Brian, Flood's partner in a small San Francisco saloon until he joined the stampede to Nevada and returned a Bonanza King, did not follow the example of others of his sort and build on Nob Hill. While the Floods were plain homely people, O'Brian's forebears in Ireland must have been well-bred and possibly distinguished. Many an impoverished young man of good family came to California to seek his fortune and took whatever job offered. One from the regnant South, too proud to work at home, landed in San Francisco with but a few dollars in his pocket and sold shoelacings on the street until another Southerner discovered him and found him a job. He prospered thereafter and became a social favorite. Unfortunately his career was cut short when one of the ferryboats blew up and all on board were lost.

But to return to Mr. O'Brian. He made a sensational entrance at a ball one night accompanied by a tall woman and two tall girls, whom he introduced as "My sister, Mrs. Coleman, and my nieces." Mrs. Coleman looked as if she had all the blood of all the Irish kings in her veins—tall, stately, elegant, with her mass of snow-white hair set off by a black velvet gown, her features as patrician as her "air." The local *grandes dames* involuntarily drew themselves up and tried to look haughty, but gave a gasp of admiration withal. The girls had none of her beauty but were slender, graceful, and also had the grand air. One of them a few years later married Harry May of Baltimore and became a social leader in Washington, D. C.; the other married the Viscount d'Andigné and lived the rest of her life in France. The son, "Jimmy" Coleman, married the beautiful Carmelita Nuttall, of the Parrott clan, whose sister, Zelia Nuttall, went to Mexico and became one of the most celebrated archaeologists of her time.

It may interest the admirers of Herbert Agar, famous author, editor and Pulitzer Prize winner, to know that he is a grandson of Mrs. Macdonough, another sister of O'Brian, a tall and stately dame with none of Mrs. Coleman's great beauty, but with great style and charm.

James G. Fair, another of the Nevada millionaires, lived in a less pretentious house than those of his brother nabobs, on the northwest corner of Pine and Powell Streets. He had two pretty daughters, "Tessie" and "Birdie," but his wife was a large un-wieldy woman with no trace of what good looks she may once have possessed. When I was a fledgling writer, Mr. S. S. Chamberlain, editor of the San Francisco *Examiner,* asked me to contribute an occasional column, and since it was my habit to utter my impressions with untempered frankness, I described Mrs. Fair as a big, slowly moving woman who looked as if she carried her millions in her stomach, and also made some allusion to Birdie's "worsted curls." I heard that my crudity displeased the Bonanza Queen, and I never met any of the family, except Mr. Fair at a much later date. He was a true product of Ireland, humorous and witty, and an interesting talker. Tessie married Herman Oelrichs of New York, Birdie one of the Vanderbilts, and California saw little of them thereafter.

Other families as well known if not as wealthy as the uncrowned kings of Nob Hill, nor, perhaps, as the older families on Taylor Street, lived on the slopes below. The "rows" of houses in San Francisco today are for the most part unsightly, but at that time they were large and sumptuous. The Adamses lived in one on Sutter Street, and I remember a "castle carpet" they brought from Europe. The castle motive ran the entire length of the double parlors, and as the colors were extremely delicate, in some places almost invisible, it amused Ella Adams and her friends to get down on their stomachs and crawl backward down the long vista, each striving to outdo the other in "finds." Mrs. Adams finally put a stop to it, for obvious reasons.

The Thorntons, Crittendens, Parrotts, McAllisters, Friedlanders, Lilienthals and other members of the "ancient aristocracy," after the glory of Rincon Hill and South Park had departed, had houses on those slopes—on Pine, Bush, Sutter and even as far down as

Turk Street (now a red-light district). Judge Sanderson built a large, formless but spacious house on the corner of Sacramento and Laguna, and there the beauteous Sybil lived until she went to Paris to become one of the famous prima donnas of her day. She entertained every opera singer that visited California, thereby incurring the disapproval of the conservative.

A block farther down, my Spanish mother-in-law built a house that began on California Street and ran halfway up the steep block on Laguna, whose architecture can be described only as weird. She gave many parties for her youngest daughter, Florence, and the friends of her elder daughters, Alejandra Rathbone and Elena Macondray, as well as those of her daughters-in-law, were also included.

There was a large central hall where the young people danced while the elders looked down from the surrounding balcony. What struck me most forcibly when I went up to that gallery to do my duty by those ladies whose dancing days were over (my eldest sister-in-law was old enough to be my mother) and I too surveyed the scene below, was the acres of revolving white (or whitewashed) flesh, for although every girl or matron who entered that house must be as respectable as the charwoman and would have shuddered at the thought of exposing an ankle, it was the fashion to exhibit the upper part of the body so far south as just to avoid the mammalian point, and those were the days when young matrons and maidens were buxom.

I would go now and then to sit for a few moments with my mother-in-law, who weighed 200 pounds, and never mingled with her guests but spent the evening in the library, where the matrons and members of the family paid her an occasional visit. Upon one of these occasions I found her alone and shaking with laughter. What, I demanded, had happened to amuse her?

"That Mrs. Mark Hopkins, she been here just now," she replied in her broken English. "She looka like the crystal chandelier. She wear so many diamonds I no can see the color of the dress. Six rows on her neck, and one necklace down to her knees, a—how you call it—stomacher?—big like a mustard plaster, a tiara and bracelets enough to fill Shreve's window. Never I see anything so funny. Why Alejandra asking her here?"

"You are a pretty good businesswoman yourself," I reminded her, "and must know that our men have their reasons for telling their wives to cultivate the new aristocracy." Here Mrs. Atherton gave a refined snort. "And," I continued, "you were reading Madame de Rémusat's *Memoirs* the other day—remember Junot's famous retort: 'We cannot all be descendants; some of us must be content to be ancestors'? Tonight you have beheld one of them."

"I no believe," she said emphatically, and in this case she was right. Of those spectacular nabobs of the 1870's only two have contributed any descendants, to California at least.

Some years later M. H. De Young, owner of the San Francisco *Chronicle,* bought an old house opposite Mrs. Atherton's and added an immense music room. They too entertained: opera singers, who visited the city periodically, and that brilliant galaxy of writers, artists, actors, editors, who called themselves Bohemians and were quite as exclusive as Society and the French Colony. When her children were old enough Mrs. De Young, an accomplished woman herself, took them to Europe to be educated, and before returning to San Francisco had them presented at the Court of St. James's. Today they are shining lights in Burlingame.

Mount Davidson, on the other side of Twin Peaks but visible from certain parts of the city, has a great cross on its summit which is illuminated throughout Holy Week, and on Easter morning hun-

dreds of the devout climb the hill to pray before it. During the
United Nations Conference it blazed all during the first and last
weeks of that momentous assembly, but whether any of the delegates took more than a distant look at it I have been unable to
ascertain.

# CHAPTER THREE

# *Here, There and Everywhere*

FOUR first-class hotels in an earlier day were the Occidental, the Lick House in Montgomery Street, the Grand and the Baldwin in Market Street. But no hotel past or present could compare with the old Palace on the corner of Market and New Montgomery Streets, world-famous in its day, whose story has been so brilliantly told by Oscar Lewis and Carroll D. Hall in *Bonanza Inn*. Conceived by William C. Ralston and finished only two days before his tragic death, it became the property of William Sharon, another millionaire out of Nevada. Seven stories high, it surrounded a great central court into which four-horse teams would race at top speed while excited guests hung over the galleries above. There was a "royal suite," but all the suites were spacious and there were immense rooms for entertaining on the grand scale.

Every person of any prominence who visited San Francisco between 1875 and 1906 registered in the Palace: General Sherman; General Grant; John Charles Frémont; General McClellan; Lieutenant Richmond Pearson Hobson of Spanish War fame; Rudyard Kipling; George Augustus Sala; Oscar Wilde and his sunflower; the Duke of Manchester; Josh Billings; James Gordon Bennett; the Hungarian Count Kinsky; Oliver Wendell Holmes; Robert Louis Stevenson; Julia Ward Howe; Mrs. Frank Leslie; Charles W. Eliot, president of Harvard University; John Fiske, expounder of Herbert Spencer; James Whitcomb Riley; Bronson Howard; Bill Nye; Henry Watterson (Marse Henry); F. Marion Crawford; Mrs. Patrick Campbell; Dom Pedro of Brazil; King Kala-kaua of the "Sandwich Islands," who died in the royal suite; his queen and his sister; Henry Ward Beecher; Bob Ingersoll; Carry Nation; the Prince of Siam; scions of the Vanderbilt, Rockefeller, Morgan, Carnegie, Pullman and Wanamaker families; Presidents Hayes, McKinley, Theodore Roosevelt and Taft; Prince Albert of Belgium; Prince Louis of Savoy; Prince Poniatowski (who married "Beth" Sperry of Stockton, a sister of Mrs. William Crocker); Prince Napoleon Louis Joseph Jerome Bonaparte; Lord and Lady Randolph Churchill, parents of the immortal Winston; Joaquin Miller; Mrs. Harry Payne Whitney, a sculptress of the first order; General Vallejo; Sarah Bernhardt, who with her entourage occupied a suite of eight rooms; Henry Irving; Ellen Terry; Paderewski; John Drew; Maude Adams; Nat Goodwin; Maxine Elliot; Lillian Russell; the Howard Coits; and for a few days before the fire Caruso, Sembrich, Plançon, Homer, Scotti.

The new Palace that rose on the ashes of the famous old structure after the earthquake and fire of 1906 is good-looking without, but there is a large dining room where the court used to be and there are no inner balconies. It is always well run and well patronized, but is no longer pre-eminent. The Fairmont and the Mark Hopkins on Nob Hill are far more desirably situated. However, it has had its dramas. In 1922 President Harding died there and the dark legend persists that his wife poisoned him to save him the ignominy of impeachment or worse.

I wonder it has never occurred to anyone to give a fancy-dress ball at the Palace, each guest representing one of those still unforgotten celebrities who spread the fame of the old Palace over two continents. Few if any are left who played a part in its first phase, so it would hardly be a nostalgic affair and could be a brilliant and memorable one. Joaquin Miller with his black broadcloth suit, the pants disappearing into boots that reached his knees, lace scarf, sombrero, hair sweeping his shoulders in a series of rattails dyed a bright orange, could be impersonated by one of those amateur actors who distinguish themselves at the Bohemian Grove. We have any number of dark-eyed handsome women who could bring Mrs. Pat Campbell to life for a night—I would suggest Constance Horn Patton. Others out of the past could be easily simulated with the aid of some make-up artist of the theater, and heaven knows we have enough fat men to get themselves up as Caruso or Oscar Wilde, and skinny ones as Robert Louis Stevenson. General Vallejo has many descendants, some one of whom could attach a pair of "stormy" side whiskers, put on one of his old uniforms and do him to the life.

Of course there would not be enough of those old celebrities to fill a ballroom, but there were many outstanding San Franciscans of that day who dined and wined at the Palace Hotel to supply the deficiency: Senator Phelan, who when he was mayor must have given many a dinner there; Raphael Weill, leader of the French colony, plump, dignified and genial; William T. Coleman, president of the Vigilance Committee that cleaned up the city in 1856 when it was "the wickedest city on earth"; William Bourne (with whom at the tender age of fourteen I imagined myself in love and planted sweet william in the back yard), owner of the Empire gold mine in Grass Valley, and extremely good-looking; James Ben Ali Haggin, who always entered a room looking as if he hated everybody, and was almost as dark as his Turkish ancestors; his partner, Lloyd Tevis, another plump one; Mrs. Haggin, tall, dark and forbidding; Mrs. Tevis, tall, stately and genial; Blanche Butterworth, the red-haired beauty who married Louis Haggin; W. H. L. Barnes, eminent attorney and a handsome dashing person who liked to ride a prancing horse back and forth before this or that fair lady's window; Hall McAllister, head of the San Francisco Bar, and his beautiful wife with her high-piled snow-white hair and exquisite features, who in the '50's and '60's was the undisputed leader of San Francisco society; Major Rathbone (who with Francis Newlands founded the now famous Burlingame) and his wife who, as Alejandra Atherton, was a "raving beauty" with her immense blue eyes and mahogany-colored hair, and still handsome after she turned the scales at 180 pounds; her sister Elena, an extremely pretty woman even after she put on too many Spanish pounds; and her brother-in-law, Frederick Macondray, who, when the wild winds shook his exposed house out in the Western Addition, piled his family into a carriage and sought shelter in the Palace; Frank Pixley, who founded the *Argonaut,* and was a quaint-looking old party; Isaac Friedlander, six feet seven, and his three handsome daughters.

The hosts should be William C. Ralston and Lily Hitchcock Coit.

Once more the character of Nob Hill changed. The fire of 1906 disposed of all but the Flood mansion, whose stone walls remained intact. It is now the home of the Pacific-Union Club. Grace Cathedral has risen (and is still rising) on the site of the formless Crocker house. On the southeast corner of California and Mason Streets there is a skyscraper of nineteen stories, whose cocktail bar, known as Top of the Mark, is the most famous on the Pacific Coast. Stanford Court, just below, is an immense and shapely apartment house. Opposite the Mark on California Street is the Fairmont Hotel, covering an entire block and built by the heirs of James G. Fair. It is a beautiful structure of white granite, six stories high, its front ornamented with six lofty columns. I crossed the Bay at night while the fire was raging and forgot the doomed city as I gazed at the Fairmont, a tremendous volume of white smoke pouring upward from where its unfinished roof had been, every window a shimmering sheet of gold; not a flame, not a spark shot forth. The Fairmont will never be as demonic in its beauty again, but San Francisco has cause to be proud of its stately elegance nevertheless. Within is a large sumptuous lobby and a great dining room commanding a superb view of the Bay and the Contra Costa Mountains beyond.

The lobby of the Mark Hopkins is uninviting and so are its dining rooms, but the Room of the Dons with its murals by Maynard Dixon and Frank van Sloun depicting scenes of Old California, when it was a Department of New Spain, is original and imposing.

It was in 1927 that Prince William of Sweden made a tour of the United States and, weary of being entertained by fashionable society, wrote to his consul general in San Francisco that it was his royal wish to meet the California literati. The consul consulted Charles Caldwell Dobie, secretary-treasurer of the P.E.N., and we gave him a dinner in the Room of the Dons. Observing the etiquette of royalty, he remained outside in an antechamber until all the guests were assembled, and at the proper moment Dobie brought him in and turned him over to me, whose duty it was, as president of the California Center, to make the introductions.

The guests, some sixty in number, filed by. I began: "His Royal Highness Prince William of Sweden." "His Royal Highness Prince William of Sweden." "His Royal Highness Prince William of Sweden." Three minutes of this. I proceeded: "His Highness Prince William of Sweden" in what seemed to me an endless repetition. I dropped to "Prince William of Sweden," and stood that until about thirty more guests had smiled and been beamed upon. Followed "Prince William," again and again and yet again.

In my intense boredom that was not far from stupefaction I might have ignominiously descended to "Bill," but it was over at last and we took our seats. Of course I still had him, but Dobie had placed Helen Wills, then in the height of her fame, on his other side since they had played tennis together in Sweden.

I recall but a few of the other guests: Senator James D. Phelan, Mr. and Mrs. Joseph Henry Jackson, Hildegarde Hawthorne, Sara Bard Field, Charles Erskine Scott Wood, Ednah Aiken, Pauline Partridge, Mr. and Mrs. Oscar Lewis, professors from the University of California and Stanford, Mr. and Mrs. Fremont Older, Lionel Stevenson, Ruth Comfort Mitchell, Templeton Crocker, Marie Hicks Davidson, Esther Birdsall Darling, Mrs. Atherton Russell, the Swedish consul general and his wife and Stewart Edward White.

It was a very gay dinner. Prince William was no trouble to entertain; he did all the talking, and I knew the complete history of the Bernadotte dynasty before the evening was over. Everybody liked the big genial man and he appeared to like us and was polite enough to say, whether he meant it or not, that it was the most interesting dinner he had attended in the United States.

There are also six large and commanding apartment houses on Nob Hill, but no more mansions. The Huntingtons, as I have related, moved to New York in the seventies. The elder Floods and Crockers died before the fire. James L. Flood built a large and handsome house of white stone in the Western Addition, and in 1939 his widow presented it to the Mesdames of the Sacred Heart to use for their grammar and high schools. The younger Crockers, like many other San Franciscans, took up their permanent residence in Burlingame, driving to the city for the opera, theater and social entertainments, or retaining a suite in one of the hotels. Mark Hopkins died in 1878. Several years later his widow married Edward T. Searles, a man twenty-two years her junior, and lived in New York. Her foster son, Timothy Hopkins, opposed the marriage with audible vigor and when she died she left the great fortune she had inherited to her young husband. Timothy contested the will, but the matter was finally settled out of court, and Timothy accepted three or four millions. He died in 1891, and the Nob Hill horror housed the San Francisco Art School until the fire took it.

The Stanfords had one son, Leland, Jr. He died of typhoid fever in Florence in 1884, and the inconsolable parents bought the old Gordon estate at Palo Alto, some thirty-five miles down the peninsula from San Francisco, and in 1886 founded the Leland Stanford Jr. University as a memorial to the lost heir. It is now one of the great universities of the world. Mr. Stanford died in 1891, but not before he had served a term as governor and another as United States senator.

The Mackays played no part in the social life of San Francisco. Mrs. Mackay preferred to live in Paris and entertain the *noblesse*. Their son Clarence married the beautiful Katherine Duer of New York and lived there for the rest of his life. The elder son was killed while boar hunting in France. His horse, taking fright, bolted into a tree and dashed out the brains of the ardent young sportsman.

That part of the Western Addition favored by the Old Set in their second migration lies between Jackson and Filbert Streets, running east and west, Van Ness Avenue and the Presidio. There are many big shapeless houses built during that period when architecture went on a prolonged spree of uglification, but happily there are now many mansions of a quiet and stately elegance. The windows of those on the hills or on the slopes facing north command a fine view of the Bay, its islands, Mount Tamalpais and the wide curve of hills beyond. Many have gardens, even trees of many kinds—in one there is a great Monterey cypress—and those on the slopes are reached by long flights of steps; but where long ago the wayfarer stumbled over rocks or plowed through sand dunes are now wide and well-paved streets. Green Street, on which I live in my daughter's house, must, in this area at least, have given the engineers a good deal more trouble than clearing out mere gullies. It was chiseled out of the side of a steep hill and while our side of the street is level the houses opposite are reached by flights of steps anywhere from sixty to a hundred in number. From my back window, which has the Bay view, I look down upon a number of gardens sloping southward which are a delight to the eye, not for the flowers, which are few, but for the mass of greenery and the splendid trees. There are palms and pine trees and immense rubber trees that look as if their leaves were polished every morning even in the long dry days of summer. A few streets down, the ground becomes level, and there is nothing to be seen but housetops until they end at the Bay. I also have a full view of Golden Gate Bridge, which is the city's pride, but which I think hideous, even if it is the longest single-span suspension bridge in the world; it is painted a rusty red and its so-called towers look like ladders.

There was a time when that noble expanse of water was gay with yachts—and ferryboats like great white swans, before the bridge was built—but in later days one saw nothing but ships of war, dark and somber, many filled with men wounded or maimed for life, a few in for repairs.

On the streets sloping south from Jackson Street as on those below Nob Hill are rows of small flats whose architecture for some obscure reason is known as Carpenter's Gothic. The projecting windows are sometimes flat, sometimes "bay," and the one is as ugly as the other.

Down the eastern slope from Nob Hill are old St. Mary's Cathedral, now the church of the Paulist fathers, and more little flats, their ugly monotony broken only by the magnificent building of the Metropolitan Life Insurance Company, which covers half a block on Stockton Street from the corner of California. The architecture is Greek, and ancient Athens would have been proud of it. Then down through Chinatown to the business district and thence to the handsome Ferry Building, the work of that fine architect, Page Brown, whose untimely death in an automobile accident was a loss to the city.

There was a time when St. Mary's Cathedral was on the corner of Dupont Street, the most disreputable quarter in San Francisco. Besides the many houses of ill fame there was a row of cottages behind whose open shutters sat women plastered with paint— French, for the most part—who solicited the passers-by. Pleasant for any devout Catholic on his way to Mass, or to some wedding or funeral, if he took the wrong turn; if he showed his discomfiture he would be followed by hoots and ribald laughter. In the course of time the red-light district migrated to Stockton Street and after the fire to Turk Street, once distinguished by stately "rows" in which members of the Old Set were not too proud to live. Today the name Dupont exists only in memory; it has been changed to Grant Avenue and the blocks between Chinatown and Market Street are the center of the shopping district—although the City of Paris is on the corner of Geary and Stockton, and is very French. On nearly every corner of downtown San Francisco, there were until recently large flower stands, whose sales rivaled those of the two leading florists, Rossi and Podesta, for San Franciscans love beauty and those masses of spring flowers, roses, lilies and chrysanthemums were a delight to the eye. But there are few left. The city—and its sidewalks—have become too crowded.

The White House, with entrances on Sutter, Grant Avenue and Post Streets, covering nearly half a block, was founded by Raphael Weill. Mr. Weill was not only the head of the French Colony and one of the city's leading merchants, he was one of San Francisco's outstanding personalities and devoted citizens. He arrived in California in the '50's and took a job in the large dry-goods store of John W. Davidson and Richard Lane. His rise was rapid; his brother Alexander bought him a partnership, and in 1884 he changed the name of the firm, then at the corner of Post and Kearny, to The White House in memory of the Maison Blanc in Paris. That building was swept away by the fire and the present structure built in 1909.

He was a rather short stout man with a beaming intelligent face. One rarely entered The White House without meeting him, for he knew all his customers personally and liked to chat with them. I cannot remember how many times he informed me that he had known five generations of my family, but he liked to divert the conversation to France, to which he was still devoted with his heart if not with his honest and enterprising head. Upon one occasion the conversation veered to Alsace-Lorraine (I think because I had told him that my paternal ancestors had come from those seesaw provinces) and then to the war of 1870-1871. He became so excited that he waved his arms and shouted, "Alsace-Lorraine! Alsace Lorraine! Stolen, raped by those German swine! But one of these days—oh, one of these days——"

I calmed him down as best I could—all business was suspended at near-by counters. "Of course, of course," I said soothingly. "Is not France mighty again? There will be another war one of these days—what is history but war?—and then it will be the destiny of France to conquer and rub Germany's nose in the dust." I knew as little about the military condition of one country as of the other (this must have been in the early 1900's), for although I had traveled a good deal I had taken little interest in European politics. But he subsided and escorted me to the glove counter.

The only other conversation I had with him that I recall was in 1916 when I was persuaded to go to Paris by those ardent "friends of France," Whitney Warren and Owen Johnson, to study the "wonderful war work of the French women" and write a book about it. While there the war relief *(oeuvre)*, Le Bien-Être des Blessés, was formed and I was persuaded, much against my will, to become the American president—which meant raising funds and sending over supplies. But as I had gone over to get the material for a book I consoled myself with the prospect of traveling in the war zone and seeing many different phases denied mere visitors to Paris. So I paid daily visits to the Ministère de la Guerre and blackmailed them into giving me the necessary permits and escort, protesting that I could interest the American public only by harrowing first-hand impressions of devastation, misery and the many hospitals in the war zone. It took some time for the French are interminable talkers and slow to make up their minds even in wartime. Finally, however, they gave their consent and then asked a favor of me in return. It was their intention to establish disabled soldiers on little farms. Would I kindly ask the United States Government to send them millions of seeds—but millions! Those poor young men; it would be their only chance to make a living, perchance to know happiness again! And France would be so poor after the war, while America was so rich.

"But, messieurs," I gasped, "I have no influence with the American Government! I don't know a soul in Washington. And if I approached anyone with a letter of introduction, he would think I was quite mad."

They replied blandly and with some irony that they were sure Madame could manage to get anything she wanted, and I walked down those three flights of stairs I had climbed so often, wondering what on earth I was to do. I had not refused outright, for that might have meant the revoking of my permit, and what would they think of me if—or rather when—I failed? Of course they had taken my consent for granted when my protests ceased.

And then, suddenly, I had an inspiration. Raphael Weill was in Paris. He would advise me. I went at once to his hotel. A page took up my card, on which I had scribbled "pressing," and returned in a few moments. Monsieur Weill (they pronounce it Vail in France) was not feeling very well but would be *enchanté* to see me if I would kindly go up to his room. I found him wrapped in a blanket dressing gown huddled in a chair and looking old and ill, but he beamed upon me as usual. *"Bien, ma chère,* what can I do for you? Always I am at your service."

I poured out my tale of woe. "They ask the impossible!" I cried. "My only hope is that you may know some member of the French Embassy and will write to him."

He waved his hand casually. "Think no more about it, *ma petite. I* will give France those millions of seeds. It is a great opportunity you have given me to do this for the ever-beloved country of my birth." And he did.

San Francisco in its forty-four square miles has streets and quarters so shabby, ugly or merely commonplace that no ambitious small town would tolerate their counterparts. But it has ever been a city of violent contrasts, even as it has ever been a city so cosmopolitan that a dozen or more foreign lands have contributed to its population: Spain, Italy, China, Japan (until Pearl Harbor), Greece, Ireland, Germany, Russia, Norway, Sweden, Denmark; and all have their restaurants, some their small crowded districts, even their churches.

Chinatown is the most famous, and so much has been written about it that I will give only a personal experience of the days when it was rather shabby and had not yet been discovered by the tourist.

In the 1880's when I was a young married woman a Chinese merchant invited my husband to dine with him in Chinatown and attend the theater afterward; and probably as an afterthought included me in the invitation. That evening made an indelible impression on my plastic mind.

There were several four-story houses in Chinatown devoted exclusively to restaurants: the ground floor was for coolies, the two above for those of moderate means—small shopkeepers and the like—the top floor reserved for the haughty aristocracy, of which our host was presumably a member in high standing, judging by the respectful attitude of the waiters, two of whom after almost bowing to the floor escorted us to our seats at a small round table. As it was in the middle of the room I had a good view of the company and of several other features.

It was a handsome room, well lighted by colored lanterns, the windows opening upon balconies, and there were two or three gold-colored tapestries on the walls. At all but one of the round tables sat men (no wives came from China in those days), middle-aged, rather stout and placid, all looking as prosperous and important as our host. The food was abundant but served in tiny portions on dishes equally minute. But I soon lost all interest in the food, and while the two men were talking business my attention was absorbed in watching a near-by table—at which there were no men. It was surrounded by girls, young Chinese girls, who looked as if they had been born old—old and hopeless. They were the entertainers, and they sang without pause in low monotonous voices. Their faces were equally expressionless, or rather those faces wore a combined expression of dolor, abject misery and hopelessness, as if there was nothing left in their starved enslaved souls but a dull resignation to their unhappy lot.

I have seen the dregs of humanity in many lands, but nothing that so horrified me as those poor little Chinese girls who had been torn from their homes in China and sold into slavery at an age when the opening mind is full of happy dreams and curiosity, and transplanted into a foreign land with nothing to look forward to but death.

At the other end of the room in a contrast that was almost violent I beheld a scene of exquisite happiness. On a couch of carved teakwood and mottled marble lay a Chinese blissfully smoking an opium pipe, a long pipe made of bamboo. Beside him was a small open lamp and a jar of opium, a thick black paste that looked like tar. Occasionally he refilled his pipe with an expression of beatitude that would have been joyous had it not been marred by gloating. He dipped a wire into the paste, twirled it in the flame of the lamp and then transferred it, bubbling and sizzling, into the bowl of the pipe. When this rite was concluded he sank back on his wooden pillow and drew in slowly and blissfully the gray-white smoke. Before we left his pipe had fallen to the table and he was in the nethermost depths of the opium paradise.

The men having satisfied their appetites with the contents of those innumerable small dishes, we descended the long flights and walked up the street to the theater. The performance, which, I was told, went on all day and all night—the audience changing every two hours or so—was accompanied by music that altered its rhythm with the change of subject. There was no scenery, the stage was almost bare of furniture; the performers were all men, some of them dressed as women. But there was no lack of action and high singsong chatter. We sat in a box and at first I gave no attention to the stage, for the audience was unlike any I had ever seen. The large auditorium was filled with men, all dressed in the cold blue denim of Chinatown and all wearing soft round hats. I inferred they were enjoying themselves, as that was what they had come for, but those faces were as expressionless as so many rows of recently opened clams.

The galleries presented a startling contrast, for there sat the prostitutes of Chinatown in all their splendor and arrogance. They wore costly brocades and jewels; their black well-greased hair was like small towers above their delicately painted faces (those towers were built up every two or three weeks and they slept on round wooden pillows that fitted into the back of their necks). They wielded large, painted paper fans and sometimes whispered to one another or laughed noiselessly. Some were very handsome; all were getting everything out of life there was in it and no doubt were accumulating bank accounts that would enable them to spend a comfortable old age in China proper.

I transferred my attention to the stage. A "woman" was lying full length on the floor, moving restlessly and groaning; another stood beside her holding a cup of tea. A man, manifestly a doctor, was prancing about her, bending down, peering anxiously, grasping her hand while she heaved in what I assumed to be her death throes. Suddenly the woman gave a violent shudder, a still mightier heave, dropped back and shuddered again. The doctor darted forward, dropped on his knees, put his hand under her skirts—and brought forth an eight-pound doll. He must have pressed a button, for it emitted a squawk. The nurse bent over the woman and held the cup of tea to her lips. The doctor waved the baby in the air triumphantly and made an exit.

There was a subdued chuckle from the auditorium, and I glanced downward. Those uniform faces under those uniform hats no longer resembled clams. That climax was unexpected and they were amused. So were the ladies in the gallery, who giggled audibly.

Our host's face was beaming with satisfaction. "We have great plays and great actors here, don't you think so?" he asked me. I responded politely that they were certainly remarkable.

There was a tap at the door. A vendor entered with sticks of sugar cane two feet long. The host bought three and presented two to his guests. I eyed mine with dismay and then glanced over the house. The ladies of elegant leisure were munching their "canes." I inserted the formidable object in my mouth and nibbled as best I could. It was hard, sticky and saccharine-sweet, but duty is duty and a host is a host. He looked his approval and I was rewarded.

And, after all, he was a considerate host. He must have guessed that I had had enough for shortly afterward he said that the best of the performance was over and he would not keep us up any longer. We thanked him effusively and went our way rejoicing.

San Francisco may have her eyesores but is redeemed by her beauty spots, and the Civic Center is one of them. Here there are really noble buildings. The wide plaza with its fountain, its acacia trees and boxed yews is surrounded irregularly by the splendid City Hall, the Public Library, the Civic Auditorium, the State Building—presented by the Pacific-Panama Exposition of 1915—the State Building Annex, and those twin structures, the Veterans' Building and the Opera House. For the most part, these are of gray granite and in the style of the French Renaissance—although the City Hall has a golden dome. It is a magnificent group and as impressive within as without, but it should surround itself with a wall ten feet high, for the neighboring streets look like poor relations and tatter-demalions.

The word "creative," so often used loosely, may be justly applied to the author of Golden Gate Park, for here literally something was created out of nothing. One thousand and thirteen acres of loose shifting sand dunes—with little hills and valleys here and there—have been converted into one of the most beautiful parks in the world. There are a million trees there now: redwoods, pines, oaks, eucalyptus, pepper trees, bamboo, palms and poplar. Every variety of flower known to man from the red-gold poppy of California and the superb and highly colored rhododendron to exotic importations from other lands, five thousand varieties of plants from all parts of the world, the most delicate in conservatories, lakes with water lilies on their surface, the home of the swan and other water fowl. Every variety of the bird kingdom from the humble swallow to the haughty peacock. Brooks, waterfalls, bridle paths, broad driveways. Meadows where sheep graze peacefully, paddocks for buffalo, elk and deer. The De Young Museum containing many treasures of art, the California Academy of Science, the Museum of Natural History, a Stadium, an Aquarium, a Pioneers' Log Cabin, picnic grounds, a recreation field for tennis and other games, a Children's Playground—and heaven knows how many busts and statues of the great (some of them not so very great).

The growth of this fabulous park was slow. In 1870 Governor Haight, after several years of appeals, demands, threats from the beauty-loving citizens of San Francisco, for "some place to drive in besides streets," appointed the first Park Commission, and three superintendents in turn wrestled successfully with the problem of converting sand into fertile soil. They shoveled away great quantities of dunes and planted acres of coarse grasses and the hardy lupin to hold down the still shifting sand. They transplanted a few cypresses and pines from Monterey, but still it did not look much like a park, although as soon as there were driveways, however crude, many drove through the uninviting expanse on pleasant afternoons in buggies, tandems, rigs, open carriages—where the ladies displayed their brightest garments and befeathered hats— and the tallyho.

I believe it was that dark and dour man of wealth, Mr. James Ben Ali Haggin, who imported the first tallyho, and I remember him as he sat proudly aloft with his youngest daughter Edith, as Turkish-looking as himself, beside him. Occasionally the whip would crack above his four blooded trotters, but he was an admirable driver—hailing from Kentucky, he could hardly be otherwise —and there were no accidents.

But although San Franciscans had a park at last and could drive through something besides streets or over rough country roads, they took little pride in it until after 1887. A young Scot, a landscape gardener, was appointed superintendent and the miracle began. The man who wrought it was John McLaren.

During the fifty years that McLaren dwelt within that park, adding daily to its beauty and novelty, he was perhaps the best-beloved man in San Francisco. Grafting bosses and dishonest mayors tried to oust him, but retreated to their lairs to think up new infamies when the infuriated public went so far as to threaten lynching. With the retirement of Abe Ruef, the last of the bosses, to San Quentin Prison, the danger passed, and under Mayors Rolph and Rossi Golden Gate Park might have been McLaren's private estate —no doubt he had long ceased to regard it as anything else. His house was just within the principal gate, and before it was an immense tree which once a year was the most gorgeous Christmas tree in all California, the delight of thousands of children, not one of whom went home without a present.

He died January 12, 1943, and lay in state for two days in the rotunda of the City Hall. There is to be a statue to him one of these days in the park he so literally "created."

Beautiful as the park is we are told by the new superintendent, Julius Gerod, that the war now being over $12,000,000 will be spent to make it the most beautiful park in all the world. Well, San Francisco has always been a city of superlatives. Why not?

The further improvement of Golden Gate Park has a double object: it is to be a postwar project, employing hundreds of war veterans for five years or more. As the sum of $12,000,000 is rather a staggering one it is hoped that the Federal Government, considering its object, will contribute!

# CHAPTER FOUR

# Romantic Backgrounds

HERE and there in San Francisco, particularly in the Western Addition, are smaller parks covering one or two blocks. Lafayette, two blocks square, was once the property of the Holladays, a family with an interesting history.

Samuel Holladay arrived in San Francisco in the early days and, disliking the turbulence of the young city, built himself a house on one of the lower hilltops in what was then a waste of sand and rock. The house in due course was surrounded by a fine garden and so many trees that it was hidden from the vulgar gaze.

But it was his wife, Catherine Georgiana, sister of the then famous General Edward Otho Cresrap Ord, who provided the family with a distinction high above mere wealth or the regnant Southerners who ruled San Francisco society for so many years. For the Ords had royal blood in their dark blue veins. They were descended no less, from the rakish King George IV of England and his morganatic wife, Mrs. Fitzherbert, an alliance that rocked Britain in its time, but upon which the Holladays placed a determined emphasis. A morganatic marriage might deny them any claim to the throne, but at least there was no bend sinister in their coat of arms. True, the cynics in the Pacific-Union Club (it was said that all the gossip of San Francisco originated in the P-U and traveled thence to wives and daughters) asserted that "morganatic wife" was merely a fancy name for "mistress," but San Franciscans, as prudish as Queen Victoria in those days, on the whole preferred to accept the Holladays

60

at their own valuation and were proud of that thin vein of royal blood in their midst—to say nothing of the romance—and disposed of the gentlemen of the P-U as old fogies.

In later years, after the two handsome daughters had married Englishmen and deserted San Francisco, and the Western Addition had become the fashionable residential district, Mr. Holladay became what is known as a "character." The city maintained that no resident had the right to monopolize two unbroken blocks and interfere with the even course of a street. A lawsuit was the result. It dragged on and on. Mr. Holladay made a vow that he would not cut his hair until the suit was settled in his favor.

His white hair grew longer and longer. It floated over his shoulders and waved in the breeze. Little boys mocked him as he took his daily constitutional but were sometimes awed by his haughty mien.

Years passed. The long-drawn-out suit finally ended in a compromise (no doubt after Mr. Holladay was weary of the constant drain on his bank account); the city bought the property for a handsome sum, but the board of supervisors, instead of leveling the hill to accommodate the missing block in Clay Street, converted the "old Holladay place" into Lafayette Square with many more trees, a tennis court, and comfortable benches for those who enjoyed sunning themselves on fogless days.

Other San Franciscans have interesting backgrounds, but the Mailliards' is the most notable.

Long ago on another continent, Joseph Bonaparte, King of Naples, King of Spain, had a love affair with one of his consort's ladies in waiting, and in order to protect her when the child was born he married her to a friend named Mailliard, a faithful subject of his Imperial brother. He named the boy Louis and, conceiving a deep affection for him, transferred him to his own household.

What ructions this may have caused in the family circle we are not told; the Queen may have been amiable or merely indifferent. When Louis grew up he also married, and his son married a sister of F. Marion Crawford, popular novelist of the '80's and '90's.

But meanwhile there was a change of scene. Joseph, realizing that Napoleon's downfall was inevitable, took passage on a ship for the United States under the title Count de Survilliers. He was accompanied by Louis Mailliard and his legitimate son Louis Napoleon, as well as by a retinue of servants. As his wife was too delicate to stand a long sea voyage she remained behind with her sister, the Queen of Sweden, and so did his daughters, although they visited him later. He and Napoleon bore a striking resemblance to each other. Before sailing he offered the tottering monarch his ticket to the land of freedom, but Napoleon declined, refusing to leave his generals.

Joseph must have been a man of foresight to transfer his considerable fortune to America when the Imperial comet began to drop, for he bought himself a handsome estate near Bordentown, New Jersey; he also took furniture and works of art that must have filled the hold of the ship. There is a legend to the effect that he lived the life of a mysterious recluse, seen by no one besides his household, and kept his royal past merely a matter of conjecture. But the truth is even more interesting. He was a genial soul and loved company; he was popular with his neighbors in Bordentown, both poor and rich. He entertained in his splendid mansion Henry Clay, Daniel Webster, John Adams, General Scott, Commodores Stewart and Stockton. Lafayette and many other Frenchmen were his guests, and poor émigrés sought him out to receive substantial proofs of his sympathy for those less fortunate than himself.

Time passed. Adolph, son of Louis Mailliard, grew up and married Eliza Ward, member of a distinguished American family:

his wife was a sister of Julia Ward Howe. Both were desirous of living in California, and as Joseph had exhausted his capital and died leaving little to his heirs, Samuel Ward bought his sister a ranch in Marin County, twenty miles north of San Francisco, a domain of some 16,000 acres, well forested with redwoods and other noble trees, and containing many acres of grazing land. There the two sons and two daughters of Adolph grew up in peace and plenty. The Mailliards waxed rich and important. The parents occasionally visited San Francisco, which welcomed them, not because of the Bonaparte ancestry of which it knew nothing for many years, but because of the Crawford-Howe connection.

But these visits came to an end when the girls grew up. Adolph Mailliard must have been an insufferable old tryant. No doubt he persuaded himself that he was the reincarnation of his collateral ancestor; as he could not rule an empire he got what satisfaction he could in being lord and master of 16,000 acres and his unfortunate family. There was no entertaining on the San Geronimo ranch, nor were his sons permitted to bring their college friends home during the holidays. He vowed that his daughters should never marry. They were his and his they should remain. If any young man who may have seen those two pretty girls during their shopping visits to town had dared to force an entrance within that sacrosanct preserve he would have been run off with a shotgun. The girls had grown up under the imperious will and submitted. I met one of them after his death. She was regal and lovely but very sad, for her youth had passed.

The boys after they left college escaped from the domestic fortress, engaged in business in San Francisco and prospered. The eldest, John—or Jack, as he was always called—very handsome and very distinguished, married Elizabeth Page, member of a large family that came to California in the '60's with a fortune made in

Chile. Today the Page-Mailliard clan is the strongest in San Francisco. Its ramifications are beyond me although I have known them nearly all my life.

These two young men, by the way, regarded the bend sinister on their escutcheon with profound disfavor and never mentioned the subject to each other, nor did Jack ever mention it to his wife and five children. But before proposing to "Lizzie" he sought an interview with Mrs. Page and told her he thought it his duty to confess that his great-great-grandfather had been the illegitimate son of Joseph Bonaparte. Mrs. Page, a woman of the world (and mother of thirteen), smiled, set his mind at rest, told him that the Americans were romantic and that he should be proud of his illustrious descent. Young Mailliard was relieved if not convinced, and the marriage was an ideally happy one. He built a house on Belvedere, a residential island in the Bay, and another in San Francisco. In that town house is a full-length painting of the brothers, Louis Napoleon and Louis Mailliard. It also contains many Bonaparte relics, including a set of china bedecked with the Imperial "B"—once the property of Napolean himself—and other objects of art that Joseph had given to his son Louis, all of which, owing to the inconsistencies of human nature, Mr. Mailliard was not too proud to possess.

His sons were handsome, his daughters beautiful. The eldest, Anita, married a distinguished mining engineer, G. Temple Bridgman, who emerged many years later from his retirement to serve the government as head of the Metal Reserve Corporation of the R. F. C. under Jesse Jones. The second daughter, Marion Lee, married Dr. Walter Baldwin, the most eminent orthopedic surgeon in the West until his untimely death.

He was very proud of his children and would have been prouder still could he have lived to follow the career of his eldest son, John Ward Mailliard, one of the leading citizens of San Francisco. He

A STREET IN CHINATOWN

A SHOP IN CHINATOWN

has been president of the Chamber of Commerce, president of the Police Commission, director of Remedial Loans, of the California-Pacific Title and Trust Company, Fireman's Fund Insurance Company, and is now (1946) president of the Harbor Commission. He has an estate of 15,000 acres in Mendocino County where he raises sheep and on which he has built two houses, one for summer and one for winter. He also manages his mother's affairs and is the adviser and stand-by of his brothers and sisters.

After Jack Mailliard's death his widow sold the house on Belvedere and spends the summers with Marian Lee in San Rafael, her winters in the town house—surrounded by the Bonaparte relics, of which, having her mother's sound common sense, she is reasonably proud. She is lively, clever and charming, the idol of her family, and has a coterie of devoted friends whom she entertains delightfully.

That family! Lizzie is veritably the matriarch of a tribe, for she stands at the head of one hundred and six children, grandchildren, great and great-great-grandchildren, nephews and nieces similarly bracketed, in California, and forty in Chile.

Her brother Arthur Page married Emmelita, daughter of the famous William C. Ralston, the beauty of her day and still a handsome woman.

Other families in San Francisco and the Bay area with notable backgrounds are descended from the Spanish families of Old California—from a time when California was a Department of New Spain, whose capital was Mexico City, and life, when they were not fighting one another, was Arcadian. The Dibblees stem from the De la Guerras of Santa Barbara, in whose fine old adobe house took place that wedding described by Richard Henry Dana in *Two Years Before the Mast,* and in one of whose rooms Concha Argüello lived for a time and wore the habit of the third order of the Franciscans, devoting herself to good works, until Bishop Alemany came from Mexico and built the convent at Benicia.

And then there is the beautiful Mrs. Harry (Ruth) Hill, descended from the Bandinis and the Carrillos of the south (one of her daughters married a Page) ; Mrs. George Brady (of the Ortega clan), known as the White Angel because she is never seen on the street or elsewhere in anything but white, and whose son, aide to General Doolittle, distinguished himself in World War II.

Mrs. Reginald Courtney Jenkins (she who has the Monterey cypress behind her house in the Western Addition) is descended from the Bandinis and the Argüellos.

And the Vallejos! Descendants of that "Lord of the North" who reigned over a hundred thousand acres until the Americans came and the infamous "Squatters' Act" reduced them to a bare three hundred. This is a clan whose numbers I make no attempt to follow, but his wife, Doña Benicia (after whom the first capital of California was named) presented him with thirteen children; his eldest daughter, Epiphania, who married Captain John Frisbie, produced twenty-two, and heaven only knows how many were contributed by his other progeny. All the Old Californians seem to have been equally prolific, and quite a number of those offspring miraculously survived.

A town on the eastern shore of the Bay was named for the old general, and a street in San Francisco. Several of his children and grandchildren have distinguished themselves. The younger Vallejos, with few exceptions, married Americans, and their blood, the blood of the last and grandest of the old Dons, runs in the veins of unnumbered San Franciscans.

On the corner of Lombard and Hyde Streets, where Russian Hill begins to flatten out, is a house before which devotees of Robert

Louis Stevenson, tourists for the most part, stand and gaze. For in that house, they have been assured, he lived and wrote.

It is always a thankless job to shatter an illusion, but the cold fact is that Mrs. Stevenson built that house after her husband's death. He may have liked the spot and talked to her of building a home there one day, and she erected it to his memory, but that is his only association with it. She sold it some years later to Mr. Frank Sullivan, brother-in-law of Senator James D. Phelan, and he presented it to the Carmelite nuns, of which order his daughter was a member. There was a large garden, but the Carmelites are a cloistered order, and no passer-by ever caught a glimpse of them. They may have taken their exercise at night, but by day that garden was empty save for a statue of St. Francis d'Assisi. This too was a shrine—for devout Catholics who lingered before the convent listening to the solemn music, hoping that a window might open suddenly to reveal a cloistered head veiled in black, but it is doubtful if they were ever gratified. Only priests, relatives or a physician could cross that guarded threshold. After a time the nuns moved to Santa Clara, and the house reverted to the Sullivans, where the son, Noel, gave many delightful entertainments—musical for the most part. The upper room was decorated to resemble a ship, and the statue of St. Francis, visible from one of the windows, was always illuminated. I heard Tibbett sing there one night, but that magnificent voice, accustomed to an auditorium, almost tore the roof into shreds.

A block farther down on the corner of Chestnut and Hyde Streets is by far the most interesting house in San Francisco for it is the oldest; other houses preceded it, but those old adobe and wooden structures of Yerba Buena have gone long since, and its only rival is the onetime residence of the Comandante of the Presidio (sacred to the memory of Concha Argüello), which is on a United States

Reservation and a relic of the old Spanish and Mexican regimes.

This house was built in 1852 by one William Squire Clark, but why is a mystery to this day, for he never lived in it and a few years later sold it to Mr. William Penn Humphreys, whose name still clings to it. This venerable mansion, built from a cargo of white oak lumber brought "round the Horn" and left to rot in one of the hundreds of deserted ships during the days of the Gold Rush, is a large square structure with a machicolated roof. It is shaded by the biggest and ugliest eucalyptus tree in the Bay area, and it is the most sinister, the most mysterious and the most haunted-looking landmark that we possess. Nevertheless, it is admirably proportioned with a wide veranda and a cupola in the middle of the roof in which Mr. Humphries used to loaf and enjoy the wide sweep of the Bay, its islands, the mountains beyond and the ships sailing through the Golden Gate.

But why the machicolated roof in the year 1852? There was not an Indian left to attack this solitary residence, and the United States had wrested California from Mexico six years before. Perhaps Mr. Clark had a wayward taste in decoration—or merely a sense of humor. Who knows? But there it stands in the middle of a wild garden, not only notable for its age but "different."

Mr. Humphreys furnished it sumptuously for its time with importations from New York and Boston. One of its heavy carpets is now in the De Young Museum in Golden Gate Park—as a sample of the luxury and bad taste of the old days. The price was $800.

That old mansion looks as if it might collapse any minute, and the picket fence surrounding the garden is in the last stage of dilapidation, but within it is comfortable and brought up to date by certain modern improvements—one bathroom and five toilets.

In 1919 the house was rented by Frank Carroll Giffen, distinguished musician and teacher of voice. Mrs. Giffen furnished the lower rooms on the eastern side of the hall with many pieces of valuable old furniture of the more comfortable period of the Victorian era, some of horsehair, some covered with *petit point,* which she inherited from her mother, as well as the Aubusson lambrequins from France. The double parlors opposite—now thrown into one—with their two grand pianos were sacred to the cause of music, and in this room the San Francisco Opera Association was born.

In 1921 Gaetano Merola came to San Francisco with the San Carlo Opera Company of which he was conductor, and Giffen persuaded him to remain and give San Francisco yearly performances of its own. The rehearsals were held in that music room, and the only flaw in Giffen's content was the gum invariably parked on the underside of the chairs brought from other parts of the house—by the local chorus. The first five performances were held in the stadium of Stanford University and were attended by a large and enthusiastic audience, for San Franciscans can never get enough of music.

And who, it will be asked, provided the funds for the Metropolitan Opera singers' salaries, the costumes of the local chorus for five operas and other incidental expenses? Now, hold your breath, for never was a great opera association so founded before. Thirty thousand dollars was contributed by the Italian fishermen, who might be heard singing any morning as they sailed back to Fisherman's Wharf with their catch. Merola had paid many visits to San Francisco, made friends with this picturesque element of the city and was president of their union. Their response to his appeal was immediate—and it may as well be stated here that they were repaid in full.

After those initial performances Giffen and Merola had no difficulty in raising the money for a permanent San Francisco Opera Association. Giffen had a number of wealthy women among his pupils, and they agreed to canvass the town and persuade several hundred others to become "Founders" at fifty dollars a head. I had formed the habit of paying my bills by return mail, not from excess of virtue but because I traveled a great deal at that time, and it saved a lot of bother at the last moment. It was owing to this habit that my check was the first to go into the yawning exchequer.

There were also many large contributions, and the first of the San Francisco performances was given in the Civic Auditorium in 1923. The opera was *La Bohême*. When the War Memorial Opera House was built it opened on October 15, 1932, with *La Tosca*, and since then performances have been given there every autumn; the opera season is the high light of the year.

Some day there will be busts of Giffen and Merola in the lobby.

# CHAPTER FIVE

# San Francisco Bookstores

TODAY there are many bookstores in San Francisco, such as those of Newbegin's, Paul Elder and Co., Gelber and Lilienthal, John Howell, David Magee, Miss Seymour's Personal Book Shop. But in the 1880's the only ones I can recall were Bancroft's, A. Roman's, Doxey's and the smaller but far more fascinating one of C. Beach in Montgomery Street in the heart of the shopping district. That shop was very distinctive with its sign portraying green waves breaking on a rocky shore and very attractive with its nice sympathetic young clerk, Alexander Robertson—to become in his own time the dean of all that were to come.

Life was a monotonous round on those country estates surrounding Menlo Park where I spent my married life; I loved reading and my only sources of supply were my grandfather's library, classics which I could have recited backward, and those an old gentleman in the neighborhood lent me occasionally. When I was about twenty-two an old ambition to be a writer, smothered by too much domesticity, awoke and I tried my hand at articles which I sent to the San Francisco *Argonaut*. They were published and I found a mild excitement at seeing myself in print. They were unsigned for I well knew the prejudices of my time, to say nothing of my immediate environment. (Several years later my Spanish mother-in-law remarked caustically, "The ladies in Spain, they no write," and Mrs. Selby of the neighboring estate, told me, when speaking of her eldest daughter, "Annie writes the most beautiful poems and

stories, but *of course* she would never think of publishing them—
exhibiting herself in print! Impossible!" The intimation being that
no lady Spanish or otherwise would topple off the sacrosanct
heights of SOCIETY to mingle with the common herd. But time
marches on.)

One day a reference in a newspaper to an old romance and scan-
dal of a family that had once lived at Palo Alto not far from Menlo
Park inspired me to write a story, filling in the few bald facts with
my imagination. It was accepted by the *Argonaut* and ran through
six numbers. When it was finished I went up to town to receive
my check, filled with a lively expectation; I had received small sums
for my articles (which had gone into the coffers of C. Beach) ; surely
I would get forty or fifty dollars for a long story.

When the editor handed me a check for $150 I nearly fainted.
Never had I looked upon a check of such magnitude before. My
grandfather had given me a monthly allowance, but when I married before my school days were over and into a wealthy family
(wealthy for that era) it naturally ceased. My husband was one
of those 100-percent males who could see no reason why a wife
should need any pocket money. Was I not well fed, well housed?
When I needed new clothes did not one of my elder sisters-in-law
take me to the White House or the City of Paris and fit me out?
Very simply it was true, but quite adequately. What was I but a
child, anyhow?

Well, I wanted a lot more. I cashed that check, and after buying some presents and a few folderols my feminine soul had longed
for I made for C. Beach and had a lovely and exciting afternoon
with young Robertson, who was nearly as excited as I was. It was
an odd assortment we selected: the speeches of Fox, Pitt, Burke and
Daniel Webster; Gladstone's *Gleanings of Past Years;* Emerson's
*Essays;* Macaulay's *Essays* and *History of England;* Kinglake's *His-*

*tory of the Crimean War* and *Eothen; Vathek;* Herbert Spencer's *First Principles* and *Essay on Style;* Pepys's and Evelyn's diaries; Taine's *History of English Literature;* Richard Grant White's *Words and Their Uses; The Moonstone* by Wilkie Collins; several of Daudet's novels. I spent the major part of that marvelous check in the bookstore of C. Beach and doubt if I have ever felt more elated in my life.

In due course Beach retired and Alec Robertson succeeded him. After the earthquake and fire of 1906 he rented a shop in Stockton Street opposite Union Square, and under the fashionable Town and Country Club. There, assisted by Miss Long and his handsome son Harry (who confided to me that he hated the sight of books and when his father retired he would retire with him and become a farmer) he continued to be patronized by the élite of the city. He not only had all the new books on his shelves as quickly as freight and express could bring them across the continent, but "everybody" had his cards, note paper, and invitations engraved at "Robertson's." He also published notable books: *In the Footprints of the Padres,* by Charles Warren Stoddard; *The Man with the Hoe* by Edwin Markham; a book of travel by James D. Phelan; *A Senator of the Fifties* (Broderick) by Jeremiah Lynch and almost all of George Sterling's poems.

That bookstore was very attractive and not only because of its long rows of bookshelves, and long tables with the most tempting of the new literary wares set forth; above the shelves running around three sides of the store was a frieze, so to speak, of paintings by local artists depicting the wild flowers of California: gold-red poppies, purple and yellow lupins, blue "baby-eyes," wild lilac, violets, pansies, blue iris, yellow buttercups and wild roses.

The members of Town and Country were intelligent women for the most part and had plenty of money to spend on books; it would never have occurred to them to go elsewhere and they had a real fondness for "Alec." Many others patronized that rather small bookstore because it was the thing to do and made them feel superior.

Alec's favorite customer was one Mr. Samson, a mild-mannered dark man with an excellent literary taste and a fascinating personality. But that pleasant acquaintance was brief. One day Alec opened his newspaper and was astonished to see the face of his interesting though somewhat mysterious friend on the first page. He was still more astonished, not to say horrified, to read that Mr. Samson was the notorious highwayman, Black Bart, who had been captured at last.

When Robertson died in 1933 Harry sold the stationery business to Gelber and Lilienthal, who took over Miss Long and all the plates, etc., of his former customers. Harry, happily married, has achieved his ambition: he is a farmer in southern California.

Before 1906 two young men, Paul Elder and John Howell, also had a handsome and popular bookstore, but the fire swept it away.

For a time after that fire Van Ness Avenue was the center of activities. All sorts of booths were erected, and one met every man he knew striding along looking full of pep, or talking eagerly in some group. And all the old conventions seemed to have gone with the greater part of the city.

One day Senator Phelan and I were strolling along eating candy from a bag he had bought at one of the booths, and like everyone else, discussing the future of San Francisco. "Now who do you suppose that is?" I exclaimed, indicating two young men some distance ahead. They were sitting on a box on the edge of the sidewalk holding a large white placard in front of them. They proved to be Paul Elder and John Howell with the name of their new firm, site and all, painted in large black letters on the white background. They grinned as we paused before them and looked as cheerful as a May morning without a fog. We shared our candy with them and talked of the new city that was to rise on the site of those ashes now being shoveled into carts.

Their faith in that future was verified. They remained together in their new shop until 1912 when Howell decided that he wanted to engage in another kind of book business and started out for himself.

But I must begin with Paul Elder, who was Alexander Robertson's only rival. His career as a bookseller has been both interesting and original for he combined a sound business faculty with the soul of an artist. He began as a clerk in Doxey's big store under the Palace Hotel during the '90's, where he assisted in publishing *The Lark,* edited by Gelett Burgess and Bruce Porter, a famous little magazine in its day. He recalls with pleasure the many visits of Mrs. George (Phoebe) Hearst, the outstanding Californienne of her time. "She usually selected the hour after the store had closed," he relates, "and in consequence had to lift her skirts as she picked her way daintily around the charwomen engaged in scrubbing the floor."

In 1898 he decided to go into business for himself and rented one of the glass-fronted mezzanine rooms in the court of Mills Office Building. But although the shop was artistic it was off the beat and patrons were few. He was relieved when a friend introduced him to a young clerk in the Bank of California, Morgan Shepherd, who had higher aspirations. They joined forces, raised more capital and moved the business to 238 Post Street. Although books were the dominant interest, pictures, pieces of pottery and metal were displayed to give the place a noncommercial atmosphere. Mr. Shepherd designed the furniture of stained redwood picked out here and there with bits of colored glass. There was a fine painting by Keith, glass cases containing precious volumes, and books still more rare were shown in an alcove at the rear of the shop. In a roofed-in back yard there was a rich display of Oriental art: pieces of brass and copper, old brocades and vases. Beyond was another old building they annexed and turned into a children's bookroom. Altogether it was the most attractive shop in San Francisco outside Chinatown. It was at this time that John Howell became a member of the staff.

Of course the great fire devoured it with relish. It was a sad loss but the young men were undaunted, and as soon as it was physically possible the architect Bernard Maybeck designed a building for them of Old English type, with massive beams, peaked roof and dormer windows. It was situated in the temporary shopping district—then designed to be the permanent center—at the corner of Van Ness Avenue and Bush Street and was as attractively arranged as the old store, although with less variety.

But San Francisco is ever capricious. As the city was rebuilt all shops in the new center were abandoned for the "old downtown district." Our young men rented a building on Grant Avenue, and Mr. Maybeck designed the interior, this time with beautiful Gothic columns and ceiling and richly carved gilt screens. The art interest was continued on the second floor. As they had already gone into the publishing business, Mr. Nash, with his type and hand press, was on the third floor. On the fourth was a gallery for authors to talk about their latest opus and lecturers to instruct the public, another innovation in the book business. One important series dealing with the campaigns of World War I were delivered by Sidney Coryn, associate editor of the San Francisco *Argonaut* (and father of that brilliant young author, Marjorie Coryn). Among other publications for which the new shop was notable were *The Love Sonnets of a Hoodlum* and *The Rubaiyat of Omar Khayyam, Jr.,* by Wallace Irwin, one of San Francisco's originals, *The Cynic's Calendar of Revised Wisdom* by Oliver Herford, and verses of Arthur Guiterman.

It should be mentioned here that one of Mr. Elder's assistants was Miss Theresa Thompson, the beautiful sister of Kathleen Norris, who later married the poet William Rose Benét.

In 1919 Mr. Elder made another move, this time to his present spacious quarters that reach from Post Street through to Maiden Lane, and once more Mr. Maybeck was the presiding genius. He designed a tall Gothic arch for the entrance and a "golden stairway" leading to the mezzanine and the great room a few steps above, whose windows are on Maiden Lane. This room is lined from floor to ceiling with books, to say nothing of many tables. Details of the Grant Avenue store—the Gothic columns and ceiling, the gold screens and the Gothic motif—appear in the new fixtures. On the mezzanine is the art room and above, the gallery for exhibitions and lectures.

On either side of the Post Street entrance is a large window with a fine display of the latest books, to be found in greater abundance in the room between the Gothic arch and the stairway. There is also a large desk where authors sit and autograph their books.

For seventeen years Mr. Elder's principal assistant was the handsome, intellectual, charming and able Mrs. Morris, who was said by all the travelers for Eastern publishing houses to be the best bookwoman in the United States. In 1938 she went to Newbegin's, where she remained for six years. She is now married and living in Denver—a great loss to San Francisco, whatever she may be to the fortunate Mr. Arthur Blackburn Copeland.

The principal members of Mr. Elder's staff are his son, who for

a time was absent in the Army, and his son's wife Eloise, who had
been conducting the details of the Art Department, and who func-
tioned admirably in his stead. Now that he is back, Paul, Jr., with
his father is managing the store, and Eloise continues to do the nonfiction buying.

Paul Elder has been a strong cultural influence in San Francisco
and the city is grateful.


John Howell has an interesting record. Born in the small town
of Healdsburg, he finished his education at the University of California, where in 1895 he founded the *Daily Californian,* the largest
college daily in the United States. After his graduation he was associated with the San Francisco *Morning Call,* then from 1903 until
1912 he was manager and vice-president of Paul Elder Company.

At the Panama-Pacific Exposition in 1915 he received the medal
of honor for the best display of books, and he was chairman of the
Bible Committee at the Golden Gate Exposition of 1929-1930. He
was first vice-president of the Booksellers Association of San Francisco and Bay counties for four years, is a charter member of the
California Historical Society, president of the San Francisco branch
of the English-Speaking Union, and is a member of Antiquarian
Booksellers, London; Authors' Club and Authors' Lodge, London;
charter member of the Delta Upsilon of the University of California, and in San Francisco is a member of the Bohemian and Commonwealth Clubs.

His large store in Post Street is the delight of collectors. He
handles current books but specializes in tomes of the past. I saw an
enviable volume there one day, a volume long, broad and deep,
with peeling leather covers and yellow-spotted pages: Lord North's
translation of Plutarch's *Lives.* I believe he got one hundred and
fifty dollars for it later.

He has no less than 7,000 rare Bibles, which he exhibits when he lectures at U. C., Stanford University, or at other colleges and clubs. He has supplied 7,000 volumes to the Folger Shakespeare Library in Washington, D. C., and many more for the famous Huntington Library in Southern California—English literature and Californiana, including the finest collection of San Francisco directories in existence. Not content with all this, he has to date published twenty-five important books, including *Seventy-five Years in California,* by William H. Davis; *Sketches of the Sixties,* by Bret Harte and Mark Twain, heretofore uncollected; three manuscripts of Robert Louis Stevenson, and *Sir Francis Drake's Voyage Around the World—Its Aims and Achievements,* by Henry R. Wagner.

His three sons served in the Navy during World War II: commander, lieutenant commander, lieutenant.

The fashionable bookstore of Gelber and Lilienthal, in Sutter Street has been doing a fine business since 1923. They too are publishers: *The Modern Writer,* by Sherwood Anderson; also books by Stella Benson, Charles Erskine Scott Wood, Hildegarde Flanner and a "small item" by Robinson Jeffers. They also specialize in finely printed books by private presses and other collectors' items. Miss Long, until lately, presided in the back of the shop and carried on the tradition of Alexander Robertson. There one may buy fine stationery and have one's calling cards engraved as well as invitations and announcements. In addition this firm carries the largest and most original cards, in the Christmas season, to be found in San Francisco.

David Magee, whose shop is almost next door to Howell's, was for a time a dealer in rare books, manuscripts and fine printing only, but in 1932 he branched out into current publications, although still as interested as ever in first editions of books long out of print. He has also expanded his business by including old prints and pictures, and he has published several books, most of them with the famous Grabhorn Press of San Francisco, said to be the finest in the world. These deal mainly with book collection and include *Original Leaves from the First Four Folios of Shakespeare;* three separate volumes of illuminated *Manuscripts of the Middle Ages,* by H. C. Schulz of the Huntington Library; an essay on Barclay's *Ship of Fools,* by James D. Hart and the monumental and beautifully printed bibliography of the Grabhorn Press.

The Magee shop is very attractive and authors are always glad to autograph their books for him.

The smallest and most novel bookstore was established by two college girls, Gladys Seymour and Isabel Wiel (a member of the distinguished Lilienthal clan, who has since left the store to travel). It is a bright spot in the bleak canyon of Montgomery Street for its window is filled with the new books in their colored jackets, and as the passer-by who may linger for more than a glance at this unusual sight in the heart of the business district has only to step over a threshold, the Personal Book Shop is seldom empty. Not only does he find there the latest publications but a tempting lending library, and he seldom leaves without a book under his arm. When a new book by a local author is "out" Miss Seymour gives an autograph party to which the regular patrons are invited. The guests have a fine time, while the author sits at a corner table behind a pile of books and plods away at his monotonous task (consoling himself with the reflection of how much worse he would feel if unwanted).

Miss Seymour was born in Seattle and, after attending the University of Washington for a time, transferred herself to the University of California where she was a member of the Alpha Phi fraternity and graduated in 1931. Returning to her native city, she opened a bookshop, and although the country was groaning under the Great Depression she accomplished the miracle of building up a fairly prosperous business in a short time. In 1934, however, being of a roving and experimental disposition, she went to New York and persuaded several bookstores to engage in what might be called a lend-lease business with their customers, the books personally delivered by herself. She pursued the same plan in New Jersey and finally opened a bookshop of her own at Spring Lake, a fashionable resort. This did well, but after a similar experience in Middleburg, Virginia, her curiosity regarding the East and South was satisfied and she concluded to settle down in San Francisco, that city to which her great-grandparents had come in its formative years.

She obtained a position in Paul Elder's bookstore as buyer for children's books and fiction, later for nonfiction, but her enterprising spirit demanded a shop of her own, and in 1941 she established herself on the eighth floor of the Bank of America, this time in partnership with Miss Wiel. A San Franciscan by birth, Miss Wiel was educated at Miss Burke's private school and at Mills College and served her apprenticeship as a bookwoman at Paul Elder's, where she had the good fortune to be assistant to the "greatest bookwoman of them all," Isabel Morris. But Miss Seymour's invitation to be a partner in a bookstore of their own was too great a temptation to be resisted. One secret of the success of these two women, aside from their ability, is that they enjoyed their business hugely. Although Miss Wiel is no longer with the store, everyone wishes Miss Seymour the same success the two achieved together.

Newbegin's in Post Street is a popular and prosperous bookstore. Cannily situated on the very waistline of a hotel center, to say nothing of office buildings and variety shops, it also faces the evergreen Union Square where sea gulls flutter about, and persons from bums to tired businessmen sun themselves on the benches. Newbegin's sells books exclusively and has a very large stock. Its telephones ring all day and the long and lofty room is crowded from nine until half past five.

The business was founded by John J. Newbegin, Sr., in 1889, with quarters in the old Flood Building on Market Street. He came to San Francisco from Montreal where he had engaged in the business of selling fine sets of books on art, wholesale and retail. His brother, R. G. Newbegin, was associated with Mark Twain in the American Publishing Company at Hartford, Connecticut.

Mr. Newbegin died in 1919, and his son, John J. Newbegin, Jr., who had been a partner in the firm since 1903, moved to the present location and has been expanding the business ever since.

Mr. Newbegin's personal interest is in old books, of which he has a large collection stowed away out of sight, and although he maintains that the interest of Newbegin's is centered on current books and their rapid sale, I notice the following statements on his letter heads: "Fine Editions. Californiana and books of the West. Out of print items secured. Import orders executed. Libraries appraised, catalogued or purchased." But all that must go on behind the scenes and after hours. Mr. Newbegin may be seen at any time sauntering about the shop with an air of complete repose while his ten clerks scurry about filling his coffers. But they all look contented and happy, proud to be indispensable at Newbegin's.

That thriving business is by no means confined to the hotels and office buildings; its steady customers are on every residence street in the Western Addition and in those flourishing subdivisions I have described elsewhere. It may truthfully be stated that not the least of its attractions is Mrs. Newbegin herself. Pretty, gracious, and always charmingly dressed, she sits at a desk in the middle of the shop and every customer tries to have a chat with her. Not only is she lively and responsive, but she can give instant information on every book that is on the shelves, which rise to the ceiling, or that is displayed on the long tables—the latest book that has come from the East, what are the prospects of this or that book as a best seller, the address of any author to whom one may wish to write a fan letter—her information is endless. Her particular job is buying the new books, attending to the correspondence, and general supervision. And she never looks tired.

I have written at length of those bookstores with which I have had personal contact and for which I always autograph my books as they come out. But there are many other notable bookstores in San Francisco that have a large following: Maritime Book Shop, Mission Book Exchange, Malcolm MacNeil, Holmes Book Company, Lieberman's Book Store, International Book Store, Town Book and Card Shop, Springer's Book Company, Central Circulating Library, Down Town Library, The Tunnel Library, Ames Book Shop, Fields Book Store, The Ray Graham Bookshop, J. W. Stacey, Inc., Technical Book Company, Warren Wright, Bookseller, Just-a-Mere Library, Metaphysical Library and Book Shop, Carl K. Wilson Book Department at Hale Brothers, Inc., and Books, Inc., in the Fairmont Hotel.

Our department stores have fine book sections and are a vital factor in the sale of books in San Francisco. These book departments have been noted for the manner in which they have succeeded in developing a personalized service so that just the book he or she wants is brought to the attention of the man or woman wishing to buy the book.

The Emporium book department is magnificent. The department in The White House is in the best Raphael Weill tradition, and the fact that Brentano is installed in City of Paris speaks for itself.

# CHAPTER SIX

# A Few of Our Illustrious Dead

SINCE to write even a brief sketch of Mark Twain and his books would be what is grandiosely called a work of supererogation, I shall confine myself to a personal experience.

When I was about nine years old and my mother had married a New Yorker, John Frederick Uhlhorn, there was great excitement in the house; Mark Twain, whom my stepfather had known in the East, was coming to dinner. Mr. Uhlhorn, although anything but literary himself, not only liked Mark Twain personally but felt that it became him to do honor to so vast a reputation. The word "author" meant nothing to me. If he had been a bandit or King of the Sandwich Islands he would have been equally impersonal; but he was someone to make a fuss over and I was determined to get a glimpse of him. When the doorbell rang the first time I slipped out of bed and hung over the banisters.

The guests were many (I doubt if there was another writer among them), and I waited impatiently to hear his name announced. He was late, but when "Mr. Clemens" floated up to me I nearly precipitated myself into the hall below—but all I could see was the top of a shaggy head.

Many years later I attended a luncheon at Delmonico's in New York, given by George Harvey, then head of the house of Harper, in honor of Mark Twain and William Dean Howells.

Thinking it would amuse him, I related this incident. "Ah—

yes," he drawled. "I remember Fred Uhlhorn. He once borrowed twenty dollars from me and never paid it back."

If I had been seated next to him I fear I should have given him an unladylike kick. It was not only abominably rude of him but probably a lie and he was merely being smart aleck. I ignored him thereafter, although he monopolized the conversation, and devoted myself to Mr. Howells, a nice little man who never was rude to anyone.

The only other personal impression I have of him is a big man clad in white linen sauntering along Fifth Avenue, quite pleased that he was attracting a great deal of attention. But although I detested him as a man I reveled in him as an author and read his big books several times, particularly his *Personal Recollections of Joan of Arc,* and the one which contains a description of the famous Indian mutiny, but whose title I have now forgotten.

I saw Bret Harte once during an afternoon reception at the American Embassy in London. I was standing near the door talking to Henry White, first secretary, when I noticed a small man walking slowly across a clearing in the middle of the room. "That is Bret Harte," said Mr. White. "Take a good look at him." And I did, with wide-eyed interest, for I loved his stories, and he owed his fame to my own California.

He was about sixty, very good-looking with dark hair and a heavy mustache, and only the word dapper, or perhaps elegant, could describe his person. His skin fitted him no more perfectly than his impeccably cut clothes. He lifted his small feet in their brilliant patent leather shoes as daintily as if conscious of their pointed perfection—and probably aware that many eyes were upon him. The ambassador, John Hay, an author himself, was hospitable to literary celebrities, but I remember no one but that dapper little man who should have looked rather absurd but did not.

Why I did not ask Mr. White to introduce me to him I forget, but I did not and so missed my one chance to meet him. Someone in America sent me a letter to him and I forwarded it immediately. I received a prompt and very charming answer—from Paris. He was on his way to the Riviera but hoped I would be in London when he returned. But I was not, and he died before I visited London again.

Ambrose Bierce came rarely to San Francisco, for he suffered from asthma and wore out one climate after another, dwelling more often than not in uncomfortable country hotels which had nothing to recommend them but the climate. He was the typical Yank in appearance—that is to say the Yank as portrayed on the stage—but he was tall, with a fine head, a genial smile and a portentous frown. In dress he was the reverse of Bret Harte.

For some reason he was worshiped by women, who pursued him from one retreat to another to burn incense at his shrine. I met him only twice and disliked him thoroughly, although I yielded to no one in my admiration of his work. His column, "Prattle," in the San Francisco *Examiner* (I believe he was the first of the columnists) was brilliant, scarifying, witty, bitter, humorous and utterly fearless. He was no respecter of persons and many of the "eminents" when honored by his notice in that column must have felt as if they were taking a long draft of gall and wormwood. We were always expecting to hear that he had been shot.

His reputation as a writer, unique in his generation, traveled far, and at one time he accepted an invitation to join the staff of a London newspaper and deserted California for four years. He was vastly popular in England, not only as a writer but socially, for he could be a great gentleman when he chose, and was a brilliant talker. But since there is probably no worse climate in the world for asthma than England's, he was obliged to return to this state of many climates, and here he remained until 1896 when he went to Washington, D. C., to fight, through the Hearst newspapers, the Funding Bill of the Central Pacific Railroad. As the climate agreed with him he remained as correspondent of the *Examiner* until 1913 when he left suddenly for Mexico and a mysterious death.

There was a report that President Wilson had sent him with a secret message to the Mexican President Huerta, that he had been forced to join the revolutionists in order to make his way to the capital and had either been killed in action or shot as a spy.

In 1920 when I was in Hollywood his daughter called and told me that in the last letter she received from him he had written that he was bound to be killed for any one of three reasons: he carried a thousand dollars in a belt; as he had no desire to kill anyone (he had killed many in the Civil War where he had distinguished himself) he fired over the heads of the enemy, and if this were noticed he would be stood against a wall and shot; or he would stop a bullet from the opposite ranks. Neither she nor anyone else ever heard from him again, so the reader may take his choice. Bierce was seventy-two when he left the United States for Mexico.

Besides his newspaper work Bierce published several volumes of war stories and horror yarns, the former surpassed by none I have ever read. He also published books of verse, fantasy and "fables" as notable for content as for style. But despite all his triumphs he was an embittered unhappy man. His wife treated him badly, and his son, in whom he took great pride, was shot to death in a disgraceful saloon row, an episode that was headlined in every newspaper in the state—a double blow, for he was a very proud man.

And he must have been a lonely one, living for the greater part of his life in country inns with no one to talk to except the foolish females who pursued him or some member of the *Examiner* staff who was recovering from a drunken spree.

Although I disliked Bierce when we met as much as he disliked me, oddly enough we had a long and amiable, even friendly correspondence. He wrote delightful letters in the most beautiful hand I have ever seen; I must have had dozens of them and would be treasuring them still, but alas, they were in a trunk in the Occidental Hotel at the time of the great fire and went the way of many other treasures.

Ina Donna Coolbrith, I am told—I am no critic of verse—was a real poet and Bierce lauded her in his column. There was even an Ina Coolbrith Society for study of her work that lasted for many years after her death.

She had another ambition, to write a history of California, and had collected a great quantity of valuable material when the fire of 1906 destroyed it. She lost everything else she possessed and was so impoverished that as soon as the city was rebuilt her friends and admirers devised several ways of making her independent. Her health was broken and she was no longer able to support herself as a librarian.

The Spinners Club brought out a handsome volume to which all the local literary lights contributed (it is a collector's item now) and it was published by Paul Elder at a high price.

There was also a benefit performance for her, an "Author's Reading," one night in the ballroom of the Fairmont Hotel, which was packed to the doors. Luther Burbank was not an author, but he was famous and I induced him to come down from Santa Rosa and read a paper. He arrived late and when his turn came he was discovered fast asleep at the back of the room. However, he read his piece and must have been gratified at the loud appreciation of his audience.

Joaquin Miller was the star performer. In top boots, lace tie, flowing white locks, and a long white beard, he recited his poem "Columbus" with such dramatic fire that when he finished the audience stood up and shouted.

Mr. James D. Phelan managed to get a law passed by the State Legislature conferring the title of Poet Laureate of California upon Ina Coolbrith, carrying with it a stipend of $1,200 a year. With the moneys raised by private contributions she was enabled to build two flats on Russian Hill, renting one and living in the other. A little money went a long way in those days, and she lived in comfort, enlivened by the constant attentions of her many friends, for the rest of her life.

I was told that she had been a beauty in her youth but she was old and ill when I met her, although her eyes were still bright and animated, often sparkling with humor, and she had a fascinating personality.

Emma Frances Dawson was another writer, of prose this time, whom Bierce praised with even more enthusiasm in "Prattle" as "this master of style and mystery." It was an enthusiasm I did not share and our correspondence was caustic at times. However, I respected his opinion and was willing to concede that he was a more experienced critic than I, so the next time I went to London I took *An Itinerant House* with me and offered it to several publishers. Unfortunately they agreed with me and once more Bierce was wroth.

But she was unique in one respect, not to say mysterious and provocative.

At one time I had an apartment in Washington Street. Opposite was a steep hill bare but for a dilapidated old streetcar on its side—the abode of Emma Frances Dawson! Many passers-by paused and gazed at that odd dwelling, hoping for a glimpse of the locally famous writer, but were never gratified. Nor was I, although I often sat at my front window filled with wonder and curiosity. There was no chimney, so she must have cooked on an oil stove. I never even saw a light after dark, for the windows were heavily curtained. When she did her marketing and took her exercise no one could even guess. Of course I could have obtained a note of introduction from Bierce and made a polite call, but I felt it would be an intrusion. If she desired privacy and seclusion that was her right. And no doubt if I had attempted to storm her fortress she would have refused to open the door.

Like so many of our literati Mary Austin was born elsewhere—in Carlinville, Illinois, but unlike many she was a college graduate. She won immediate recognition with her first book, *The Land of Little Rain,* a volume of short essays portraying the desert and its Indian tribes, and written with an exquisite simplicity and charm. Her deep and permanent interest was the American Indian, and she lectured on him all over the country, at universities, colleges and clubs, and established herself as a leading authority on the subject. She was a born essayist, but less successful with fiction.

She came to San Francisco early in her career and lived for a time on Russian Hill. Later she joined the literary colony at Carmel, where she did her writing up in a tree, and when her long hair became entangled with leaves and twigs the poet George Sterling, then at the meridian of his fame, would scramble up the trunk and liberate the tresses one by one. Carmel was a subject of frantic discussion for a number of years and she certainly contributed to its notoriety. But *The Flock* and other small volumes she conceived in that inspiring atmosphere were written with the same evidence of commanding intellect and delicate art.

Later she went to New York to live and there fell in with a group striving to become superintellectuals (which they were not) and lost her early simplicity and distinction of style. Nevertheless her intellect continued to develop and she wrote many valuable essays and articles for the more literary newspapers on other subjects besides the American Indian, and New York was as proud of her as California had been and still was. She was immensely flattered and run after. H. G. Wells praised her, and as she was but mortal her ego became somewhat inflated. "Of course," she said to me one day, "*I* am the greatest woman writer living." "The hell you are, Mary!" I replied. But she did not smile. There was no room in that massive intellect for humor.

After a time she moved to the literary colony at Taos and again wrote and lectured on the American Indian. Apparently in the best of health, she died suddenly in her sleep at the age of sixty. Every newspaper of consequence in the country gave her a grand send-off —which she richly deserved.

Kate Douglas Wiggin was born in Philadelphia and educated in Maine, but in 1873 she moved to Santa Barbara where she taught school until summoned to San Francisco five years later to establish the first free kindergarten in the West. She soon became an outstanding figure, not only for the brilliant success she made of her work, but because she was a great favorite socially. She was pretty, witty, charming and had a flair for dress.

Above all, her contacts with children and her deep sympathy for them inspired her to write certain little books, which like the well-known brook, bid fair to go on forever. *The Birds' Christmas Carol, Rebecca of Sunnybrook Farm,* and the *Penelope* series brought her a rapid and world-wide fame, and they were translated into many languages.

Her first husband was Samuel Bradley Wiggin (who looked like a large white frog), a clever lawyer and her equal intellectually. Several years after his death she married a really handsome and charming man, George C. Riggs of New York, but retained the pen name she had made famous, Kate Douglas Wiggin.

Riggs was a wealthy man and they lived in one of New York's handsomest duplex apartments; she had beautiful clothes, which she knew how to wear, for she had style, a tall slender figure and a fine carriage.

At that time there was a "Literary Set" in New York, quite as notable as Mrs. Astor's. Its hub was the ultra high-brow *Century Magazine,* edited by the poet, Richard Watson Gilder, who had married one of the fashionable DeKays. They established a salon and sought out the most cultivated and gifted men and women in New York. Others of the chosen followed their example, and salons finally expanded into that Literary Set, as exclusive as it was brilliant.

Of this set Kate Douglas Wiggin became the most popular member, for she was not only famous but amiable and fascinating and her wit and vivacity made her the shining light of any party.

I saw a good deal of her both in San Francisco and New York and never could make up my mind whether I liked her or not, nor was I ever certain that she liked me, despite her professions. She was full of little affectations, rather snobbish, and I had my doubts of her sincerity in general. I also disliked the way she swished her skirts. But I respected her for her accomplishment and for her gallant spirit: all her life, and despite her activities, she was a semi-invalid.

I often wondered what difference it would have made in her character—and possibly her health—if she had had children of her own. She must have loved children or with all her art she never could have written about them so enchantingly. She was a curious anomaly. If a complete stranger to both her and her work had been told that she was a famous author, he would have assumed that she was a writer of light, sparkling and highly sophisticated novels.

And she inspired a lasting affection in two fine men.

A contemporary and friend of Bierce, Charles Warren Stoddard in no wise resembled him save in a high order of mental capacity. A gentle, rather melancholy creature, he had a beautiful mind full of sympathy for unfortunate humanity, but he also had humor, a talent for good-fellowship and many interests. A poet by endowment and a writer of delicate prose, he traveled around the world from 1873 to 1878 as correspondent for the San Francisco *Chronicle*. At other times he was professor of English literature at the University of Notre Dame and the Catholic University of America.

But the greater part of his life he spent either in San Francisco or in the Hawaiian Islands where the lepers—of all things!—inspired some of his most beautiful prose. His published works include *In the Footprints of the Padres, The Island of Tranquil Delight, The Lepers of Molokai* (his most famous book) and a volume of poems, *South-Sea Idyls.*

He had a noble head and fine profile and would have been handsome if he had shaved off his bushy beard.

The untimely death of that gifted and versatile author, Sidney Coe Howard, was a loss to American letters and is still deeply lamented by his native state. Born in Oakland, California, on June

26, 1891, he was graduated from the University of California in 1915, and spent the following year at Harvard. During World War I he served with the American Ambulance Corps and was later a captain in the United States aviation service. From 1919 to 1922 he was on the editorial staff of the old *Life,* and in 1933 he was a feature-story writer for Hearst's *International Magazine.* But it was not long before he entered upon his distinguished career as a playwright. In 1921 *Swords* was produced. This was followed in rapid succession by *Bewitched* (in collaboration with Edward Sheldon), *They Knew What They Wanted* (Pulitzer Prize play for 1925), *Lucky Sam McCarver, Ned McCobb's Daughter, The Silver Cord, Alien Corn, The Late Christopher Bean,* and some thirteen others. He also translated and adapted plays from the Spanish, French, German and Hungarian. His screen adaptations were *Bulldog Drummond, Arrowsmith, Dodsworth, Gone with the Wind,* among others. He also published a volume of short stories.

In the full tide of his brilliant career he met with a violent death on August 23, 1939.

Frank Norris, that gifted disciple of Zola, was born in Chicago in 1870, came to San Francisco when he was fourteen and attended high school and the University of California.

Of course he lived on Russian Hill and there wrote most of his books. *McTeague* was the first to attract nationwide attention. It was a powerful but loathsome novel to read, but Dobie many years later made it into a thrilling play excellently acted by a company of amateurs, one of whom, George Skaff, should have adopted the stage as his career.

As everyone knows, his other two books that swept the country were *The Octopus* and *The Pit,* the first two volumes of an unfinished trilogy.

I never shared the enthusiasm for Frank Norris. He had talent, power, sincerity and was as merciless in his realism as he was fearless. But he was long-winded, discursive, melodramatic and often dull. He never mastered craftsmanship. No doubt if he had lived long enough, maturity would have corrected these faults and he would have attained first rank as a writer. But he literally wrote himself to death and tossed his obol to Charon at the age of thirty-two.

I never met Jack London and I do not know his books very well but he was outstanding in San Francisco. And so I consulted Mrs. Oliver Remick (Laura) Grant, leading authority on Jack London, about him and she wrote this appreciation of him for me.

Jack London will always be a challenging and controversial subject. He cannot be casually dismissed as wholly a product of his time and environment, though both contributed to his development. His brilliant, restless mind, his craving for dangerous adventure, his natural kindliness, his unselfishness, his faith in his fellow man, his generosity—these were not the result of environment or period. They were the real Jack London, a man of amazing contrasts, of inner conflicts, whose spectacular success kept him constantly in the ruthless spotlight of publicity, a man who plumbed the depths and scaled the heights of human experience but never lost his vision.

"I retain my belief in the nobility and excellence of the human. I believe that spiritual sweetness and unselfishness will conquer the gross gluttony of today, always before my eyes the Holy Grail, Christ's own Grail." This was his design for living.

He was born in San Francisco, California, January 12, 1876, with a background of substantial middle-class American forebears.

*Courtesy of Californians Inc.*

THE SAN FRANCISCO OPERA HOUSE

RHODODENDRONS IN GOLDEN GATE PARK

His family was poor; in his boyhood he knew the grueling toil of canning factory and jute mill; saw life along the Oakland water front in all its sordidness and caught rare glimpses of another world of gracious living. This early realization of cultural, social and economic inequalities humiliated him and he determined to level such differences.

He had a brilliant mind that drove him pitilessly, remarkable courage, boundless faith in himself. Though quick-tempered and extremely sensitive, his appealing boyishness and basic shyness easily won friends. He was of medium height and rather stocky build, with a magnificent head, a mass of golden-brown wavy hair, a sensitive mouth, firm chin and direct gray-blue eyes.

His struggles and almost phenomenal success are rich in drama: newsboy, factory hand, laborer, oyster pirate, member of the Fish Patrol, seaman, prospector, tramp, ardent Socialist, war correspondent, agriculturalist, humanitarian—all merged in the author, who before his twenty-eighth year was internationally recognized.

In sixteen years he wrote fifty books, among them eighteen of compiled short stories. Many have been translated into twenty languages and twenty-six Russian dialects and are being regularly published and filmed. His powerful stories of Alaska, among them the incomparable *The Call of the Wild,* long a classic, have placed him beside outstanding ethnologists. What Bret Harte did for California, Jack London did for Alaska in his unforgettable pictures of the primitive Northwest. Others, equally powerful, deal with the vital problems of his own time.

Criticized for his "disgusting realism," he says: "Life is full of disgusting realism. I know men and women as they are, millions of them still in the slime age, but my love for the human (in the slime though he be) comes from knowing him as he is and seeing the divine possibility ahead of him."

Jack London died on his ranch in "The Valley of the Moon" at Glen Ellen, California, November 22, 1916, in his forty-first year, during World War I, yet years before he predicted the chaos of today: Germany's plan for world domination, Japan's treachery, Russia's emergence from imperial bondage, the stabilizing roles of the United States and Great Britain.

Several writers have attempted his biography, but after years of study, I consider his widow Charmian's *The Book of Jack London* the most accurate and sincere. From it the film version of his life was recently made.

Bierce, Charles Warren Stoddard, Mencken, Robinson Jeffers and many others have proclaimed George Sterling a great poet. As I have remarked before, I am not a critic of poetry, so I am willing to take their word for it, although personally the word "great" is an adjective I hesitate to apply to anyone, whatever my enthusiasm. Has it ever occurred to our critics who apply that word so freely to authors and poets who command their admiration that there is no word greater than great? Is not that the final word for "Homer," Aeschylus, Sophocles, Euripides, Virgil, Shakespeare, Milton, Goethe, Dante? Wonderful, magnificent, stupendous and superb are weaklings beside those five letters that spell GREAT.

When an Oxford or a Harvard professor, let us say, is about to deliver a lecture on that immortal group, does he utter "We will now consider the nine greatest poets in all literature"; or would that pundit whose knowledge of words is as profound as his lore, substitute "tremendous," "magnificent," "wonderful"? The very thought would make him shudder. "Great" is the accepted, the ultimate word, and that is that, although other adjectives, more particularly "sublime," may be used incidentally.

Those great poets have stood the test of the centuries; a few more must pass on those that have coruscated since.

But to return to Sterling. Whether time will award him the laurel wreath or not, I am glad he was acclaimed as great during his lifetime, for, modest as he was, it must have given him many thrills of pleasure—although, since he had a sense of humor, I am willing to wager his mind rippled with laughter as he stood before the architrave of the Panama-Pacific Exposition and read those deeply carved lines of poetry signed Shakespeare, Milton, Sterling. But great or not, he was a serious poet and would have sacrificed life itself for his Muse.

Of his eighteen volumes thirteen were published by Alexander Robertson. There was no second edition: the demand for poetry was limited then as now, but, although the sales were confined to California, many of his poems were republished in Eastern magazines and newspapers, and in 1925 Henry Holt brought out a small volume of his shorter poems.

He was always poor, but money was the last thing he thought of—except when some other indigent writer asked for a loan, and then he either begged or borrowed to supply a need greater than his own. For many years he gave his services without remuneration to his friend, Miss Virginia Lee, editor of the *Overland Monthly,* and even induced such eminent poets as Robinson Jeffers and Edgar Lee Masters to write for it, to say nothing of a number of lesser poets and writers of fiction, now for the most part forgotten, but popular in their day.

If he had inherited a fortune he would have given it away, and he was no less prodigal of his time. Miss Lee relates that "he reviewed over six hundred volumes of poetry for an amazingly large group of tiny publications scattered over the country. He reviewed prose work for the newspapers, and just before his death a miscellaneous assortment of volumes for the *Overland Monthly*. He is the author of seventy-odd short stories and a tremendous amount of variously-sized prose sketches in the Carmel *Pine Cone* and the New York *Times*. Newspapers, menus, catalogues, fair bulletins, anthologies, pamphlets, magazines, book forewords, parades, public campaigns—he wrote everything from hymns to advertising. Every committee started in San Francisco wanted something from him to aid their cause. Friends with the autograph phobia, little poetry magazines, motion-picture magazines and druggist pamphlets—all extracted some contribution from the author of *Testimony of the Suns*."

An appalling waste of a poet's time! But it serves to emphasize his immense popularity and importance. He also had other demands upon his time. Women ran after him, and perhaps he loved too many. He was also extremely convivial, sometimes to the point of dissipation.

I met him several times at Montalvo, Mr. Phelan's country place. He was the ideal poet in appearance, tall, gracefully built, with a mop of dark hair that fell over his forehead (but properly cut), large gray eyes "that had an eternally burning softness," a beautifully curved mouth, which was generally smiling, but upon which I detected at times a fleeting expression of scorn.

But he observed none of the sartorial vagaries of the traditional poet. In fact he wore black broadcloth, well cut, well fitted, well pressed.

He was always gay and friendly in company and wholly without affectations or mannerisms, a delightful talker, and as popular with men as with women.

Life offered him a brimming cup and when he had drained it he found the dregs too bitter, and on November 18, 1926, he drank of another cup and was found writhing in death throes on his bed in the Bohemian Club. Genius oft carries a curse about its neck.

Whether time will give him a place among the immortals or not, his long dramatic poems are enchanting to read and it is to be hoped that one of these days, when the war god is amusing himself on another planet, some New York or Boston publisher will take over from Harry Robertson the copyrights of *Wine of Wizardry, The Testimony of the Suns, The House of Orchids* and *Lilith* and give them to another generation.

William Chambers Morrow, a handsome, accomplished and delightful gentleman, was one of the most popular writers of the short story in his day. He attended the College and the University of Alabama, but in early manhood, like many others, he succumbed to the lure of California and his stories were written in San Francisco. *The Ape, the Idiot and Other People* rivaled Bierce's most bloodcurdling efforts in horror.

He trained many young writers in the art of the short story while Director of Creative Writing in the Cora L. Williams Institute in Berkeley, but his friends were in San Francisco and he continued to live there until his death in 1923.

Like Bret Harte with his "Heathen Chinee," Edwin Markham woke up one morning in San Francisco to find himself famous. Published in a morning newspaper, "The Man with the Hoe" set the town ringing before noon. Travel was slow in 1899 but that hoe might have had wings, so swiftly did it travel over two continents—to be hailed as "the battle cry of the next thousand years."

Markham's early years in Oregon and California were not

poetical. He was farmer boy, blacksmith, cattle and sheepherder. Nevertheless, he managed to acquire an education, first at a public school, then at the State Normal School of San José (California), and specialized in ancient and modern literature. He also attended three Eastern colleges and won a Litt.D. from the University of New York.

After his return to California he was principal and superintendent of schools until 1899. All this time he was writing poetry, published in many Eastern magazines, but he was forty-seven before "The Man with the Hoe" won him universal recognition. After that it was all he could do to cope with the demands for more and more, and until his death in 1938 he wrote constantly for the leading magazines and newspapers and published eight volumes of poems, as well as a series of magazine articles on child labor, in book form entitled *The Children in Bondage.*

Cincinnatus Heine Miller (born in Wabash, Indiana, 1841) led a roving and turbulent life during his early manhood, but in 1863 he became owner and editor of the *Democratic Register* in Eugene, Oregon. It was during this period that he so warmly defended the Mexican bandit Joaquin Murietta that he was nicknamed "Joaquin," and liked it so well that he later adopted it as his pen name. The *Register* was suppressed by the United States Government during the Civil War because of his support of the Confederacy. For a time he practiced law and published several volumes of poems, *Songs of the Sierras* meeting with instant success. But he was still something of an outcast, not only because of Confederate sympathies but on account of his personal eccentricities, and he decided to try his luck in England. There he became the lion of the season. London was often unappreciative of Americans who were too much like themselves (or tried to be)—

but here was the real thing! A genuine product of the wild and woolly West, with his chaps and sombrero which he wore on all occasions, indoors and out, and always willing to delight them at any moment by reciting his poems with such dramatic effect that comedians of the theater trembled for their laurels. London set its seal upon Joaquin not only as "the greatest personality that had ever visited them" but a genius of the first order, and his poems outsold the "penny dreadfuls."

When he returned to the United States he settled in Oakland, California, and built himself a house which he named "The Hights" (his eccentricities including spelling).

As to the worth of his prolific pen I quote from a speech delivered by William A. Morgan on Treasure Island, during the Exposition there, on June 13, 1939. "This unique personality introduced beauty and daring into American literature. He did not subject his work to meticulous discipline either in thought or expression, but he was a great literary trail blazer. In some of his best efforts, as in his 'Columbus,' he reached great heights both in dramatic beauty and in verve of expression."

In 1898 he was elected a member of the National Institute of Arts and Letters. He died in 1913.

Born in Milwaukee, Charles (Augustus) Keeler was for several years an ardent traveler, visiting Alaska, Tahiti, New Zealand, Australia, Samoa and the Hawaiian Islands, but finally made his home in Berkeley where he wrote his many books and poems: *San Francisco and Thereabouts, San Francisco through Earthquake and Fire, The Victory, Sequoia Sonnets, An Epitome of Cosmic Religion.* He was the founder of the Cosmic Society, and director of the California Academy of Science. He made a world tour to read his poems before audiences in Japan, China, India and every capital in Europe. He married twice, his second wife being Omeida Curtis Harrison, who has been one of the most active members of the California Writers' Club.

Charles Caldwell Dobie died in 1943 and we are not yet resigned to his passing. He was only sixty-two and should have lived many years longer to add to the enjoyment not only of his readers but of his many and devoted friends. He was a gallant gentleman, a man of personal and intellectual integrity, and he was as popular socially for his keen brilliant mind, his humor and goodfellowship as he was with the reading public for his admirable stories and such valuable and enduring works as *San Francisco: A Pageant* and *San Francisco's Chinatown*.

In his early youth he was able to attend primary and grammar schools only, for his family was poor, and he was forced to earn. After several jobs he went into the insurance business.

But he was determined to educate himself and, consequently, read and studied the best in literature. It was not long before he felt the impulse to write and practiced assiduously the difficult art of the short story. He prowled about this cosmopolitan city and "discovered" the Italian colony, the Greeks herded in a small area south of Market Street, the Mexican and French groups, to say nothing of the long-renowned Chinatown.

For several years he met with only local recognition, but the day came when the all-powerful H. L. Mencken accepted one of his stories for the *Smart Set,* and shortly after he appeared in the pages of *Scribner's* and the *Atlantic Monthly.* After these initial triumphs it was almost impossible to meet the insistent demands from other publications. William Dean Howells praised him. Dobie was made.

He retired from the insurance business and entered into the

more congenial—and lucrative—partnership with his typewriter.

His stories received other recognitions. That exacting annual publication of Edward O'Brien, *The Best Short Stories,* included his more frequently than those of any other writer. He was invited twice in one year to contribute to Harper's *Prize Short Story Collections,* the only writer so honored. He received two awards from the discriminating Commonwealth Club of California for the best short story of the year.

How he managed to turn out such a mass of work and dine out every night excited the wonder, admiration and envy of other writers. During the summer he spent many week ends at Montalvo to the delight of that perfect host, Senator James D. Phelan, and the other guests.

In 1920 the only P.E.N. Center was in New York. I happened to be there during the winter of that year and received a message from John Galsworthy asking me to found a center in every state in the Union. That was a large order and I dismissed it, but wrote that I could promise him one in California.

When I returned to San Francisco I sent for Dobie, the most prominent of all the younger California writers. Full of energy, enterprise and ambition, he was never too busy for anything new and interesting. It was decided that I should be president and he secretary-treasurer, and together we made out a list of members, agreeing that it would be wise to be extremely exclusive. That would so infuriate the ignored that they would abuse it loudly and so make the P.E.N. the most famous club in California.

It was a success from the start. Fortunately, Mr. Phelan had published a book of travel and was eligible for membership. Through his influence we were able to hold our dinners in the Bohemian Club—and he paid for the cocktails until Dobie put a stop to it.

The Club gave us the use of two rooms, one for the dinner, and the Owl Room adjoining, with many comfortable chairs and a cheerful fire, where we could loaf afterward, split into groups and enjoy ourselves generally.

I made but one stipulation at the start: the women must wear formal evening gowns. I had attended several P.E.N. dinners in New York where some of the women had worn street clothes and hats and looked like frumps. Otherwise, Dobie did all the work with no interference from me. All I did was to preside at the dinners. After our first conference he admitted new members when he thought best. He also invited many distinguished guests who happened to be passing through the city. The dinners were pleasant reunions, sometimes brilliant, despite the fact—or because of it—there were no speeches.

There was only one flop. A distinguished New York poetess paid a brief visit to San Francisco and all her evenings were engaged before she arrived, but Dobie gave her a cocktail party—I believe at his own expense; I was in Europe at the time. It was a very large party. Besides our sixty members Dobie invited a number from the world of fashion who were delighted to do him honor. The hour was five. At half past four the poetess arrived and said she would like to take a nap. Dobie gallantly escorted her to the dressing room, which fortunately had a sofa, and posted a guard at the door. At five o'clock she sent for Dobie, informed him she had quite forgotten she had to catch a train and departed. That was probably the most brilliant cocktail party ever given in San Francisco. The guests enjoyed themselves immensely.

We gave six or seven dinners a year until 1940, when Dobie's health began to fail, and after that they became more and more infrequent. Finally, in order to keep the interest alive I gave cocktail parties in the house of my daughter, Mrs. Russell (with whom I live), and have continued the practice ever since, although sherry has taken the place of bourbon and Scotch for well-known reasons.

Dobie was the "family friend." For many years he had dined with us on Christmas, Thanksgiving and birthdays, and often between.

We miss him.

# CHAPTER SEVEN

# *Our Literati*

SOME of our luminaries have deserted us for the south: Dr. Sidney L. Gulick, Jr., associate professor of English at Mills College, in 1945 accepted a call to the San Diego State College; Dr. Lionel Stevenson, poet, author of *The Showman of Vanity Fair* (a biography of Thackeray) and now instructor of English in the University of California at Los Angeles, more recently president of the Los Angeles P.E.N.; Inglis Fletcher, who is growing more and more important with her historical novels of the Colonial South; and the unique Idwal Jones, who promises to return to us.

But we have plenty left. In this fertile soil they sprout overnight. It is possible to mention only a dozen or two—for the most part members of the P.E.N. I had intended to arrange them in alphabetical order to avoid any suspicion of favoritism, but there were so many "inserts" that I gave it up. Here they are.

Julia Cooley Altrocchi, although she spent most of her unmarried life in Chicago, was born in Seymour, Connecticut, under a family tree with many historic names decorating its branches: Cleveland, Hawthorne, Wooster, Willard, Wolcott, Kingsley, Chapin, Gardner, Trowbridge, Chatfield, Norton and Putnam. Inheriting the gift of poesy from her mother, she was "discovered" at the age of ten by Richard Le Gallienne, who wrote an introduction to *The Poems of a Child* and sent the manuscript to Harper's. It was accepted at once. In Chicago, where her father, Harlan Ward

Cooley, was an attorney and civic leader (Yale 1888), she attended the public grammar school and the University High School. In 1914 she was graduated from Vassar, and in 1920 married Rudolph Altrocchi (Harvard 1908), author of many scholarly articles for the *North American Review,* the *Nation* and other intellectual magazines, besides notable poems in *Poetry.* His verse has appeared in three anthologies. He is the editor of three textbooks, and in 1944 published (Harvard Press) the witty and scholarly *Sleuthing in the Stacks.* For many years he has been professor of Italian at the University of California.

Meanwhile, Mrs. Altrocchi in her Berkeley home continued to write poems and articles on European history and literature, which were published in *Yale Review,* the *Atlantic Monthly, Harper's Magazine,* the *Classical Journal, Poetry,* and in many anthologies. In 1936 she published *Snow Covered Wagons,* a narrative epic in blank verse that brought her national fame. It is the terrible story of the Donner party, immigrants on their way from the Midwest to the Promised Land, who were marooned in the Sierra Nevada Mountains and suffered such hardships as the human frame has rarely been called upon to endure. The snow was waist-deep, there was no vegetation; after their supplies were exhausted they ate the horses (there is a legend that they put Mrs. Donner in a pot and boiled her down for soup, but this incident Mrs. Altrocchi wisely omitted), and there was little left of the survivors but skin and bones when finally rescued. It is a story of unrelieved horror, yet, in Mrs. Altrocchi's rendering, somehow pervaded with beauty, a secret known only to a poet. It was awarded a medal for General Literature by the Commonwealth Club of California.

Her next book was a historical novel of the Midwest, *Wolves Against the Moon,* also highly dramatic and absorbing. It went through a number of editions both here and in England—where,

by the way, she was asked to drop her husband's name and sign
herself merely Julia Cooley—World War II was on and Italians
were unpopular. In 1937 she received the $100 Browning award
from the Western Writer's Guild in Los Angeles for a poem,
*Review of American Poetry*. In 1945 the Caxton Press published
her latest book, *Old California Trail: Traces in Folklore and Fur-
row*.

Besides writing, rearing two sons and entertaining the intellectuals, Mrs. Altrocchi has traveled throughout the nation lecturing
at universities, colleges and clubs on historical and literary subjects.
She is a member of the P.E.N., of the Poetry Society of America,
the Society of Midland Authors, the California Writers Club (of
which she has been president), the Town and Gown Club, and
the Berkeley Interracial Committee. She spends her summers at
"Singing Sands" in Harbert, Michigan.

The reader of this brief biographical sketch no doubt pictures
Mrs. Altrocchi as worn to the bone, nervous and irritable. She is
a beautiful woman with a tall commanding figure, sparkling dark
eyes, chestnut hair, a clear white complexion and an expression
of charming serenity. And as she dresses herself in lovely pastel
colors she is a highly ornamental figure at any gathering.

At a banquet given in honor of Professor Herbert Eugene
Bolton of the University of California, on December 28, 1945,
Edward J. Lynch, grand president of the Native Sons of the Golden
West, reminded the 200 guests that "forty years ago the lack of
assembled data on early California history prevented teaching of
the subject in schools," and that "today schools in every California
county give instruction on that subject. Professor Bolton was the
guiding spirit in the necessary research." Professor Paxton asserted
that the University of California's department of history, now out-

standing in the country, was built by Dr. Bolton and that although he was now professor emeritus, he was still regarded as "the livest of us all." President Sproul paid a handsome tribute to Dr. Bolton's scholarship and historical writings, which in 1932 won for him among many other honors the presidency of the American Historical Association.

Herbert Eugene Bolton was born in Wilton, Wisconsin, July 20, 1870. He was graduated from the University of Wisconsin (B.L.) in 1895, and he has subsequently received degrees (Ph.D., LL.D., Litt.D.) from the University of Pennsylvania, St. Mary's College and the Catholic University of California, the University of San Francisco, the University of Toronto, the University of Santiago de Chile, Marquette University, and the University of New Mexico. He taught history at the University of Texas and at Stanford and finally came to anchor in the University of California in 1911. He took time out to make extensive researches in the archives of Mexico, and in 1931 was traveling in Europe for the Native Sons of the Golden West and Del Amo Foundation. His honors and activities fill an entire column in *Who's Who in America,* and I refer the reader to that reliable authority for further information.

Professor Bolton has published sixteen volumes as learned as they are interesting; of these perhaps *Anza's California Expeditions* is the most widely known. For *Outposts of Empire* and *Rim of Christendom* he received gold medals from the Commonwealth Club of California (more precisely of San Francisco).

It should also be added that in 1924 he was decorated Comendador de la Real Orden de Isabella Católica by the King of Spain.

Until recently Royce Brier has been known chiefly for his column "This World Today" in the San Francisco *Chronicle,* although he had written three short novels, *Crusade, Reach for the Moon,* and *Boy in Blue,* the last a story of the Civil War and notable for a portrayal of the blind confusion of warfare that I, at least, have never received from any other novel on that overwritten subject. His column, however, overshadowed his fiction for a time. Unique, and brilliant in style, it would be remarkable alone for a profound knowledge of history that encircles the globe and ranges from Adam to Hitler. This knowledge, never obtrusive, gives his column a fascination and importance unequaled by any other column in the United States.

In 1943, however, he published *Last Boat from Beyrouth* and rose to a definite position among the young novelists of his time. It is a terrible story and a beautiful one; a story of the horrors of war and the passionate intensity of love between a man and a woman whose fate it was to find and know each other on a doomed ship that steamed out of Beyrouth a week too late to escape Mussolini's "stab in the back."

I raced through this entrancing novel, but guessing that I was missing many subtleties I read it over again at once, determined to capture those subtleties as well as take more time to enjoy the masterly prose. It remains in my mind as the most fascinating novel of World War II. His latest book is *Western World, A Study of the Forces Shaping Our Time,* a work as profound as it is important. Anyone who begins it will read to the end whether he understands it or not, for this author has the Magic Touch.

Royce Brier was born in Wisconsin in 1894, the son of an eminent educator. He did not take kindly to formal pedagogics but enjoyed reading history and was able to gratify his taste in his father's extensive library. While in college he discovered he had the rotten spot in the brain that turns out fiction, and wrote stories of the desert and South Seas for *Adventure.* Later he was ill for several

years, but during a voyage around the world, while his love of
history waxed, his health was restored, and he decided to adopt
California and took a job on the San Francisco *Chronicle*. In 1934
he won the Pulitzer Prize for his reporting of a peculiarly sensational and abominable kidnaping and lynching case. Then he spent
another year in Europe as well as the Near East, studying the symp-
toms of the impending war, and preparing himself to write a page-
one interpretative column for the *Chronicle*. This column has now
run for nine years and the immediate admiration and interest
it commanded have never slackened.

Brier is very good-looking, with regular features, hair as black
as an Indian's, and looks no more than thirty-eight or forty. He
has a winning personality and, it may be added, is a spick-and-
span dresser. His wife is also handsome and charming. They live
in their own house in San Anselmo with their little girl twins.

William Martin Camp is a young man of tremendous energy.
At one time he was night city editor of the *Chronicle,* instructor
of journalism at the University of California, and was writing two
books at the same time. He wisely retired from journalism in
1944, devoting his energies to his class and his books until he
joined the Marines.

He looks a mere boy, but one must gather from his record that
he is somewhere in his thirties; we are told that up to date he has
had sixteen years of newspaper experience—in China, Honolulu,
Washington, D. C., as well as in San Francisco. He was in the
Orient in 1932 and witnessed the bombing of Shanghai from a
roof top. When he returned to the United States he did his best
to convince men in authority of the eventual designs of Japan on
the peace of the world, but like Senator Phelan and Homer Lea
before him he met with no success. While in Washington and

working on the *Star*, later on the *Times*, he attended Washington College of Law during his spare time, receiving his LL.B. in 1938.

His first novel, *Retreat, Hell!* published in 1943, is a dynamic performance, with hair-raising details of the war in the Philippines after the incident at Pearl Harbor, and raw enough to please the admirers of Hemingway. But it is a valuable piece of history, and written with such flaming credibility and knowledge of every inch of Bataan that it is difficult to believe it was not a personal experience.

*Retreat, Hell!* is a man's book—there is no "love interest"—but it went through three printings and its quality was recognized by the discriminating both here and in Britain, where it appeared in a wartime edition.

His latest novel is *Skip to My Lou,* a tale of people of the Ozarks in California.

The San Francisco P.E.N. is very proud of Dr. Joseph Catton. In fact it prides itself on his membership, for he has a nationwide reputation as a psychiatrist, and he seems to give an added touch of drama to the most sensational cases. As a matter of fact he barely escaped being an actor.

He was born in New Haven, Connecticut, on March 10, 1890, but he is a true San Franciscan, for his family moved there when he was seventeen years old. Six years later he had completed his academic and college course and was practicing medicine before his twenty-third year. But in grammar, high school and university ("Cal"), some part of that active and precocious mind was always on the theater. He took part in many productions in the Greek Theatre at Berkeley. Debating and public speaking also became a part of his activities for they gave another outlet to his dramatic cravings.

And why did he not become an actor? Well, he was still very young and had been taught obedience by strong-minded and intelligent parents. They were determined that he should become a doctor, and had visions of his being a celebrated diagnostician, with a hospital of his own. So he finished his course in medicine at the university and received his Bachelor of Science degree as well as Doctor of Medicine—but no general practitioner for him! He had his own way on this point and specialized in psychiatry, which with its relationships to education, literature, delinquency and crime, made an irresistible appeal both to his intellect and his love of drama. Neurologist, psychiatrist, alienist, in a short time he won his reputation and was called in on the most important cases. Here are a few of them: Dorothy Ellington (matricide), Winnie Ruth Judd (trunk murders), William Edward Hickman (kidnaper, slayer), Irene Mansfelt, musician and society matron, who obeyed the unwritten law.

And all these and many others have given outlet to that undying urge for drama. When he makes his appearances in court, he, not the defendant, is the notable figure. It is as impossible for the actor in him to refrain from giving a performance as not to give conscientious and memorable testimony. Sometimes he explodes at both judge and jury, then apologizes handsomely and is gladly forgiven. Needless to relate, his gift of oratory and debate causes him to be in heavy demand for public addresses of all sorts and kinds.

In laying out his life work he included among many other things: "Write at fifty." He felt that the satisfaction of this urge should await maturity, although through the years many scientific articles flowed from his pen, written for the most part on demand. But it was not until 1938 that he said to himself, You are making a more or less successful appeal to the public through the ear, why not through the eye?

So he went to work on his famous book *Behind the Scenes of Murder,* and published it two days before his fiftieth birthday. Like himself it lost no time in achieving success. It was an alternate selection of the Book-of-the-Month Club, it sold all over the country—and still sells—and had notable reviews. The *Journal of the American Medical Association* pronounced it "an important contribution to modern scientific criminology, and at the same time one of the most interesting works that have been developed in its field." But with all the laudations the doctor confesses that the one he liked best was the *New Yorker's* "Fascinating stuff."

He has now in preparation a book on sex and a novel. He hopes gradually to cut down his practice and find the time to place between book covers the story of some thirty-five years of experience with the mind and mood of man. It is safe to predict all his books will be best sellers.

Dr. Catton has a beautiful, intelligent and companionable wife, and as she is almost as tall as he is they make a striking couple at any gathering. They have six children.

That writer of beautiful prose and poetry, Stanton Coblentz, was born in San Francisco on August 24, 1896. His father lost his business in the disaster of 1906 and moved with his family to Stockton, where young Stanton attended the high school. In 1913 some of his verses won for him a trip to Yosemite Valley in a state-wide competition. He entered the University of California in the same year where he took a prelegal course. In 1919, after studying law for two years, he renounced the legal profession in order to enter upon his career as a writer. Hardly had he made this decision when a four-line poem won him a twenty-five-dollar prize in a contest conducted by the San Francisco *Chronicle,* and as a result of this stroke of fortune he was invited to write book reviews for the *Argonaut,* which helped him to pay his expenses while studying for his master's degree. He also wrote daily feature poems for the *Examiner.* In 1920 he left for New York where he remained for eighteen years as a free-lance writer, among other activities interviewing for *Success Magazine* such personages as Einstein, Tagore, Chesterton, Philip Gibbs and many others. He reviewed books of every type, from cookbooks to psychological treatises, for the New York dailies, the *Bookman,* and other magazines. He gradually veered toward writing books himself, turning out everything from a sociological treatise, *The Decline of Man* (1925), to *Villains and Vigilantes* (now regarded as a valuable contribution to Californiana), and a juvenile, *The Wonder Stick,* which, much to his surprise, was accepted not only by a publisher but by the Junior Literary Guild. In addition to writing books of his own and editing three anthologies of poetry, he has been editor since 1933 of *Wings,* which he founded and has ever since managed as a labor of love.

Finally the pull of California was too strong to be resisted any longer and he returned to his native state, where he lives most appropriately in a redwood grove under the shadow of Mount Tamalpais. There he wrote *When the Birds Fly South,* the story of a young American geologist lost in the mountains of Afghanistan. Not only has this remarkable book a high fiction value but the style, rich and chromatic, is a poet's prose (*not* "poetical prose"), and the descriptions, wild, varied and magnificent, are unsurpassed by any I have ever read. There is no doubt in my mind that *When the Birds Fly South* will survive as a classic.

He too has a handsome and charming wife, and they take daily tramps through the woods and over the hills.

We all know that Life gives with one hand and takes with the other, and one of the most noteworthy exemplifications of this truism is Alice (Nourse) Tisdale Hobart. Well born, well educated, uncommonly bright, with intelligent and understanding parents, she suffered a lumbar injury in early youth that left her a semi-invalid for life. After three attempts she renounced her ambition for a college degree and lived a quiet life, part of the time in a luxurious home on the edge of the prairie not far from Chicago. Her only companions were her parents, her brother Edwin and her elder sister Mary. When their mother died Mr. Nourse took her place as well as a man could and life went on at the same even pace. There were carefully selected books to read; her father was a fine musician and a master of the art of conversation. And during all that time—with its many idle hours—there was not a stirring of the gift planted among her otherwise active brain cells that was to make her one of the most brilliant and original novelists of her time.

It was during her freshman year at college that her father died suddenly, and the pleasant home life was over. Edwin went out into the world to seek his fortune, and Mary accepted a position as a teacher in Hangchow. After her two final attempts at a collegiate education Alice went to China in 1908 to live with her sister.

And it was there that her drowsy imagination woke up, shocked into active life by the staggering contrast between the prairies of the Middle West and the aged East with "its raw color, smells, swarms of un-understandable, unpredictable people. The soft green of southern China, the hard red-brown of the North, the scrolled architecture of the Imperial City. The East of the trade routes and the camel caravans, of ships and dark water fronts, and seas whose place names come to the tongue as pungently as the taste of spice. The East that made Conrad, remembering it, cry out for youth, golden and glorious. This was the country to set on fire a daughter of clipper-ship captains [to say nothing of an ancestress who had been burned as a witch], a girl whose imagination had been lying fallow in the flatlands of the Middle West."

But fiction was still dormant. She began to write little essays and descriptive letters to her friends at home. And then she had another and still more exciting experience. She fell in love and in 1914 married Earle Tisdale Hobart.

Mr. Hobart worked for an American oil company. "There was no end to the territory he covered, no spot too remote to send one of the young men. Earle and Alice Hobart would live for a time in a frontier village until a job there was done and then move on to another, establishing in each place a temporary home. They traveled any way they could, sometimes by mule cart, sometimes by junk. Once in a while, fresh from some town in the interior, where they had been the only white people, they would be sent down to one of the big cities where they could have a few weeks of luxury and a flurry of parties and gaiety." In quick succession they lived in a Chinese palace, a warehouse, a vacated sing-song house, an English terrace house, a thatch-roofed, half-Chinese, half-white-man's house, a junk turned into a houseboat.

A fine life for a semi-invalid! How she survived what would have tried the constitution of a healthy woman one may only imagine. Alice Hobart not only survived but in 1922 managed to write a tale, *By the City of the Long Sand*.

"In 1927 came what the newspapers called the Nanking Incident. Earle Hobart had become manager for the company, and they lived in the great house that stood high above the Yangtze on Socony Hill. China was more than usually torn by civil war, racked by

famine and poverty. Nationalism became a watchword and a uni-
fying cry. The expulsion of the foreigners who owned the treaty
ports was demanded. The danger grew.

"Open violence broke out. The foreign powers had warships in
the river below the Hobarts' house. On the land side Chinese
soldiers massed. All the foreigners who could get there took
refuge with the Hobarts. The Chinese opened fire. A siege
began. . . .

"Finally the attack came. The Chinese soldiers rushed the house.
When the little foreign community barricaded in the house saw
they were to be wiped out they signaled the American warship for
help and a barrage was put down around the hill where they were
imprisoned. The soldiers drew back long enough for the foreigners
to knot sheets together and slide down the city wall and so escape
to the boats."

It was a shattering experience. All of their possessions were
swept away, with the exception of a manuscript saved by a devoted
houseboy. Their job was gone too. After a year in France and Germany they came to anchor in Washington, D. C., where Mr. Hobart
became an employee of the Federal Farm Board.

And there it was that Mrs. Hobart wrote *Oil for the Lamps of
China,* a book that swept the country, was translated into many
foreign languages and made a powerful moving picture. Then
Mrs. Hobart's sorely tried body rebelled and she had a long spell of
illness that included the dread arthritis. But nothing daunted her.
During her convalescence she began work on *Yang and Yin,* and
as this demanded firsthand knowledge of the new China, and as her
husband's business would not permit him to leave, she went alone
and once more endured incredible hardships. Once more she survived and returned to her husband, now established in California
as secretary of the Berkeley Bank for Co-operatives, a government

institution. She finished *Yang and Yin,* a mystically beautiful novel. *Their Own Country* followed with but a moderate success, and it was not until they bought an almond ranch in the lovely area of Mount Diablo that she had another inspiration, and triumph that equaled *Oil for the Lamps of China,* and *Yang and Yin.* *The Cup and the Sword* is a story of the vineyards and the disparate races that live in the valleys of Napa and Sonoma. It seemed to her that all the races of the world had settled in those California valleys. "They had brought with them their own cultures and their own ideals of beauty." A profoundly interesting study for a mind ever on the alert for new impressions, and gifted with sympathy and understanding. And in her own romantic and beautiful valley she found not only happiness in her new book but quiet, peace, and rest for her tired body. And she had the unruffled companionship of her husband—for five years. In December 1941 that phase of her life was over. Mr. Hobart offered his knowledge of the Orient to the Army and was sent to the Far East. This time Alice Hobart, who had gone with him to the wildest corners of Mongolia and Manchuria, had to stay behind. It was the second time they had been separated in twenty-five years of marriage.

"She turned again to hard work as an anodyne. To the south lay Mexico, an old country of conflicting races. There, as in China, foreign corporations—American, British, German—were building up an economic empire. And there, as in China, the life of the people was dislocated and profoundly altered; strong forces had been let loose to drive out the economic invader. In Mexico she could go on with her study of the Latin temperament begun in *The Cup and the Sword.* The country attracted her. Alone, she went there to travel and live, and learn the feel of the country."

After her long experience in China there was little she did not know about the ways of corporations and the lives and minds of businessmen, and Mexico with its romantic background, its dying aristocracy and its modern aspirations made a powerful appeal to her imagination. *The Peacock Sheds His Tail* was the result, a novel as valuable as it is'fascinating, the finest as well as the most important novel of Mexico that has been written. Its success was immediate and sensational.

At the war's end Mr. Hobart, now treasurer of his bank, bought a house in Oakland, and there they expect to live for the rest of their lives.

Mrs. Hobart still spends three hours a day on her back (writing all the time) but I never saw anyone look less like an invalid. It may be added that she has a tall handsome husband, and they certainly make a striking couple.

Hildegarde Hawthorne is just about the most active person physically or mentally I have ever known. I doubt if she herself remembers how many times she has crossed the Atlantic Ocean and, when not writing, has tramped all down the English coast of Cornwall to Land's End, climbed the Welsh and Scottish hills, the mountains of Switzerland, or practically covered France on foot.

In 1918, however, she went to France for another purpose. At Selles-sur-Cher, near a large cantonment, she took charge of a place where men could come and relax, read, write letters, play a piano, and refresh themselves with coffee and sandwiches—to say nothing of her lively companionship.

During the ten years she lived in California she took long hikes every August in the Sierra Nevada Mountains, even more formidable than those in Switzerland. Her home was in Berkeley and when her long hours of work were over she went for a tramp in the hills. Once she met a wildcat, but nothing daunts her. When she was living in New York or Connecticut she spent the summers in Colorado where she climbed mountains either on foot or horse; she is as fond of riding as walking. She mentions superfluously that her hobby is the out-of-doors, and she loves swimming and sailing a boat.

She married John Oskison, a Stanford man and editor of *Collier's Magazine,* and the marriage lasted a dozen years.

She has written some thirty books, many of them involving research in libraries, and with all her physical activities they bear not the slightest evidence of fatigue or haste. Their style, if sprightly, is both balanced and smooth.

She began her long career by writing book reviews for the New York *Times* and *Tribune,* poems and articles for *Saint Nicholas, Harper's* and other magazines, but it was not long before she found herself writing serious books for young people. I believe that her first was *Romantic Rebel,* a biography of her grandfather, Nathaniel Hawthorne, which was taken by the Junior Literary Guild. Other books of the same nature (and all of which have a permanent sale) are *Rising Thunder* (Jack Jouett), *Youth's Captain* (Emerson), *Poet of Craigie House* (Longfellow), *The Happy Autocrat* (Holmes), *Concord's Happy Rebel* (Thoreau), *Phantom King* (Napoleon's son), and *The Long Adventure,* one of the most fascinating and valuable biographies of that greatest of modern statesmen, Winston Churchill, for readers of any age. And these are but a few.

Her most important books for adults to date are *Romantic Cities of California, California's Missions, Williamsburg, Old and New,* all illustrated by Suydam. They are standard works and brought out in a format that adds to the dignity and importance of any private library.

And all of these I have mentioned and many more were written between 1934 and 1945!

I am happy to say they were also written in Berkeley, California. I have known Hildegarde for something like thirty years and during that time her thin brown face has remained unchanged, and so has her thin wiry body. Needless to say, in society she is always the liveliest person present, and I have never seen her show the slightest trace of fatigue nor even languor. I infer that she sleeps at night.

Oscar Lewis, author of *The Big Four,* served a long apprenticeship before he reached his present eminence. Born in San Francisco in 1893, the son of a popular architect who, he admits, was responsible for many of the horrors in the Western Addition, he was suddenly plunged from affluence into what is politely known as reduced circumstances, during the depression of the 1890's. The family moved to a ranch in Sonoma, where he attended a country school, thence to Berkeley where he continued his education in the public high school. It was during his senior year that he amused himself by writing a story which he sent to a favorite boys' magazine. For this he received a check for fifteen dollars, and was so elated when, upon presenting it at the bank, he beheld three five-dollar bills all his own, that he adopted the career of author then and there. During the next five years he wrote 500 boys' stories which were published in practically all the juvenile magazines and Sunday-school journals in the country. He also tried his hand at writing stories for adults but found no harbor except in the now defunct *Smart Set,* which accepted some fifteen or twenty of them. Then came World War I and he served for two years in the Army. When he returned to Berkeley he abandoned fiction for articles which by 1922 had enabled him to save enough money for a trip to Europe and North Africa. During this period he wrote travel and political articles that appeared in the *Outlook,* the *Independent,* the New York *Times,* the *Christian Science Monitor,* the Kansas City *Star* and other newspapers and magazines.

When he returned to California he continued to free-lance, writing both fiction and nonfiction for *Harper's Magazine, Scribner's* and the *New Republic,* and fiction for the pulp magazines. California history had begun to interest him and he mapped out a story about an imaginary railroad king who had built one of those mansions on Nob Hill that would have horrified even his father.

And then it was that he became so interested in those railroad monarchs and their mighty enterprises that he abandoned the novel and wrote the book which, first published in part in the *Atlantic Monthly* under the title "Men Against Mountains," then in book form as *The Big Four,* had an immediate and nationwide success and established him firmly in the top rank of nonfiction writers; not only had he something new to tell the public, but owing to his long apprenticeship with fiction, he knew every device of attack and presentation, in other words how to interest as well as inform. *The Big Four* won him a medal from the Commonwealth Club.

In the following year, 1939, he published in collaboration with Carroll D. Hall (curator of Sutter's Fort, who collected the material) *Bonanza Inn,* a lively and fascinating story of the old Palace Hotel, once the most famous hotel in the world. Its success was equally sensational.

Then he remembered his discarded novel and went to work on *I Remember Christine,* which, despite certain faults in craftsmanship, is the best novel yet published of the Bonanza kings who perched themselves on Nob Hill in the 1870's. For this he was rewarded by the gold medal from the Commonwealth Club.

At present he is engaged in gathering material for another nonfiction book on lives of the four men who made their colossal fortunes in the Nevada silver mines—Mackay, Fair, Flood and

O'Brian—a companion volume to *The Big Four*. His latest novel is *The Uncertain Journey*.

Besides the four books that have given him so enviable a reputation, he also wrote a history of San Francisco for a subscription house in Chicago, *Hearn and His Biographers, The Origin of the Celebrated Jumping Frog of Calaveras County* and *Lola Montez in California*. He was secretary of the Book Club of California for many years, and is now a member of the San Francisco Art Commission. In 1925 he took time out to marry an extremely clever and attractive girl, Betty Mooney.

Quite a full life—no? as the Spanish say.

In 1941 one of the most striking and popular books of the season was *Storm*. It took a powerful imagination to write an entire book about the adventures of a storm wind, but Professor George R. Stewart accomplished the feat. Those who read the condensation in the *Reader's Digest* hastened to buy the original; they wanted more. It was a Book-of-the-Month Club choice. He also wrote an authoritative account of the Donner party in *Ordeal by Hunger; East of the Giants,* a story of Old California; *Doctor's Oral;* a biography of Bret Harte; and recently *Names on the Land,* a historical approach to place names in the United States.

He was born in Sewickley, Pennsylvania, in 1895; was graduated from Princeton in 1917; got his master's degree at the University of California in 1920, his Ph.D. at Columbia in 1922. He taught English at the University of California in 1920, at Columbia in 1921, at the University of Michigan in 1922-1923, returning to the University of California where he has remained ever since, although he has taught during the summer season both at Duke and Michigan Universities. In 1942-1943 he deserted "Cal" for the time being to be Resident Fellow in Creative Writing at Princeton, which is quite an honor in academic circles. He served in World War I, and has won both a silver and a gold medal from the Commonwealth Club. He married Theodosia Burton whose father had been president both of Smith College and the University of Michigan, and has two children.

Needless to relate, he lives in Berkeley.

Idwal Jones is a baffling author to write about. He occupies a solitary niche in letters, for he belongs to no school either of thought or fiction. When I read one of his novels, deeply interested in the story as I am, I have the impression that somewhere in the depths there is another story moving like a slow undercurrent, mystic and haunting, and never to be fathomed. Perhaps one should be content with the dissimilarity of his creative faculty, his melodious prose and a vocabulary surpassed by no modern writer. It is said that Shakespeare had a vocabulary of 16,000 words. I would be willing to bet that Idwal Jones has 16,400. A woman once said to me plaintively that she had just read one of his book reviews and been greatly impressed with it but that she intended to read it over again with the help of a dictionary!

Like many another writer who has reached the heights, he began life as a newspaperman, writing book reviews for the San Francisco *Chronicle*. Thence he went to the *News* as critic of music and drama. His next move was to the *Examiner* where he took on the double job of columnist and dramatic editor. Meanwhile, he had married Miss Olive Vere Wolf, who had been a teacher in Hawaii and at Miss Burke's fashionable school for girls in San Francisco. They were active members in the Bohemia of the 1920's and 1930's and kept open house once a fortnight in their "aerie" at the corner of Hyde and Greenwich Streets overlooking the Bay.

He has a tremendous capacity for work. Besides his regular newspaper chore he wrote some 200 articles on California geology, folklore, characters, history, mining and viticulture, to say nothing of traveling in Europe and devoting no little time to the study of metaphysics, theology and Dantean literature. One wonders when he found time to write his novels and stories, but he has published nine works of fiction, and they are outstanding.

His first, *The Splendid Shilling,* is a picaresque tale of a gypsy in the California Gold Rush days; *Steel Chips* is a deep study of life in an engineering works and the impact of the machine philosophy on the mind and soul of men engaged in routine work. The critic James Oppenheim asserted that "the background is as good as that of Faust," and it was the only novel he included in his "The Plight of the Poet in the Machine Age." *Whistlers' Van,* a tale for the young of gypsies in Wales, still goes on and on as all captivating books for children do and was a Junior Literary Guild Selection.

*China Boy and Other Stories* appeared first in the *American Mercury,* and the title story has been reprinted in various anthologies. Mencken wrote of it, among other comments, "It took the humblest thing in creation, an old Chinaman in a dead mining camp, and made him a symbol of the spirit triumphant against the world." The two Japanese tales in this book, "Miss Mori" and "A Party at Mr. K. Nagoya's" (the latter a study in atmosphere of San Francisco), are required reading in certain schools.

*Black Bayou,* on its surface is a boy-and-girl romance in the swamps of Louisiana, but the real protagonist of the tale is "the active-contemplative philosophy of St. Theresa de Avila, with the thesis of the superiority of the balanced faculties as the true key to the life of the spirit in a world of turmoil and evil." It is a

THE GIFFEN-HUMPHREYS HOUSE

LAGOON AT FISHERMEN'S WHARF

profound book all right and bears out what I said about haunting undercurrents.

*The Vineyard,* so far, is his masterpiece, as it is the classic story of the extensive grape industry in northern California, for, when one finishes this book, there is nothing he does not know about every variety of grape, how to select and cultivate it, the process of converting it into wine—in short, a complete course in viticulture.

Nevertheless, even here, the story is the thing. The heroine puzzled me, for she gave the impression of being two women in one: a quiet competent woman who managed her large vineyard in a manner that compelled the admiration of her masculine rivals—and yet was somewhere else at the same time. I was not surprised therefore when Mr. Jones told me that the woman he had in mind was the Lady Julian of Norwich, the fourteenth-century anchoress and mystic. Also, that his object in writing *The Vineyard* was to give a full emanation of California, to make the region apperceptive to all the senses of the reader. The vine is symbolic, being Nature, the link between man and the infinite.

He certainly did get down to brass tacks, but this triumph of symbolism is little more remarkable than the fact that he spent exactly one whole day in Napa Valley—the scene of his vineyard—several years before he wrote the book! And yet the picture of that beautiful valley is as complete in every detail as if he had spent his life there. "But," says he, "I just sat on a log and looked hard and long at the scene." Well! He is Idwal Jones. Nothing more to be said.

He is working now on *Vermillion,* a tale of a California quicksilver mine which might be the once famous New Almaden but is not. It is the story of the decay of a great mine and the hierarchical family that owned it, its theme the continuity of life. *High*

*Bonnet,* a fling at humor and serious fantasy, is an autobiography of
a high priest of the French cuisine, his arduous toils, exaltations,
his discipline and aesthetics—yet all struck off lightly. Mr. Jones
is nothing if not various. He is now contemplating a history of
California during the Mission era and a novel of San Francisco
in the plush-and-ormolu days of the 1870's.

He calls himself a conservative, a rigid medievalist. Critics have
called him a genius.

For fifteen years Joseph Henry Jackson has been literary editor
of the San Francisco *Chronicle,* and he wields a mighty power over
the immediate destinies of authors and books. His daily reviews
on the editorial page of the *Chronicle,* and his leader in the Sunday supplement, "This World," are so thoughtfully balanced, so
caustic at times, so hearty in their praise at other times, that his
wide public either hastens to bookstores and libraries or dismisses
the unfortunate victim with a shrug. For eighteen years he also
reviewed once a week over the radio and reached an even greater
public. The only fault I have to find with him is that he is sometimes carried away by the prose of certain short-story writers who
are all style and no content; stories that in the unfascinated evoke
a vision of an exquisite Paris gown floating about, with no bones,
no guts inside of it. But all critics have their little weaknesses, and
sometimes forget that no book in which style and content are not
evenly balanced is worthy to be called literature.

Of late years Mr. Jackson has won another reputation—several,
to be exact. He has written introductions to books by Stewart
Edward White, John Steinbeck, Ambrose Bierce, Ben Lucien Bur-
man, and others. He has also contributed articles to the *Yale
Review,* the *Saturday Review of Literature,* the New York *Herald
Tribune* "Books," and other publications of the same status.

But his lasting reputation will derive from his own books. After a motor trip through Mexico with his wife he wrote *Mexican Interlude,* a travel book so lively and fascinating, so filled with the *joie de vivre,* that others hastened to follow his trail. After this came *Notes on a Drum, Tintypes in Gold,* and then his opus, *Anybody's Gold.* This large volume of 445 pages is the most comprehensive and important book that has yet been written about the old mining towns of California. From Mariposa in the south to Weaverville in the north he gives the history of every town of the Mother Lode, born of the Gold Rush of '49 and after. And these pages include all the personalities, legends and anecdotes of that exciting period of California history, to say nothing of scenery. It is a book that required enormous research and many months of travel and interviewing the sons or grandsons of those old pioneers. In consequence *Anybody's Gold* is one of the most valuable "items" of Californiana that we possess. Quite naturally it won the gold medal from the Commonwealth Club.

His book *Continent's End* is an anthology of the more recent of the many California writers, with four exceptions, and has already gone into Braille. His latest anthology is *The Portable Murder Book.*

"The World of Books," literary section of the San Francisco *Chronicle,* was the 1945 winners of the Publishers' Ad Club award for the best book page of the year. The section was chosen for "its scope in coverage of books, its professional make-up, and its excellent editorial direction in the choice of books reviewed and in the quality of the reviewers." The judges were the literary editors of the New York *Times,* the New York *Herald Tribune,* and the Chicago *Sun* "Book Week."

In his own way, Mr. Jackson is as good-looking as his wife. He has a pale patrician face, rather aloof and haughty at times, but he can thaw when he feels like it and is the most genial of hosts. His pretty, clever daughter Marion is a pupil at Smith.

For fourteen years after her marriage Charlotte Jackson was known as the stunningly handsome wife of Joseph Henry Jackson, a young matron with a brilliant mind, a vivid personality, whose gowns and hats were as smart as they were becoming to her dark Italian type. She was born in the Mother Lode (Big Oak Flat) country.

But she is no longer merely Mrs. Jackson; she is now known to the reading world as Charlotte Jackson, for she has published a number of children's stories and has a reputation of her own.

She had taught kindergarten in her girlhood and when she went to Guatemala in 1936-1937 she visited the kindergartens there and became so interested in all she saw and heard of the youngsters that she was later inspired to write a story about them.

She had a little girl of her own, who like all bright children outgrew the toy age early and buried her nose in storybooks. When she had exhausted these and demanded more, Mrs. Jackson found herself "making up" stories, and these Marion liked so much better that it was then Mrs. Jackson wrote and rewrote *Tito, the Pig of Guatemala* to see how it would look on paper. Finally she summoned up courage to send it to a publisher, who accepted it promptly. It had an immediate success and ever-widening popularity. The story was not only dramatic and original, but with her personal knowledge of the scene she could give it the descriptive authority of a historic background. Any grownup may learn something from this book and find it lively reading as well. Her latest book is *Around the Afternoon.*

Her other books, *Sarah Deborah's Day, Roger and the Fishes,* have met with the same enthusiastic reception. Charlotte Jackson has a long future before her, and with her gift for characterization and drama may capture another public one of these days with a novel or a play.

One of the best sellers of 1941, and greatly admired by the most intelligent of our many "publics," was *Sir Richard Burton's Wife,* written by Jean Burton, a collateral descendant of the author of *The Anatomy of Melancholy,* to whose family Sir Richard was also related.

I was living in London in the early 1890's when Lady Burton's life of her dour, erratic, reprehensible but gifted husband was published, and I read it with both interest and curiosity, for the purely personal reason that I had recently seen a portrait of him in one of the galleries and wondered how any woman could have had the courage to marry him. That was a long while ago, but, as I recall that book, the author was a woman of original ideas (for her time), a forceful personality and almost as erratic as her husband. It had nothing of the sparkle, verve and brilliance of Miss Burton's remarkable performance, possibly because the one was Victorian *au fond,* the other a product of the Age of Speed. Miss Burton also makes her heroine a good deal more interesting than she made herself. Indeed, it is not too much to say that Lady Burton's biographer understood her far better than she understood herself. *Sir Richard Burton's Wife* is a book to buy for one's own library, and experience a pleasant sense of possession.

Her other books, *Elisabet Ney* (with Jan Fortune) and *Heyday of a Wizard* are equally fine, but the subjects less important. Her most recent work, *Garibaldi,* a book for young people, deals with an exciting subject and no doubt will be vastly popular with another public.

Jean Burton was born in Abernethy, Saskatchewan, of British

parents. She was educated at St. Alban's College, University of British Columbia (B.A.), and at the University of Alberta (M.A.). For several years after her graduation she was on the editorial staff of the *Canadian Mercury* of Montreal, and of the *New Frontier* of Toronto. Before writing her opus she contributed to Canadian magazines.

The reason she is included in "Our Literati" is because she is now not only an American citizen but lives in the San Francisco Bay Area—in Berkeley, to be exact.

Burlingame is not in the Bay Area but, after all, it is a *faubourg* of San Francisco, and I am proud to include its most illustrious resident, Stewart Edward White.

His own favorites of the thirty-five books he has published are *The Long Rifle, Ranchero, Folded Hills, Stampede, Gold, The Gray Dawn* and *The Rose Dawn,* samples of each era in California, so to speak. Other books are *The Unobstructed Universe,* and his latest opus, *Stars Are Still There.*

I once read an article in the *Revue des Deux Mondes,* which could not say enough in his praise. *The Gray Dawn* it pronounced the greatest of all the novels that had come out of California. I was jealous for a time, but got over it.

Mr. White is not only a novelist of the first rank but a mighty hunter. He was in Africa for fourteen months in 1910-1911, paid a second visit in 1913 and a third in 1925. Escorted by savages he penetrated country hitherto unexplored by any white man, and not only brought down all the varieties of African big game but during his second visit made prismatic compass sketch maps of the terrain. As this was in a German colony he was fortunate in departing just before the outbreak of World War I. If he had been detected making maps he would have written no more books. As it was, those maps were of considerable value to the British.

He was explorer as well as hunter, and he was interested in natural history, but this did not interfere with his ardor in tracking down big game and laying it low. He certainly had no reason to complain of the elusiveness of game: in one day alone he saw 300,000 wild animals—which seems to me a more formidable experience than running across a few Germans.

Mr. White is a member of the P.E.N. and of the American Academy of Arts and Letters.

In 1934 San Francisco was startled by the immediate success of a biography of Sutter, written by a mere infant, one Julian Dana, heretofore unknown, for he was still in his twenties. Dobie lost no time in "corralling" him for the P.E.N., and Joseph Henry Jackson interviewed him on the radio, an honor extended to few. He became personally popular as well as famous, for he was a good-looking, engaging youngster, modest but poised, and possessed a keen sense of humor. We learned that before venturing into the ambitious realm of biography he had worked on a newspaper, the best possible training for any writer; nothing serves the tyro like a city editor's blue pencil.

One reason for the success of *Sutter of California* was its informality. To be sure, some of the critics panned it for that reason, but others did not and the public took to "a biography that read like a novel." Whatever its youthful imperfections and divergences from the normal, he made Sutter come alive, for he not only had that particular gift but he had devoted many months of conscientious research in the Bancroft Library of the University of California.

Other books followed: *Gods Who Die,* a novel of the South Seas; *The Man Who Built San Francisco* (Ralston) ; another novel, *Lost*

*Springtime; The Sacramento* (Rivers of America Series) ; *Giant of the West* (the banker Giannini), as yet unpublished.

For the Giannini book he traveled 50,000 miles by air, visited forty-seven states, had interviews with everyone from J. P. Morgan and Jesse Jones to F.D.R. and local bank janitors. Julian is nothing if not thorough, but occasionally he takes a rest and travels up and down the state lecturing at women's clubs. As may be surmised, he is very popular with the ladies.

For a long time he did his writing in a cabin high in the Sierra Nevada Mountains with a bulldog and a cat for sole company. His diversions are hiking, fishing, golf and tennis.

Mary Collins, a brilliant member of the northern group, has won a wide reputation as a writer of unusual mystery stories: *Fog Comes, Dead Center, Sister of Cain,* etc., but no doubt will graduate before long into a full-fledged novelist. She has imagination, as distinct from invention, a remarkable flair for character psychology, style and magnetism. And atmosphere. The scene of action of *Sister of Cain* is that weird old Humphrey-Giffen house on Chestnut Street, and the sinister atmosphere she caught in such perfection that the book drove many readers to loiter past it and enjoy a renewal of those shudders beloved by the mystery fans.

In 1944 Mary had a baby, and that form of creation drives the loftier faculty into a remote brain cell and padlocks the door— and that padlock has to be wrenched open and the poor dormant "creative faculty" dragged out, coaxed, petted, implored, scolded, abjectly apologized to, before it finally condescends to pour its light through the upper story and get back on the job.

Mary is lovely to look at. She is tall and slender, has charming manners and knows how to dress.

I am not in the habit of reading books for children, but Katherine Wigmore Eyre having married into the Atherton clan, I felt obliged to read at least one chapter of the book—her first—that she sent me, intending to write her a polite note without betraying my lack of interest.

I read *Lottie's Valentine* from cover to cover. I fancy any grownup would find it as interesting as I did. Kay is a born writer. There is not a trace of the amateur in her work. She has a graceful, fluent style and the craftsmanship of an old hand. *Lottie's Valentine* had an immediate success, to be repeated by *Susan's Safe Harbor* and *Spurs for Antonia*. The last, aside from its absorbing story, gives an authentic picture of ranch life in the California of today. And it won her a medal from the Commonwealth Club.

Born in Los Angeles of one of the few old American families of that once Spanish-Mexican city, she married Dean Atherton Eyre and came to San Francisco to live—although she spends the summer months on her husband's ranch. She has two children, and certainly they have both educated and inspired her.

Esther Birdsall Darling, author of that famous book, *Baldy of Nome,* has lived a remarkably interesting life. Although her father's business interests were in Nevada he made his home in Sacramento, and lived in the house where Sibyl Sanderson, San Francisco's own prima donna, spent her childhood.

Esther attended the public school, graduated from Mills College in Oakland, and then for several years traveled with her parents in Europe, the Orient, the Hawaiian Islands and Mexico. Mr. Birdsall, who had interests in California's Placer County, came to the conclusion that it had the same soil as Italy and planted a tract of land—"Aeolia Heights"—with olive trees. Then he took his family once more to Italy. There he visited oil mills at Lucca and studied olive-growing conditions in that region. After returning to California he built a mill on the Heights.

His expectations were fufilled. "And there," relates Mrs. Darling, "among the silvery gray-green leaves, one looked on one side toward the snow-covered Sierras, and on the other across the Sacramento Valley to the distant Coast Range."

She met Charles Edward Darling in San Francisco during the upheaval of 1906 and married him in the following year. And then life changed in more ways than one. For ten years the Sacramento Valley was but a fond memory. Her new home was in the bleak and faraway hamlet of Nome, where her husband had been president of a mercantile company since 1900.

Nome had a population of between 3,000 and 4,000 in summer when the huge dredges were in operation, less than 2,500 in winter. From the middle of October until the following June they were iced in by the great floes that drifted down from the Arctic Ocean and extended to Siberia 140 miles to the west. Their mail during that shut-in period came by dog team from Valdez, the nearest open port, a distance of over 1,000 miles.

Nevertheless, she thoroughly enjoyed those ten years in Nome. Her interest was aroused by the remarkable dogs of that God-forsaken region, and she became a partner in the kennels of A. A. (Scotty) Allan, secretary of her husband's company. They entered teams year after year in the All Alaska Sweepstakes, a race sponsored by the Nome Kennel Club. The course was 408 miles across long stretches of unbroken snows, often run through raging blizzards, and in a temperature of from 40 to 50 degrees below zero—rather a test of endurance for both men and dogs!

Mrs. Darling writes of it with enthusiasm as the most democratic sporting event in the world: lawyers, doctors, miners, mechanics, men of all occupations were owners and drivers of the teams in the contest. One of the successful rivals of the Darling-Allan team was the Hon. Charles Fox-Maule Ramsey, younger brother of the Earl of Dalhousie and brother-in-law of Princess Patricia of Connaught, while others were longshoremen, pick-and-shovel men, prospectors, whose good dogs and whose skill in handling them were traditional throughout the north. In 1916 over a hundred Nome sled dogs were taken to France to serve in the transportation division of the French Army of the Vosges where the deep winter snows made transportation too difficult for men, horses and mules. The use of these dogs had been suggested to his superiors by Captain René Haas, a mining engineer who had driven dog teams in Alaska and knew their capabilities. He came 10,000 miles for the Nome dogs, who, with others from Labrador and Canada, were awarded the Croix de Guerre for their valuable services with the Alpine Chasseurs. Captain Haas sent the cross to Mrs. Darling as he had used twenty-eight sons and grandsons of her old racing leader, Baldy of Nome, in the daring event that won the decoration.

"I had never done any writing up to that time," writes Mrs. Darling, "but there was a dramatic story fairly laid in my lap. At first my idea was merely to write a *Main Street* of dogdom, using ordinary sled dogs as characters, but Baldy and his associates became heroes in spite of their modest start as workers; there was not a pedigree in the entire kennel. It was their records and accomplishments that I used in the other stories that followed *Baldy of Nome.*

"In two novels, *Breakup* and *No Boundary Line,* I tried to recreate the social life of Nome, where previous experiences, gained elsewhere in any other places in the world, had to be discarded as not fitting the fantastic conditions there. It was a tabloid cosmopolis. One met such famous explorers as Amundsen, Stefansson, Sir Hubert Wilkins, soldiers of fortune, scientists, high Army officials on tours of inspection, gamblers, bartenders, college graduates, and they were all on the same social level.

"I look back upon my ten years in Alaska as the most colorful and exciting period of my life. Leaving there in 1918 we settled in Berkeley, where my husband died in 1923, and where I still continue to live. A far cry indeed from the vivid adventurous life in a frontier mining camp in the Arctic."

Besides the three books mentioned Mrs. Darling's other published works are *Navarre of the North; Luck of the Trail; Boris, Grandson of Baldy; Up in Alaska* (verse) and many short stories and articles.

Clifford Franklin Gessler has a multiplex reputation: lecturer, critic, traveler, schoolteacher, student of Polynesia, journalist— and poet. I must dismiss this last accomplishment with the assurance that his poems are held in high esteem by those who know, and that his collected works include prize poems which won awards from the Beulah May Sea Poems Contest, the *Gypsy* Annual Awards, the *Poetry World* Contest, and the Poetry Society of America. For my own part, all I can say is that I read the poems in *Tropic Earth* with pleasure, and one line—"The hours reel off the golden spool of time"—struck me so forcibly that I may, with his permission, use the last five words as the title for a novel, unless someone else snatches it first.

Mr. Gessler was born and educated in Wisconsin (M.A., University of Wisconsin, 1917). While working on the Chicago *Daily News* he found time to take a lively interest in the Chicago Group of Poets, and also married Margaret Hull, pianist, a young lady so handsome and charming that when he introduced her to Carl Sandburg that eminent critic, editor and poet could only gasp, "Cliff, you *are* a good picker!"

But his stay in the Noisy City was brief. In 1921 he was offered the position of night editor on the Honolulu *Advertiser,* and being of a roving disposition, he accepted. Two years later he moved to the Honolulu *Star-Bulletin* to act as news and arts and letters editor, and this more congenial position he held for ten years. During that period he became interested in Hawaiian and Polynesian lore generally, and accompanied an expedition of the Bishop Museum to southeastern Polynesia, studying the life and mentality of the people, particularly those of the Tuamotu Islands. Learning to speak Polynesian and having what must have been a natural sympathy with that strange race, he became so interested in its life and thought that this experience has given a unique character to much of his verse.

In 1935 the young couple transferred themselves and their interests to Berkeley, California, a cultural center they find so congenial and stimulating that they intend to make it their permanent home. He is now associated with the Oakland *Tribune.*

Among his numerous and varied publications are *Kanaka Moon* (poems); *Road My Body Goes,* the English edition of which was called *The Dangerous Islands,* a narrative of life in the Polynesian Islands; *Hawaii, Isles of Enchantment; Pattern of Mexico* (illustrated by Suydam); *The Leaning Wind* (narrative of the expedition with the Bishop Museum party); *Tropic Landfall: The Port of Honolulu; Tropic Earth;* and other volumes of poems.


Really, the gods have been too kind to Dr. George D. Lyman. It is hardly fair. Listen to this record.

He is the handsomest man in San Francisco (and that means something, for San Francisco has always been notable for its handsome men and beautiful women). He is very tall, gracefully built and has snow-white hair above regular features and dark eyes full of humor, kindliness and intelligence. When he enters a room all heads turn; nor have the passing years affected his looks in the slightest degree. As Ruth Comfort Mitchell once said, "He trims up a room."

The only thing we have against him is he was born in Nevada (1882), but as he long since adopted California we have forgiven that oversight. He received his medical education at Bellevue Hospital and at Columbia University (College of Physicians and Surgeons); then took a postgraduate course at the Universities of Munich, Berlin and Vienna in his chosen field of pediatrics. When there was nothing left for him to learn in pediatrics save by experience he settled in San Francisco and soon built up an immense practice as the city's leading "baby doctor."

He is on the visiting staff of Stanford University Hospital and St. Mary's, the Shriners' Hospital for Crippled Children; chief of staff of St. Luke's Hospital in San Francisco; director of Friends of Huntington Library in Morino; Fellow of the American Academy of Pediatrics; member of the American and California State Medical Associations and of the California Academy of Medicine; member of Sigma Alpha Epsilon, Omega Club (College of Physicians and Surgeons); president of the California Historical Society, 1943-1945.

*And*—he is the author of *John Marsh, Pioneer; Saga of the Comstock Lode* (for which he received the gold medal of the Commonwealth Club); and *Ralston's Ring,* three books so powerful, informative and fascinating that they sat down squarely in the front row of American nonfiction. (Of course he has written a number of medical books also.)

He is the owner of a large private library of western Americana.

Need I add that he has a handsome and charming wife and two lovely daughters? That he is a popular member of the Bohemian Club, the San Francisco center of the P.E.N., the Menlo Park Country Club—and somehow manages to find time for a happy family life and social diversions?

What more could a man ask? Truly, he seems to be a prime favorite on Olympus.

Virginia Rath, born in Colusa County, California, one of the "cow counties" of the Sacramento Valley, began her education in the country schools and was graduated from the University of California in 1925. For a time she taught school in Portola, "a rough-and-tough wide-open railroad town," at the head of the Feather River Cañon. She had intended to save her money and go to Europe, but a year and a half later married Carl Rath, a railroad telegrapher, and remained in Portola for five years.

She began collecting rejection slips from magazines before she was sixteen, but after she stopped teaching, her first mystery story was accepted by one of the pulps, and in 1935 the Crime Club published her first novel, *Death at Dagton's Folly.* As her talent was definitely for the mystery or crime story she renounced her ambition to write a "serious novel," and *Murder on the Day of Judgment; Ferryman, Take Him Across; Anger of the Bells; An Excellent Night for Murder* (all with a mountain background) established her as one of the most popular writers in that genre.

Then she invented a *"couturier*-detective," Michael Dundas, for *The Dark Cavalier,* and she has clung to him ever since.

Mrs. Rath now lives on Russian Hill, the scene of her later books, and she knows every terrace, lane, alley, odd old mansion and steep flight of steps on that rocky outpost. Odd as it may seem, she and her rival, Mary Collins, are the best of friends.

Professor Arthur Gilchrist Brodeur, the distinguished author of *The Pageant of Civilization* (popular history) and the novel *The Altar of the Legion* (in collaboration with Farnham Bishop), was born at Franklin, Massachusetts, September 18, 1888, and left Harvard in 1916 with the degrees A.B., M.A. and Ph.D. And yet despite these honors his devouring ambition was to be a gentleman-farmer and specialize in poultry! He wrote romances for *Adventure* and other pulp magazines and was even more passionately devoted to music, his favorite composers being Gluck, Mozart, Beethoven, and Sullivan. It would be difficult, I fancy, to name a more variform and catholic mind!

In addition to the above he translated *The Prose Edda* from the Old Norse (American-Scandinavian Foundation) and other works that have appeared in the *American-Scandinavian Review,* as well as many technical professional articles, published by the University of California Press and professional journals. And with it all he has been a highly esteemed Professor of English in the University of California since 1916—and manages to raise poultry in Berkeley. He finds time for fishing, and is proud of having "the finest collection of friends in existence." They must be as varied as his tastes, diversions and abilities!

Mrs. Margaret Harrison is a member of the P.E.N. by virtue of her fine book, *Captain of the Andes.* And as a traveler and explorer she knows Mexico, Argentina, Peru, Chile, and other Latin-

American states almost as well as she knows her native Berkeley
—another member of whom we are very proud.

During the '90's San Francisco was enlivened by three brilliant
young writers, William and Wallace Irwin (born in Oneida, New
York, but graduates of Stanford), and Gelett Burgess. All three
have long lists of books to their credit in *Who's Who,* but Will is
best remembered in San Francisco for *The City That Was,* which
in April 1906 he dashed off in four hours for the New York *Sun*
(it was afterward published in book form and is now a collectors'
item). He also wrote (in collaboration with Gelett Burgess) two
books of linked stories—*The Picaroons* (San Francisco) and *The
Reign of Queen Isyl* (San José fiesta). Wallace Irwin is known
for *The Love Sonnets of a Hoodlum* and *The Rubaiyat of Omar
Khayyam, Jr.* Inez Haynes Irwin, Will Irwin's novelist wife, first
visited San Francisco in the 1910's and fell in love with it; the
result was her witty little book, *The Californiacs,* which had an
immense sale.

Of the four Gelett Burgess has had the most interesting career.
Born in Boston in 1868, he received the degree of S.B. from the
Massachusetts Institute of Technology, then came to San Francisco,
worked as draftsman for the Southern Pacific Railway, and
taught topographical drawing at the University of California,
1891-1894. His first appearance in the literary field was as assistant editor of the *Wave,* a weekly publication where he was associated with John O'Hara Cosgrave, Will Irwin and Frank Norris,
whom he succeeded when that still famous author retired to write
*McTeague.*

Then Burgess founded the *Lark,* and immediately the whole
country was ringing with a nonsense verse that appeared in the
first number:

I never Saw a Purple Cow;
I never Hope to See One;
But I can Tell you, Anyhow,
I'd rather See than Be one.*

A thousand or more newspapers copied it, and it is still unforgotten. It has given its name to tearooms, restaurants, a college magazine or two, an Army fighting plane and an ice-cream machine.

The *Lark* was printed on bamboo paper whose stenciled edges, when the sheets were dampened for printing, streaked the pages with red and yellow. Although it always carried a serious poem, an essay and a fiction story, it was in its very atmosphere youthful and gay; it was irresponsible and spontaneous and depended for interest upon neither timeliness nor local color. It was unlike any other magazine ever written before or since. Gelett Burgess' associates on the little magazine—which published twenty-four numbers and an Epilark—were (off and on) nine active youngsters known as *Les Jeunes:* Bruce Porter, Porter Garnett, Yoné Noguchi, Ernest Peixotto, Herbert Van Vlack, Willis Polk (who afterward made a great reputation as an architect), Florence Lundborg, Carolyn Wells, Juliet Wilbor Tompkins.

In the last number of the *Lark* Burgess burst into a bitter protest:

Ah, yes, I Wrote the "Purple Cow"—
I'm sorry, now, I Wrote it!
But I can Tell you, Anyhow,
I'll Kill you if you Quote it.

But it was no use and there were many parodies. One night (after he and the Irwins had basely deserted San Francisco for New

---

* Quoted from *The Burgess Nonsense Book* (New York: Frederic A. Stokes Company), by permission of the author.

York) Sidney Porter (O. Henry), while making an omelet for his guests chanted:

> I Never Beat a Rotten Egg,
>   I Never hope to Beat One,
> But I can Tell you, Anyhow,
>   I'd rather Beat than Eat One.

Theodore Roosevelt went so far as to shout "Purple Cow" whenever he met the unfortunate author. President Wilson publicly quoted it. F.D.R., whose birthday fell on the same day as Gelett's, once wrote him, "I gladly leave to others the merits of the forty-year-old controversy over the relative advantages of visibility and being in the bovine manner of speaking, and offer as a slogan: Long live the Purple Cow!"

There is no doubt his kind wishes will be realized—and Burgess has written thirty-odd books, among them the popular *Goops,* and reconverted the word "bromide" into an equally popular substitute for platitude and cliché. In 1907 his novel *The Heart Line* was concerned with some of the many charlatans and fake spiritualistic mediums of San Francisco.

But he wrote something else which has further endeared him to San Francisco. He immortalized the cable cars in "The Ballad of the Hyde Street Grip," which Edgar M. Kahn quoted as a foreword in his admirable book, *"Cable Car Days in San Francisco."* It should be quoted in every book on San Francisco, so here it is again.

> Oh, the rain is slanting sharply, and the Norther's blowing cold;
> When the cable's strands are loosened she is nasty hard to hold!
> There's little time for sitting down, and little chance for gab,

For the bumper guards the crossing, and you'd best be keeping
    tab,
Two-and-twenty "let-go's" every double trip—
It takes a lot of doing, on the Hyde Street Grip!

Throw her off at Powell Street, let her go at Post,
Watch her well at Geary and at Sutter when you coast!
Easy at the Power House, have a care at Clay,
Sacramento, Washington, Jackson—all the way!
Drop your rope at Union—never make a slip—
The lever keeps you busy, on the Hyde Street Grip!

Foot-brake, wheel-brake, slot-brake and gong,
You'd better keep 'em busy or you'll soon be going wrong!
Rush her on the crossings, catch her on the rise,
Easy round the corners when the dust is in your eyes—
And the bell will always stop you if you hit her up a clip;
You are apt to earn your wages on the Hyde Street Grip!

North Beach to Tenderloin, over Russian Hill,
The grades are something giddy, and the curves are fit to kill!
All the way to Market Street, clanging up the slope,
Down upon the other side, clinging to the rope!
But the view of San Francisco, as you take the lurching dip!
There is plenty of excitement on the Hyde Street Grip!

If you had to drive a penny bus from Chelsea to the Strand
You'd see Westminster Abbey, and you'd say that it was grand!
If you had to pass the Luxembourg and Place de la Concorde
Atop a Paris omnibus, no doubt you'd thank the Lord!
But the Frenchy'd give his chapeau and the cockney give his
    whip
For a sight of San Francisco from the Hyde Street Grip!

Oh, the lights are in the Mission and the ships are on the Bay,
And Tamalpais is looming from the Gate, across the way;
The Presidio trees are waving, and the hills are growing brown,
And the driving fog is harried from the ocean to the town!

How the pulleys slap and rattle! How the cables hum and
   skip!
Oh, they sing a gallant chorus to the Hyde Street Grip!

When the Orpheum is closing and the crowds are on the way,
The conductor's punch is ringing and the dummy's light and
   gay;
But the wait upon the switch above the beach is dark and
   still—
Just the swashing of the surges on the shore below the Mill;
And the Flash from Angel Island breaks across the Channel rip
As the hush of midnight falls upon the Hyde Street Grip!*

Harold Lamb was born in Alpine, New Jersey, and attended
Columbia University and the Pulitzer School of Journalism. Besides
his B.A. degree he also received from Columbia the H. C. Bunner
medal. His other awards include a Guggenheim Fellowship in
1929, a decoration from the Persian Government for scientific research in 1932, and twice the silver medal of the Commonwealth
Club of San Francisco. Among his many books are *Genghis Khan*
(1927), *The Crusades* (1930), and, recently, *Alexander of Mace-
don*. For years he was a frequent visitor in the clubs and byways of
San Francisco.

During the 1920's Lawrence Rising, Peter B. Kyne, Ednah
Aiken, Frederick O'Brien and B. H. Lehman, professor of English
at the University of California, wrote a number of good novels
and it looked as if they had come to stay. But either their interest
or their inspiration gave out, for they have not been heard from
since.

Two young writers, Kathleen Winsor and Margaret Parton, have
recently illuminated the literary horizon with *Forever Amber* and

---

* Published in *A Gage of Youth* (Boston: Small, Maynard and Company).

*Laughter on the Hill,* but whether they will live in memory as comets or planets remains to be seen. The untimely death of Linnie Marsh Wolfe, biographer of John Muir, cut short a promising career.

The living poets of this area are Sidney Coblentz, Marie de L. Welch, Josephine Miles, Muriel Rukeyser and Clifford Gessler, besides others I have already mentioned.

---

As this book goes to press two California novelists, Kathleen Norris and William Saroyan, have become residents of San Francisco.

# CHAPTER EIGHT

# Some of Our Best Citizens

ONCE upon a time I lived in England and knew many people in many different "sets": literary, fashionable, middle-class, political, frivolous, academic, and humble villagers. I had an immense curiosity about England and was determined to know it from apex to base. In looking back over that long experience—which included many visits at later periods—I cannot recall that I ever heard anyone use the word Jew. And I met many Jews. They were as much a part of the social order as of the body politic. (There was even a statue of Disraeli in Westminster Abbey.) I thought nothing of it at the time, but a good deal in later years when I was older, still more observing, and opportunities were still more varied.

I have lived in or visited many lands, as well as many American cities—and the only parallel I have ever found to this differentia in England is in San Francisco. In other centers of civilization, particularly in the great cities of the United States, there may be two or three prominent Jewish families whose names are listed in the Social Register, but the majority, no matter how wealthy and accomplished, herd together to form a distinct and separate group.

I hope I may be forgiven if I quote a few lines from a novel of mine, *The Horn of Life:* "San Francisco has always prided herself on having the finest class of Jews of any city in the United States. They are, and always have been, highly educated, traveled, dignified, elegant, public-spirited and of outstanding ability; eminent at the bar, on the bench, in finance, in business, in all the profes-

151

sions. They and their wives are active in charities, generous patrons of music, art, literature, education, lectures. San Francisco attracted only the best, she told herself proudly. The women patronize the fashionable dressmakers in San Francisco, New York, Paris. Their children attend the exclusive private schools. And although they are clannish and form an inner group of their own, they are welcome members of the 'best society.' Their dwellings are as handsome as any, both in San Francisco and Burlingame, but without ostentation."

I may add, for the benefit of those who care about that particular "angle," that their names are on practically every page of the Social Register.

To quote a Jewish friend of mind who prefers to be nameless: "Ever since San Francisco has existed, its citizens, Protestants, Catholics and Jews, have worked together in harmony. There is no activity in which these groups, be they educational, cultural or philanthropic, are not fairly represented. They are on the boards of universities and colleges, the San Francisco Opera Association, the San Francisco Musical Association, the Community Chest. This is as it should be, but alas, is not so in most of our large American cities, where lines of cleavage are more sharply drawn."

My friend was not exaggerating when she said that Jews were intimately associated with other groups even while San Francisco was still in its youth. One of its noblest, most enterprising Jews, and the first to make a national reputation, was Louis Sloss. Born in Bavaria, orphaned early, obliged to make his own way, he migrated to the United States in early manhood, and for some unknown reason settled in a small town in Kentucky. He did not remain there long, however; when gold was discovered in California he joined the stampede. The "diggings" held no lure for him and he founded a mercantile house in Sacramento, "Louis Sloss

and Company." His partners, Lewis Gerstle and Simon Green-
wald, were equally enterprising and the firm prospered, but after
the great flood of 1861 it was moved to San Francisco, now a full-
grown city if still a small one.

The business flourished, but the interests and energies of Louis
Sloss were not confined to money-making. With the true spirit of
the pioneer he was concerned with the welfare and advancement
of the ambitious young city. He was one of the founders of the
still important Society of Pioneers and served as president in 1884
and 1885; and the future and prestige of that society owed much
to his wisdom and foresight. (Here I make a personal and purely
feminine contribution to the career of Louis Sloss in San Francisco.
He must have been a handsome and attractive man for when I
was a child I used to hear the women raving over him!)

In 1867 he transferred his pioneering activities to a new field
(although he never lost his interest in San Francisco). After the
purchase of Alaska by the United States, and while the rest of the
country was sneering at "Seward's Folly," he saw the possibilities
of that vast region which others regarded merely as a bleak and
barren waste, and inspiring a number of his friends—John Parrott, William Kohl, Gustav Niebaum, John F. Miller, among
others—with his enthusiasm, organized the Alaska Commercial
Company to engage in the fur trade.

The company through Mr. Sloss's personal efforts secured a lease
of the Pribilof Islands for twenty years from the United States
Government, and later he went to St. Petersburg and obtained a
lease of the Komandorskie Islands off the Siberian coast. Both
of these groups abounded in seals whose skins made a fortune for
the great Alaskan Commercial Company.

Anything sponsored by Louis Sloss charged ahead with typhonic
speed. Trading ports and stores were established at various points

and an extensive trade in furs and merchandise was quickly developed. There were other activities of shipping and of extensive fisheries, and when the seals were exhausted (or had cannily moved elsewhere) there grew up a larger business in exploitation and trading after the discovery of gold along the Yukon River and its tributaries. When the gold seekers trooped in, the company established stores and depots over a region covering thousands of miles, and built and operated many vessels.

When the famous career of Louis Sloss had run its course the following tribute appeared in a San Francisco newspaper: "A noble, kind, and gentle soul was called from earth when Louis Sloss passed away. He envied the possessions of no man; he saw the wealth of the waste places of the earth and went forth to take some of it. He was a pioneer in California, Nevada, Siberia and Alaska, and, better than William Penn, he traded with the Indians without cheating them. We sincerely trust that his life will influence the lives of all the young men in California. If Louis Sloss had been in great haste to make money, and to get it had done mean things in his early life, his declining years would not have been blest with the happiness and serenity that are God's greatest and best gifts to man."

When in 1931 the Society of California Pioneers inaugurated a series of ceremonies in commemoration of the character and achievements of the men who laid the foundations upon which the great Commonwealth of California has been built and did so much to aid in its development, their first "salute" was to Louis Sloss.

Marcus C. Sloss, the youngest son of Louis, is today one of the predominant members of the San Francisco Bar. He started in life with every advantage; born of an illustrious and wealthy family, a graduate of Harvard (A.B., A.M.), his is no Horatio Alger story and no doubt will offend those who believe that the deservedly successful should travel to that goal by the Hard Way. But luck combined with uncommon ability has always been with him. And he certainly has been a great and useful citizen of San Francisco.

Aside from his profession as attorney, Judge of the Superior Court and Associate Justice of the Supreme Court of California, here are some of his most notable activities: He has been director and officer of various Jewish benevolent organizations, local and national; trustee of the San Francisco Public Library, 1918-1933; arbitrator in various labor disputes, including the longshoremen controversies in 1934 and 1936; chairman of the Citizen's Relief Committee during the depression of the 1930's; first chairman of Budget Committee of the San Francisco Community Chest; president of the Harvard Club in 1907; trustee of Stanford University since 1920; member of the Board of Directors of the National War Fund since 1942; member of the American Law Institute; member at various times of governing boards of the San Francisco Bar Association and of the California State Bar; member of the American Bar Association Special Committee to report as to proposals for the organization of the nations for peace and war.

And a charming gentleman to meet, withal. I never saw him look hurried or burdened.

And Mrs. Sloss! She is an intellectual and has a profound knowledge of her two favorite arts, music and poetry. She is a brilliant conversationalist, witty, humorous and sometimes caustic. She radiates magnetism and charm—but before letting a strong personal preference run away with me, perhaps I had better begin again and more soberly.

Mrs. Sloss (Hattie Hecht) was born and educated in Boston. She met Marcus Sloss when he was attending Harvard Law School, and after their marriage she became as ardent a San Franciscan as if she had been born on old Taylor Street with roots in Rincon Hill. From the first she was a great favorite, and as she put on no Boston airs her superiority was not resented. In her youth she loved society and all its gaieties, but as years passed she had less and less time for it. Here is the roster of her activities: She was the founder of the San Francisco section of the Council of Jewish Women and its first president. She was appointed by Governor Stevens to serve on the California State Board of Charities. At one time she served on the Community Chest Committee and is past president of the Children's Agency. She served on the Women's Board of Directors of both Expositions. At present (1946) she is on the Executive Committee of the San Francisco Musical Association, and on the board of the San Francisco Opera Association and is literary director of the Browning Society.

But her initiative is too strong to be content with serving, no matter how prominently, with groups. Several years ago she went on the air once a week for fifteen minutes and gave the public the benefit of her own love and deep perception of poetry. Many of her eager listeners heard for the first time the great poems that throughout the ages have made the world a pleasanter place to live in. Today she has two weekly broadcasts: "Know your Symphony," and "Poetry and Prizes." During the season she analyzes in simple nontechnical terms the symphony our music-loving public will hear a few days later, and sometimes interviews one of the artists.

"Poetry and Prizes" has been a revelation to her as well as to the public. She offers a ten-dollar prize for the best original poem submitted to her during the preceding month. Some of the offerings, of course, are doggerel, but an astonishing number show genuine talent, imagination and a natural sense of rhythm. A few are beautiful and as perfect in form as they are original in concept. Most of the aspirants are young, but she received one poem from a woman of eighty that was exquisite.

Probably nothing has interested Mrs. Sloss more than this truly creative work of hers, and certainly no one has done more to foster cultural development in San Francisco and its surrounding area, particularly in the fields of poetry and music.

Munich was one of the most beautiful cities in the world. Half surrounded by the glittering Alps, the tumultuous beryl-green Isar flowed through it, separating the city from the Englischer Garten, that wide and splendid park, with its woods, lakes, hayfields, its drives and pathways. The Ludwig-strasse, as wide as the Champs Elysées, was rebuilt by Ludwig I in the style of the Italian Renaissance. But there were fine old Gothic buildings as well as many handsome churches, thirty royal palaces of different periods, besides the Residenz (palace of the reigning Wittlesbachs until the end of World War I), a great university and library, the National-Theater (opera house), galleries and museums that were an education in art, classic and modernistic, if one never entered another. Munich was a Catholic city, and religious pictures were painted on many of the houses, while statues to the Virgin were on many street corners.

In that city of 500,000 inhabitants there was no poverty, not a slum, little crime. And the sky was a deep rich blue with floating masses of snow-white clouds. (The Bavarian uniform and flag were blue and white, no doubt chosen with an eye to harmony, for Munich was artistic or nothing!) It is situated on a high plateau, and the air blown down from Alpine snow fields is so light, so tonic, that one feels as if one has wings on one's feet and can barely refrain from dancing.

And in this loveliest of European cities was born in 1816 a man destined to be the pride of a clan whose roots ran back into the seventeenth century, a man whose descendants are eminent citizens in San Francisco today.

Until 1818 the Jews in Bavaria were subject to many restrictions, and only a limited number of families were allowed to live in Munich—the first synagogue was not dedicated until 1827. In 1822 a law was passed by the Bavarian Government permitting the organization of schools on modern lines. Previously Jews had been educated in private schools by mediocre teachers.

Max Lilienthal, eldest son of Loew Seligmann Lilienthal, attended the University of Munich and obtained the education that enabled him to be a rabbi under the new conditions. He graduated in 1827, receiving the degree of master of philosophy. His record was so brilliant that he was offered a position in the diplomatic service. He was tempted, for he was anxious to retrieve the family fortunes which had been greatly reduced by a disastrous fire—apparently there were no insurance policies in those days. He renounced that ambition, however, when told that he must qualify himself further by becoming a member of the Catholic faith. Once more he decided to be a rabbi.

Two years later he was invited, at the suggestion of the Russian Ambassador at Munich, by the Russian Minister of Education to superintend the new school at Riga, the founding of which was the first step in the task of modernizing the Jewish schools in that great but backward empire. The young Jews were growing restless and ambitious. They despised their teachers and resented the miserable schools they were forced to attend, where they were taught nothing but the rudiments—and in Hebrew at that! When Dr. Lilienthal arrived to teach them Western culture he was received with acclaim and his success and popularity were immediate.

He remained in Russia for six years, visiting practically every Jewish school in the empire, nor did his duties end there. With the recognition in high places of his great abilities, more and more was demanded of him. "Everything is put on my shoulders," he wrote in one of his letters. "I am director of the Society of Orphans, member of the School Commission, of the Board of Directors of the synagogues, keep the records, attend to the bills of the school (that takes an immense lot of my time), preach a sermon every three weeks, give five hours' instruction to the confirmation of boys, and five to the girls. In order to do this I begin my duties at five in the morning, and go to school at eight; then, with the various societies, I am occupied until four. At four o'clock I give instructions to the confirmation class, and attend whatever meetings there may be. At seven o'clock I *must* visit either the bishop, the director, the pastors, or the superintendent, and—what is still more tiresome—receive many callers, who remain with me until nine o'clock. Only then can I take my supper."

In another letter he writes: "The Jews here are, without exaggeration, 600 years behind the Germans in culture."

But although he devoted himself to his work not only with a high sense of duty but with ardor, he was not a happy man. He had left his beloved Pepi behind him and even as the years passed and his fame increased, he could not send for her, for his pay was small. He received many honors and the Czar sent him a diamond ring surrounded by emeralds, and other jewels from time to time, but it never seemed to occur to His Imperial Majesty, nor to anyone else in authority, to pay him adequately for his manifold activities. His only consolation was Pepi's frequent letters. His replies are curiosities to moderns. Never did a man write more impassioned love letters to his betrothed—and he signed them "Yours, Dr. Max Lilienthal"!

The long separation came to an end at last. He returned to Munich in 1845 and in August of that year married his Pepi, whose devotion had been as unswerving as his own.

During this period of his life he was very thin and, like his brother Samuel, had red hair, blue eyes, and a clear white complexion. He was six feet tall, an unusual height for a Jew. Pepi Nettre was very lovely. She had soft brown eyes, an olive skin, ebon-black hair which framed her oval face in two smooth panels. Once, when she was walking alone on a shopping street in Munich, the King pinched her cheek as he passed and gave her an approving smile. The patron of Lola Montez was a connoisseur in beauty, and Pepi, if somewhat startled, no doubt was equally elated.

Not long after his marriage Max followed the example of Samuel, now a physician in New York, and left for America. There he soon established himself as a rabbi and also conducted a boarding school for boys.

The financial struggle at first was a hard one, and Pepi, who had been reared in luxury, did all the housework and even made the clothes for the five children born in New York. But they were very happy and both became ardent Americans. Max defined the American Jew as "a monotheist in creed, a Hebrew, Israelite or Jew in descent, and in all other private or public relations an American citizen."

In 1855 he accepted a call to Cincinnati and remained there for the rest of his life. In that smaller city he soon became a distinguished figure and was invited from time to time to preach in Christian pulpits, an honor never before extended to a rabbi. As his fame spread he was invited to neighboring cities both by Jews

CABLE CAR ON CALIFORNIA STREET

and Gentiles. He accepted these invitations willingly for they gave him the opportunity "to state before a Christian congregation the sublime doctrines of our religion. Few visit our temples and hear our doctrines expounded there. The masses in general hear Judaism decried so much that a fair and impartial judgment can scarcely be expected. I always seize the opportunity when it is offered to preach in churches and to speak on Judaism and its liberal tendencies."

As Dr. Lilienthal grew older and his shock of hair turned white he was even more imposing in appearance. With his genial manner and practical mind he was drawn into civic affairs, served on a number of boards and committees and became the most dominant personage in the city. When President Hayes visited Cincinnati in 1877 he was one of the reception committee that met him at the station. The President paid him a singular honor. He walked over to him, shook his hand and said, "Dr. Lilienthal, I am happy to meet you." The other members of the committee received merely a bow. On the balcony of the Gibson House where Hayes made his speech Dr. Lilienthal stood beside him and gave the introductory address. When it was over the President began, "Dr. Lilienthal—and fellow citizens," and the mass of citizens in the street below cheered.

Meanwhile his family of seven—Eliza, Theodore, Philip, Esther, Jesse, Albert and Victoria—had arrived at various stages of maturity. Theodore had gone to New York and taken a position in the clothing firm of Werner Brothers. (Eliza had married a Werner.) When that firm failed he obtained a position with the banking firm of Seligman and Company, and this move no doubt laid the cornerstone of the House of Lilienthal in San Francisco, for Philip went there to take a position in the Anglo-California Bank, a firm controlled by the Seligmans.

Pepi died in 1867. Although inconsolable, Dr. Lilienthal lived until 1882, when he died at the age of sixty-six more full of honors than of years.

Albert and Theodore prospered in New York, but we are concerned at present only with the fortunes of Philip and Jesse, in San Francisco.

Philip Lilienthal was an uncommonly handsome man, six feet tall with a fine figure, regular features and great charm of manner. Many women fell in love with him, but during a visit to New York he was captured by Bella Seligman and they were married in 1879. She was warmly welcomed in San Francisco both by Jews and Gentiles and is described as "a fine woman, highly cultured and intelligent, yet very simple in her ways." Both she and her husband were lavish and generous by nature. She was the first president of the Emanu-El Sisterhood in San Francisco. They had four children: Joseph, Elsie, Philip and Theodore. In 1906, shortly after the earthquake and fire, she was rushed to New York for an operation. Philip was unable to go with her for he was now general manager of the Anglo-California Bank and obliged to remain in San Francisco and supervise its rebuilding. But he did obey a hurried summons to New York later and was with Bella when she died. He returned a broken-hearted man and met with a tragic death himself two years later.

He had taken a party of friends on an automobile trip out of the city, and on their return a runaway horse crashed into them, striking Philip on the chest with its hoof and throwing him from the car to the street. He was rushed to an emergency hospital but died before his family could reach him. His death was mourned by many more than his family. Among the usual expressions of sorrow the words "Oh, how I loved that man!" were heard again and again.

Jesse Lilienthal, third son of the famous rabbi, studied law at Harvard, but owing to severe headaches was unable to finish his course and was sent to Europe in the hope that change of climate and many distractions would effect a cure. Harvard accorded him an honor never heretofore bestowed by that exacting seat of learning: Jesse received his degree without the formality of graduation.

He too was very handsome, although in no way resembling Philip. He had the dark hair and olive skin of the Nettre family, chiseled features and a beautifully shaped head. It was the delicate health of his wife that brought him to San Francisco, where he soon established himself as a lawyer of the first rank, as well as a leader in civic affairs. During the years 1914-1916 he was president of the San Francisco Bar Association. He was also at the head of the United Railways, which, at the time he became its president, was in "very bad shape," but he succeeded in re-establishing its reputation and in making it a financial success. An activity in which he took an intense interest, and of which he was one of the prime movers in San Francisco, was the Boy Scouts; he was the president of the San Francisco Council. During World War I he was an active member of the Red Cross as well as of all other patriotic movements of that time.

Although his family knew that he had a slight heart affection, they were totally unprepared for his sudden death which occurred while he was addressing the Knights of Columbus at a public luncheon. He was given a public funeral, attended by men and women of all creeds, and flags were at half-mast in his honor.

Dr. Samuel Lilienthal, who also had married a Nettre, had two sons, Ernst and Leo. They too went to San Francisco, inspired no doubt by the enthusiastic letters of Philip, and built up a large commission business, Lilienthal and Company. Ernst married Bella Sloss, daughter of Louis Sloss. Leo married Bertha Gerstle, thus allying themselves with those Alaskan pioneers whose fame had long since traveled to the East.

In 1877 Theodore, eldest son of Dr. Max, met Sophie Gerstle in New York and followed her to San Francisco a year and a half later ostensibly on business but with the secret purpose of discovering whether he was really in love with her or not. He had been attracted by many pretty girls, but no other had haunted his imagination. When they met again it took but a short time to make up his mind, and she had made up hers long since.

Theodore is described as "the perfection of grace. He was about five feet ten inches in height, slight of build, with beautiful hands and feet." Sophie was a schoolmate of mine, and I remember her as a pretty little thing, vivacious and clever. He wore a mustache and a short beard extending from ear to ear, black like his hair, but despite that eyesore he was a handsome man.

The wedding which took place in 1879 was a grand affair. The Gerstles had a house in Sutter Street, and in an empty lot adjoining, a large hall was built for the occasion. The walls were decorated with mirrors, pictures and flowers, and crystal chandeliers hung from the ceiling. On three sides of the room were tables for the wedding feast, and after the ceremony, performed by Dr. Max who had come from Cincinnati for the occasion (this was three years before his death) and two local rabbis, the 150 guests sat down to a repast which was typical of that era, but whose menu of thirty-nine dishes is appalling to the modern eye. Theodore and Sophie survived it, however, and lived happily ever after.

When the Mother Superior of the Dominican Convent in San Rafael was alive it was the habit of my daughter Muriel Russell and myself to pay her and our two favorite nuns, Sister Dominic and Sister Mercedes, a visit on the last Sunday of each month. Those visits will never be forgotten, for although at times those three women seemed to be pure spirit, almost mystical, they were also keenly interested in the outer world. They subscribed to the daily newspapers and the best of the magazines and listened to the radio news. And they were not only women of the highest intelligence but full of gaiety and humor. Although I am a heathen (Muriel is a devout Catholic) I have never had more devoted friends and shall ever cherish the memory of the two that have gone.

One Sunday afternoon as we were having our monthly confab two handsome and distinguished-looking callers were ushered in, Mr. and Mrs. Milton Esberg. They too were great friends of Mother Raymond and received a warm welcome. We passed a delightful afternoon and although I never saw Mr. Esberg again— he died soon after—I retain a vivid memory of him for I have seldom met a more charming man. And he was one of our most public-spirited citizens, a leader in many civic and social enterprises, and popular in club and political circles as well. Mrs. Esberg, a daughter of Ernst and granddaughter of Dr. Samuel Lilienthal, made her house in San Francisco known as a cultural center and entertained her friends of all creeds with co-ordinated simplicity and elegance. After her husband's death she sold the house and has lived in Ross, on the northern side of the Bay, ever since.

The beautiful Mrs. Sigmund Stern was the daughter of Eugene Meyer, at one time president of the London, Paris and American Bank, now known as the Anglo-California, and is a sister of Eugene Meyer, Jr., owner of the Washington, D. C., *Post*. Her own record is one of the most interesting of the many public-spirited women of San Francisco. In 1919 Mayor Rolph appointed her as a member of the Playground Commission, now called the Recreation Commission. She is on the board of the San Francisco Opera Association, the Musical Association and the Woman's Board of the Museum of Art. For many years she was a member of what was then called the Associated Charities, now the Children's Agency.

But her crowning achievement is the Sigmund Stern Grove.

John McLaren, besides being superintendent of Golden Gate Park, was an ex-officio member of the Recreation Commission, and he and Mrs. Stern often drove about the city looking for new playground sites. One day he said to her, "I want to show you a place that you should have," and he took her to an "enchanted vale" whose beauty so impressed her that she bought it forthwith and presented it to the city as a memorial to her husband, and to be used as a recreation spot under the jurisdiction and control of the Recreation Department. Later the city added land on either side.

The Sigmund Stern Grove, sheltered from fog and wind, is in a natural amphitheater with unusually fine acoustic properties. The floor of the little valley is planted in grass, and old fruit trees—a mass of white blossoms in the spring—afford shade for the audiences that attend the midsummer festival. Eucalyptus trees, planted all the way up the slopes, have grown to a great height, and beneath them is a dense growth of native ferns, through which are paths leading to the surrounding streets. This property was owned and developed by George Greene, a pioneer, who named it the Trocadero Rancho, and built the famous inn of that name, which for nearly twenty years was the scene of many notable gatherings, respectable and otherwise. (It was also the last hideout of Abe Ruef, "hero" of the Graft Prosecution of 1906.)

In 1938 Mrs. Stern, having interested a number of music-loving citizens, formed the Sigmund Stern Grove Festival Committee. Its purpose was to provide, free for all who would care to come, the very best in symphony, opera, ballet, drama and concert, and only the best performers and conductors were invited to entertain and instruct the large audiences (rarely less than 10,000) in those romantic surroundings at the foot of the western slope of Twin Peaks, and waft them to another sphere where politics, war, business and crime are not. No cultural entertainment in San Francisco has ever attained such a tremendous and unvarying success, nor so well deserved it.

To return to the illustrious dead. One who left an indelible impress on the city of his adoption was Adolph Sutro. Born in Germany and trained as an engineer, he came to San Francisco in 1850. The most exciting period of his life, however, was in Nevada where for nearly ten years he fought Ralston, Sharon, Mackay and others with his determination to build a tunnel four miles long through the Sun Mountain, a tremendous engineering feat which would be of great practical value to the Comstock Lode. That historic battle is told with dramatic power by George Lyman in *Ralston's Ring* and need not be related here as we are concerned only with Sutro's career in San Francisco. Suffice it to say that he built the tunnel, made a fortune in the Comstock Lode and kept it, which is more than can be said for most of the wild speculators of that era, and returned in the early 1870's to the city of his choice. He bought a part of the old Rancho San Miguel on its western rim and immediately planted that sandy waste with eucalyptus trees. They grew to a great height, and that large expanse is now known as Sutro Forest. The trees also cover a large hill which he called Mount Parnassus but renamed it at a later day Mount Sutro. On "Sutro Heights," commanding a view of the Pacific Ocean, he built his home, a stately mansion with wide verandas and surrounded by formal gardens—and hideous statues, following the fashion of his time.

His Sunday luncheons became famous. Notables of the city and visiting celebrities were entertained there besides his family and friends. Mr. Hittell, the California historian, took me to one of them. There were some fifteen or twenty guests and no doubt many of them were notables, but I remember no one but Sutro himself. He was an old man then and his hair and beard were white, but I was impressed by his black flashing eyes and the constant play of expression on his intelligent mobile face. In his early manhood he was strikingly handsome. Here is Dr. Lyman's description of him in *Ralston's Ring:* "Tall, dark-haired, massive physically, with the look of a dreamer, and the burning eyes of a seer. Resolution, determination, ambition exuded from every pore."

Well, he must have realized all his ambitions—besides that still renowned tunnel. He was mayor of San Francisco in 1894-1898, and he has had few peers in that office. With Edward B. Pond he planned and carried out the present system of boulevards west from 33rd Avenue to the beach. The famous (and at one time infamous) Cliff House was on his estate and he rebuilt it twice after destruction by fire. Close by then as now are the Sutro Baths, a large covered enclosure where the humblest are welcome.

He left Sutro Heights and Sutro Forest to the city but his heirs disputed his will and after years of litigation the suit was decided in their favor. However, his brilliant daughter, Dr. Emma Sutro Merritt, carried out his wishes.

One day I was called to the telephone by a woman prominent in civic affairs and treated to a high-pressure talk about a man of whom I had never heard but who was running for Congress and *must* be elected. When she finished I gasped, "Why! I never knew we had a man in this town possessed of so many virtues," and consented to be one of his sponsors. As I was writing a book at the moment and have a one-track mind, it never occurred to me to ask the name of his opponent. She had taken good care not to tell me, and when I heard too late that it was Mrs. Kahn I was furious.

Julius Kahn was a member of the House of Representatives from 1899 to 1903, was elected again in 1905 and served continuously until his death. In 1925 his wife, Florence Prag Kahn, was appointed to succeed him and California has never had a better representative in the House. She should be there yet, but if the public made a stupid mistake she is by no means forgotten. During the great Exposition on Treasure Island in 1939 a luncheon was given to the twelve most outstanding women in California and she was one of them and sat on the right of Marshall Dill who presided. Her mother, Mary Goldsmith Prag, also played an active part in the life of the city: she was for long the head of the history department in a girl's high school and was the first to suggest state teachers' pensions.

Albert Bender was one of our "characters." A dark stocky little man with a radiant face, and bursting with energy, good will and affection for innumerable friends, he loved to boast and brag and strut and only refrained from thumping his chest. Sometimes one felt one could stand him no more, but he was such a good soul he was always forgiven. (He bought twenty or thirty of my books when they came out, and wouldn't a writer forgive murder and arson by a man who did that?)

He was born in Dublin in 1863, the son of a rabbi, and educated there and at Beaufort College in England. In 1882 he began his life in San Francisco as an errand boy in an insurance business, worked his way to the top in short order and in a few years was a moderately rich man. But ninety percent of his income rolled into philan-thropic, educational and creative channels, the acquisition of local works of art and the encouragement of young artists claiming a good part of it. Every worth-while artist and writer was his friend, every art museum in San Francisco the beneficiary of his gifts or loans. He gave a room, with many valuable manuscripts and books, to Mills College (which had given him an A.M.) and founded a room in the Dublin Art Gallery in memory of his father. He was a Chevalier of the Legion of Honor, and a Chevalier of the Crown of Italy. He was a trustee of Mills, a member of the San Francisco Public Library Commission and of the Art Commission and a di-rector of the San Francisco Symphony.

All eminent writers and artists who visited San Francisco brought letters to him, and he entertained them royally in his modest apart-ment.

I think no man was more sincerely loved, and when he died the synagogue was as crowded as a first night at the opera. The flower shops were cleaned out, and the offerings, as he would have wished, were sent to the hospitals.

Of the three Michelsons, Charles is the most widely known. Born in Virginia City in 1869, he came to San Francisco in his early manhood and started his newspaper career as a reporter on the *Evening Post.* Thence he went to the *Examiner* and later to the *Call.* In due course he departed for New York and Chicago where he served on the Hearst papers, but he achieved his national repu-tation when he became editor of the Washington Bureau of the New York *World,* and in 1929 director of publicity for the Demo-cratic National Committee. He was also director of Public Rela-tions of the NRA in 1933 and 1934.

His elder brother Albert was an eminent physicist, and his sister,

Miriam Michelson, who wrote *In the Bishop's Carriage,* was for several years a popular novelist.

Mrs. I. Lowenburg was born in Alabama and educated in a convent at Cape Girardeau, Missouri, but came to her early womanhood in San Francisco and played an active and varied part in its life. She was one of the founders and later president of the California State Federation of Women's Clubs, vice-president of Emanu-El Kindergarten, member of the executive board of the San Francisco chapter of the American Red Cross, director of the Peace Committee, president of the women's auxiliary of the California Prison Commission, vice-president of the San Francisco Association for the Blind, and president of the Pacific Coast Women's Press Club. She was the originator of the Panama-Pacific International Exposition's Congress of Authors and Journalists. She found time to write two books, *The Irresistible Current* (a plea for a universal religion) and *A Nation's Crime,* dealing with universal divorce laws.

The noted surgeon Leo Eloesser, born in San Francisco in 1881, graduated from the University of California, went to Heidelberg and later served as surgical assistant in hospitals not only in Heidelberg but in Kiel and Berlin. Returning to his native state, he was assistant in surgery at the University of California Hospital from 1910 to 1912. But Germany called him again, and he was surgeon in reserve hospitals in Ettlingen and Karlsruhe. During World War I he was a major in the medical corps of the United States Army. After 1913 he was a clinical professor at Stanford Medical School and chief of the Stanford Medical Service, also consulting surgeon of the United States Veteran's Bureau and of the United States Marine Hospital. In 1937 he went to Spain and for two years was chief of the Mobile Surgical Unit of the Loyalist army in Barcelona. He has also been prominent in liberal circles and contributes frequently to medical journals.

Jessica Peixotto was an intellectual and an active citizen. Born in New York in 1864 of an old Sephardic family, she came to San Francisco in 1869. A brilliant scholar, she was the first woman to receive a Ph.D from the University of California and was a student at the Sorbonne in 1896-1897. Returning to California she became professor of social economics (first woman full professor) at U. C. and was head of the department for twenty years. In 1925 she became professor emeritus.

She was a member of the State Board of Charities and Corrections from 1912 to 1923.

Her brother, Ernest Peixotto, was a noted illustrator of books on California and was associated on the *Lark* with Gelett Burgess. Sidney Peixotto was deeply interested in the education of boys and formed the Columbia Boys' Club, where he trained them in football and other sports. Those that showed signs of talent he educated in one of the arts.

The brothers Herbert and Mortimer Fleishacker have played a prominent part in the city of their birth. Mortimer has been president of the Anglo-California Trust Company, president of the Truckee River General Electric Company and of the American River Electric Company. He was Federal mediator for labor troubles and head of the Exemption Board during World War I, and a regent of the University of California.

Herbert has been president of the Anglo, Paris and National Bank, afterward merged with the Anglo-California National. He was president of the Park Commission, and the Fleishacker Pool was named in his honor. He presented the Children's Playground and the building on it to the city in memory of his mother and was an ex-officio member of the Art Commission for several years. Both brothers are noted philanthropists.

"I dreamt that I dwelt in marble halls . . ." That line of an old forgotten opera always runs through my mind when I hear Mrs. M. S. Koshland's name mentioned. In her house on Washington Street is a great central hall of white marble (floor and all), and in it many of the Metropolitan songbirds have warbled during our own opera season. And so have many young aspirants, to whom Mrs. Koshland has given encouragement—and something more substantial when needed. Her musicales are famous in San Francisco, and her house is a center of musical culture.

After the period of mourning for President Roosevelt was over she was one of the first to open her doors, and the California Branch of the English-Speaking Union gave a reception there to Lord and Lady Cranborne. Cranborne was not only a delegate to the Security Conference but president of the English-Speaking Union of the British Empire, and Mrs. Koshland enabled the local branch to honor him properly, for the reception was magnificent. And quite as much admiration was bestowed upon the gracious handsome hostess personally.

When Edgar Walter died the San Francisco *Examiner* paid him the following tribute:

"Death yesterday closed the notable career of Edgar Walter, San Francisco's sculptor and 'spokesman of artists.' Deeply cultured, widely traveled, and engagingly friendly, Mr. Walter achieved a record that placed him in the front rank of American sculptors. In 1936 he topped his already outstanding career with the completion of a monumental stone group in Washington, D. C. In San Francisco Mr. Walter assisted in designing the Federal Building in the Civic Center.

"Although his position placed him on the national stage, Mr. Walter realized the full life of a citizen in his own city. He was president of the Art Commission when he resigned last year because of the press of business and failing health. Illustrative of his facility on all art subjects was his invitation to speak on 'Jewish Art.' Accepting, he thought no more of the matter until he stood up to talk, then realized there was no such thing as Jewish Art, since the art of Jews is the art of the country in which they live. As he cleared his throat he thought hard, then delivered a polished lecture on 'Why There Is No Jewish Art.' "

Born in San Francisco in 1877, he studied at the Institute of Art in his own city, then went to Paris where he was a pupil of Cromon and Perrin. His rise was rapid for he not only had a rare gift but was an indefatigable worker. His works have been exhibited in the Metropolitan Museum of New York, the Toledo Museum of Art, San Francisco Institute of Art, the Panama-Pacific Exposition and the Paris Salon, from all of which he received Honorable Mention. He made the Seligman Memorial Fountain in New York and the "Bear and Faun" fountain in Morningside Park, New York. San Francisco is very proud of him.

In the days of its youth, and for long thereafter, San Francisco was undoubtedly the most generous, hospitable—and tolerant—city in the world. Moreover, in that omnifarious community so numerous and so various were the types of humanity that a man had to be outstanding in his oddities to attract more than passing notice. But they did have one original who is still unforgotten. Joshua Abraham Norton attracted little attention when he arrived in San Francisco in 1849. He was a dignified, quiet, good-looking English Jew and brought $40,000 with him. He engaged in some mercantile business, and in 1852 his capital had increased to $250,000. Then, between one of San Francisco's disastrous fires and an attempt to corner the rice market, his fortune was swept away with many another. He disappeared for a time, no one knew where nor ever will know. When he returned it was evident that he had lost more than lucre. His tall imposing figure was clad in a shabby blue uniform, decorated, however, with heavy gold epaulets, and on his head was a general's cap with a heron's plume. In his buttonhole was a red carnation. He solemnly proclaimed himself Emperor of the United States of America, and his colossal dignity would have abashed the Emperor of all the Russias.

San Francisco was delighted with him. Instead of treating him as a figure of fun, with ribald hoots or silent contempt, or committing him to an insane asylum, it accepted him at his own valuation and cheerfully paid him the tribute he demanded. Indeed, San Franciscans took an immense pride in him, assuring one another that no other city on earth could boast so original a lunatic.

The freedom of the city was formally granted him. No bill was ever laid beside his plate in any of the restaurants where he took his three meals daily—save by some stupid waiter, and then apologies by the management were profuse. No ticket was ever demanded of him at any theater or other place of amusement he deigned to honor with his presence. He never asked for money. He demanded it when he needed cash in his pocket. The Chinese laundries refused to conform to the spirit of the town, and he was generous to his more indigent subjects. Also, he always contributed a bill to the plate passed in the church which he attended regularly, as he did the theater and prize fights.

He walked majestically into banks, stores and mercantile houses and presented formal bills for taxes. The sums were small and were paid with good-natured humor. They were acknowledged by a formal receipt decorated with a great seal and inscribed, "Norton I, Emperor of the U. S. A." The City Council voted him one of the expenses of the city treasury.

Cigar stands were honored to accommodate His Majesty; the stores gave him "credit" for underwear, handkerchiefs, etc., and when his uniform attained its final degree of shabbiness he inserted a notice in the newspaper that Emperor Norton I needed a new one, and subscriptions were immediate. When one of his two beloved dogs died, he gave it a public funeral, and the attendance was large and properly demure.

To quote Mr. Theodore Kirchhoff, in the *Quarterly* of the Society of California Pioneers: "His innumerable proclamations and fulminating governmental decrees, couched in terms of sanity and composed in superior English, in which he expressed his displeasure over political conditions, and about war and peace and municipal affairs, as well as his commands to foreign potentates and ministers, were never refused by any of the local papers, and they were read with due attention by young and old. To General Grant he sent a firm telegram during the convention at Chicago, not to accept a third-term nomination, and perhaps Garfield was indebted to our illustrious Emperor for his nomination."

Later he assumed another title: Protector of Mexico "upon the special request of our sister Republic, which is so often endangered by pronunciamentos and longs for a stable government." In 1869 he issued a proclamation ordering San Francisco to build a bridge across the Bay, but it was sixty-seven years before that enlightened command was obeyed.

Emperor Norton I died in 1880 at the age of sixty-five and received one of San Francisco's historic funerals. To quote Mr. Kirchhoff again: "The funeral of 'The Emperor' was an event that induced all the newspapers of San Francisco to print long editorials [...] f the deceased. As a fitting tribute a [...] ll their readers. Since the fortune of [...] ly a few dollars, a collection was taken [...] fine coffin procured in which he was [...] and persons, from laborer to million- [...] good old 'Emperor.' More than two [...] came, who thus offered a last tribute [...] a great friend of children."

[...] ned the funeral procession out to the [...] and for many days San Francisco was [...] ity ever could be.

[...] t of the biography of San Francisco [...] n Norton. Myself, I have a dark suspicion [...] st man in that generous but gullible City by

[...] ine) Roos was born in Epinal, France, and [...] l to San Francisco in 1872. He was one of [...] n of Roos Brothers, and when he died she [...] hille, one of the best-known merchants in [...] portsman as well. Like others of her creed she was notable for her unostentatious philanthropies.

Mrs. Roos was what is known as a character. She refused to identify herself with any "set," was somewhat unpredictable, had the "grand manner," and was more French than American. Although she entertained lavishly it was only when notables were in town, and when President Taft paid a visit to San Francisco at the invitation of her son Robert, she acted as his hostess and gave the President a reception that is still remembered.

---

## An Author's [...] Graces P. E. N.

**ZILFA ESTCOURT**

Center of interest at the recent [...] b members from all over Northern [...] Mrs. Atherton Russell, was a be[...] ther, Gertrude Atherton, the club's [...]

The portrait, painted a number [...] Francisco author's climb to fame [...] tly presented by an old friend to [...] . Russell. It had hung for some [...] e in the Paris Salon.

[...] he pose shows Mrs. Atherton's [...] e in profile, her pale gold hair [...] French twist piled high on her [...] d.

[...] rs. Atherton stood near the [...] nting to receive the guests at the [...] t P. E. N. meeting since her seri- illness last spring. Receiving [...] h her was tall, slender, blue-eyed [...] e Tisdale Hobart, author of "Oil [...] the Lamps of China" and other [...] able books. Mrs. Hobart, who [...] makes her home in Berkeley, [...] one of the most recent additions [...] ocal P. E. N. membership.

She lived to a great age, and died in 1945 leaving three sons, three grandsons, one granddaughter and seven great-grandchildren to inherit her fortune. A son and three grandsons served with distinction in World War II, Colonel Robert A. Roos, Captain John Roos, A.U.S., Lieutenant Leslie L. Roos, U.S.N.R., and Captain Robert A. Roos, Jr. The former was awarded the Legion of Merit for "unusual initiative, organizational ability, leadership and planning."

The social and civic activities of the Hellers, Hellmans and Ehrmans are in many respects similar to others I have mentioned, so I will spare the reader too much repetition. Suffice it to note that Mrs. Heller is especially known for her devoted work with the Children's Hospital. Mrs. Hellman is a member of the board of Mills College and chairman of its musical committee, which not only plans musicales for the college but makes some of them available for San Francisco. Mrs. Ehrman is notable for her splendid work with the Red Cross.

There are many, many more. I have merely selected those best known to the public. My own particular favorites are Annie Kline (born in Texas, but an ardent San Franciscan) her witty and handsome daughter Larie, who made a brilliant record at Bryn Mawr and graduated with high honors, and her equally handsome and charming son-in-law, Benjamin Boas. The young man of the family, First Lieutenant Roger Boas, served in World War II under General Patton and received two decorations, the Bronze Star for meritorious conduct and the Silver Star for gallantry in action.

# CHAPTER NINE

# *Clubdom*

BUSTLES. Tight lacing. Tiny waists. Opulent bosoms. Swelling hips. Long skirts daintily held up on the street. Trains thrown over one arm at dances. Ruffled petticoats. Hats with long feathers, rolled up on one side. High-necked and long-sleeved nightgowns. Dainty lingerie run through with blue or pink ribbons. Sidesaddles, sweeping skirts and top hats. No cause for wonder that in remote California until the late 1880's there was not a single woman's club in San Francisco.

Women of leisure read the latest novels but little else. A few embryonic intellectuals subscribed to the *Atlantic Monthly, Harper's Magazine* and "discovered" Henry James, but the majority were content with *Harper's Bazaar* and *Godey's Lady's Book,* Rhoda Broughton, Ouida, and The Duchess. Even the first group rarely opened a newspaper.

When plays wandered as far as San Francisco they crowded the theaters, nor were they indifferent to vaudeville and "Negro minstrels."

During the summer those who owned country houses entertained the less fortunate. Their diversions were driving, riding, tennis, paying calls, picnics and long hours of gossiping and embroidering on verandas, and there were many informal dances.

True, they loved music. It was said there were more first-class amateur musicians in San Francisco than in any other city in the

Union. Operatic companies were rare but concerts and bands were a trifle more frequent and occasions for rejoicing.

It was somewhere in the late '80's, in 1887 I think, that the more intelligent women began to wake up and grow restless and dissatisfied with their aimless lives. Those who had visited New York or Boston recalled what they had heard of women's clubs devoted to cultivation of the intellect and general culture, the "advancement of womankind," and the study of world affairs. They talked to others of this strange departure of women from the orthodox way of life and it was not long before quite a number humbly admitted that the East had run ahead of them and discovered many things worthy of interest and study. Enthusiasm spread and there were frequent meetings to discuss the possibility of forming such a club in San Francisco and realizing their new ambition.

But how to go about it? Just how would women's clubs differ from men's—the Pacific Club, the Union Club, the Concordia, Argonaut, Bohemian? And—they had a vague idea that all the men did in those clubs was to drink whisky-and-sodas, gossip, doze in deep leather chairs and sit at the windows and watch for the wind to reveal a pretty woman's ankle. No such feeble inanities for them! The poor creatures deserved relaxation after a hard day of banking, business and the excitement of the Stock Exchange, but what *they* wanted was work, the hard work of self-improvement and usefulness; they had had enough of leisure and relaxation.

But how? How?

In 1888 their problem was solved. The great and famous Julia Ward Howe arrived from Boston on a lecture tour and to visit her relatives the Mailliards. Mrs. George Hearst and Mrs. A. A. Sargent besought her to enlighten them and she graciously consented.

So stimulated were the women by the eloquent address she gave them, with much practical advice as to drawing up a Constitution (with Articles I, II, III, IV), bylaws, regulations and programs, that they went to work in earnest. They elected Mrs. Hearst president, Mrs. H. L. Campbell, Mrs. L. L. Baker, Mrs. John Burnett, and Dr. Emma Sutro Merritt vice-presidents. There were also a recording secretary, a corresponding secretary, a treasurer and an auditor. Associate directors were Mrs. Sargent and Miss Sarah H. Hamlin, whose *very* exclusive girls' school exists to this day although she has departed to a sphere where presumably clubs are not. It may be interpolated here that all private-school teachers were "real ladies in reduced circumstances," whose altered fortunes, however, in no way affected their social position. Money has never been all in San Francisco.

There were 172 names on the first roster of the Century Club, and many of those names are familiar to the present generation: Adams, Alvord, Baldwin, Bancroft, Beaver, Block, Borel, Cohen, Cooper, Crocker (Mrs. Will), Cadwallader, Denman, Easton, Hearst, Hittel, Kaufman, Kellogg, Holladay, McKinstry (Laura), Montgomery, Monteagle, Moody, Moore (Austin), Otis, Parrott, Pierce, Pinkard (Belle Eyre), Pixley, Redding, Redington, Shafter, Sperry, Stanford (Mrs. Leland), Whittell.

The honorary members were Julia Ward Howe and Ina Donna Coolbrith—who had dared to write poetry and publish it.

On succeeding rosters we find other familiar names: Sloss (Louis), Buckingham, Brownell, Cheesbrough, Crockett, Dean, Dodge, Folger, Goodrich, Hathaway, Kohl, Lent, Lilienthal, Livermore, MacEnerney, Newhall, Tallant, Tucker, West, De Pue, De Vecchi, Howard, Hunt, Irwin, Jordan (Mrs. David Starr, wife of the president of Stanford University), Sloss (M. E.), Knight, Palmer (Silas), Pillsbury, Russell (Muriel Atherton), Smedburg, Sulé, Whitney.

It may be asked why my name does not appear on that first distinguished list. Well—I was living in England at the time and although my name was put up by two intimate friends, Ella Adams and Belle Pinkard, it was voted down promptly. In the first place that serial I had written for the *Argonaut* was "simply shocking." Such scenes! Such caricatures of some of the most eminent women in San Francisco, thinly disguised! How *had* the Athertons, so correct, so conservative, so *un*sensational, permitted me brazenly to admit the authorship—and not only that but two novels I had written since my flight after my husband's death were downright *immoral,* condemned by every critic in the country.

Those poor little jejune performances! I have long since consigned them to oblivion, and wonder why instead of being vociferously condemned they were not ignored by the almighty critics, also, why they were called "immoral." They would be regarded as kindergarten stuff today. But time marches on. Long after, when all the original members were dead, and Mrs. Earle Brownell, daughter of one of the founders, was president, I was elected an honorary member of the Century Club, still the most outstanding club in the West, and have had some charming experiences there. They gave a dramatization of my novel, *The House of Lee,* in their auditorium, at another time a birthday luncheon when all rose and sang "Happy birthday to you," followed by a long critique of another novel, *The Horn of Life,* by a professional lecturer on the same platform.

However—to return to a more important subject. The less official part of the constitution may be inferred from the following committees: On Art and Literature, On Practical Questions of the Day, On Science and Education, On Formal Debate, On Business Meetings.

A mighty task these ladies had set for themselves, and for a time the club limped and there were doubts and confusion. With all their intelligence, these women, with the exception of the school-teachers, had had little or nothing to do with the practical side of life. It was comparatively simple, under Mrs. Howe's guidance, to draw up a constitution in proper legal form, a general program, and elect officers, but after her return to Boston they felt almost helpless. The multifarious details, the problems of administration were beyond them. If their club were merely to be for pleasant afternoon gatherings to discuss the latest important nonfiction, they might hope to expand gradually, almost automatically, but they had elected to begin at the top, to have at once a club that would in no way be inferior to those in the East and add to the prestige of San Francisco—a colossal and perhaps a too ambitious job.

They received no help from their men, who disapproved of this unwomanly venture. Why addle their dear little heads trying to be intellectual, sweating over bylaws and what not? They quoted the son of Victoria, the famous Prince of Wales: "Bright women, yes, but no damn intellect." Go out and buy a new hat.

But nothing could deter those ardent ambitious women and their courage never wavered. They persisted, and in time they conquered.

Meanwhile there was another serious impediment to progress. They were obliged to hold their meetings in one another's houses, and as membership increased and programs grew more elaborate they were cramped and thwarted. They wanted a clubhouse and they could not afford to build or rent one, to say nothing of furnishing it. Many were only moderately well off, and although the wealthy could run up bills at the fashionable shops and with expensive dressmakers, their pin money was scant and when they asked their husbands for a more liberal allowance they were reminded that their wants were all handsomely provided for and they had no use for a full purse. As for a clubhouse—had they reduced what little brains they had to pulp? Damn Julia Ward Howe!

But a good angel came to the rescue. There was one of their number who had money to command, and being convinced that the women were in earnest and determined to succeed or die in the attempt, Mrs. Hearst (who was accustomed to the role of fairy godmother; it was well known that aside from her numerous philanthropies and her donations to the University of California, no less than twenty-three girls bought their hats at Miss Coglan's and charged them to her account), offered to put up $125 a month (a goodly sum in those days) for a year if they could find a suitable building. They canvassed the town and found a large house in Sutter Street with rooms for offices and entertainment and four bedrooms for members above. (A few lived out of town the year round—at Menlo Park, Ross or San Rafael.) On the fourteenth of August 1889, the club, now really a Club, not merely a horde of peripatetic females, was opened with due formality and soon became the most famous club west of Boston.

A large room was converted into an auditorium with a platform and reasonably comfortable chairs. Professors from the universities of Stanford and California, distinguished strangers visiting the city, lectured on that platform, and the members took notes and digested and discussed those learned discourses at later meetings. Members also stood up on that platform, timid at first but with growing confidence, and talked on subjects in which they were profoundly interested—encouraged by respectful attention and spontaneous applause.

They read the newspapers and held debates on world affairs.

They also took a deep interest in their city and played their part in raising the standard of education and general welfare. Here are the titles of a few of the subjects upon which they exercised their intellects in formal debate: Child Saving, The Higher Education of Women in Colleges and Universities, Etchings and Engravings, Science and Physiognomy, Current Literature, The Practical Side of the Jewish Religion, The Kindergarten in Its Relation to Moral Training, The Servant Girl Question, The Decorative Arts, Organized Charities in Cities, The Modern Newspaper, Literature of Children, The Imperial Family of Russia, Domestic Economy, Manual Training in Children's Schools, Thorvaldsen, Alaskan Indians, The Legal Status of Children, Crime and Its Cure in the United States, Immigration and Nationalization, Louis Agassiz, The Ear, Single Tax, Study of the Classics, Old England in the New World, Chemistry of Plants, Art, Bacteria, Flower Farming and Perfume Making, Literature of Philosophical Thought from Thales to Hegel.

And many more. But these titles may give an idea of their wide range of interests. They were intellectual, all right.

Every Wednesday they had a luncheon followed by a lecture, a dramatic performance, or music, and tea was served afterward.

Their musical afternoons were the high spots. Accomplished members enchanted them with programs applauded sincerely by professional guests. And of course they accumulated a library with many old-fashioned "sets," and notable works on modern topics. Current novels, however, were not excluded.

Time passed and the club grew wealthier (possibly the men loosened up or died and left rich widows). In 1904 they bought their present handsome quarters on the corner of Franklin and Sutter Streets. Here they have a large auditorium with perfect acoustics, and this they rent occasionally for coming-out parties, balls, weddings and other social affairs, all of which adds to their income.

This is not a club like Town and Country, the Francisca or the Woman's Athletic, where the members may drop in for luncheon or tea. Meals are served on Wednesdays only and reservation must be made well in advance. But members use the library at will, at other times hold their business meetings at the club, or committees foregather to discuss future programs.

The telephone directory today lists sixty-five clubs, many of them women's, but the Century maintains its proud position at the top and its activities increase with the years. The members are a fine set of women, and it rivals the men's Commonwealth Club in intelligence and influence.

The California Club of California, founded in 1897, may be called a younger sister of the Century, as its constitution, bylaws and some of its purposes are the same. The second Article of Incorporation reads: "The purposes for which this corporation is formed are to aid through organized effort such worthy causes as may enlist its sympathies, and to create a center of thought and action among the people for the promotion of whatever tends for the best interests of the city and state." And among its bylaws: "The qualifications for membership shall be character and intelligence without regard to religion or politics."

This club is active, public-spirited, businesslike and important. Among the bills it has forced through the state legislature are those for the improvement of juvenile courts, for the preservation of meadow larks, and of old Spanish names of cities, towns and villages, to create a state forest fund, a department of music in the University of California, a tenement-house bill, two white-

slave-traffic bills, and one providing for equal domestic rights in
the relation of both parents to children. They also managed to
get a million dollars out of the United States Congress to be ex-
pended for the public schools of the state.

In the auditorium of their house in Clay Street such subjects as
civics, education, out-of-door art, social science, important current
books, philanthropy, compulsory health insurance and endangered
wild life, to mention but a few, are discussed by members and
guests. Plays are given by a well-trained company among the
members, orchestral and other musical performances. There is a
monthly luncheon in the large tearoom, to which guests are invited. At times they let the entire clubhouse for weddings, dances,
teas and other festivities. Of course the members of the various
committees meet frequently to work out programs and discuss
business affairs.

They are an intelligent, determined and persevering body of
women who hold high rank in the club history of San Francisco.
Their number is 350.

I felt very proud when elected an honorary member.

On September 27, 1890, the Pacific Coast Women's Press Association began its active and useful life. Its first president was Nellie
Blessing Eyster (grandmother of Paul Elder), and I quote her
statement recorded in the Historian's Book of the P.C.W.P.A.:
"Why should there have been a Pacific Coast Women's Press
Association? Because over this empire of a state were big-brained,
whole-souled, cultured and level-headed women, some of high
literary and artistic ability, each in her often very limited sphere
working out the travail of her soul alone and unsupported by the
knowledge and sympathy of her fellows. Some of these women
had already won, by their pens, a national reputation, others were

young and aspiring debutantes, but all needed to be united by
the cohesion of that quality of love which 'suffereth long and is
kind,' and which 'worketh no ill to his neighbor.' A knowledge of
facts weighed upon the heart of a young, enthusiastic and brilliant
woman of San Francisco, Mrs. Emily Y. Swett Parkhurst, daughter
of the eminent educator, Mr. John Swett. She caught the idea of
producing an organization of these various women and immediately proceeded to develop it with an enthusiasm that knew no
bounds. Hundreds of letters were written to the various known
writers throughout the state, and an enthusiasm was kindled which
culminated in the organization of the Pacific Coast Women's Press
Association."

The members were by no means confined to San Francisco.
They came from San José, San Diego, Santa Barbara, Sacramento,
Los Angeles and Pasadena, in California; from Portland and Salem
in Oregon, and from Carson City, Nevada. Their first meeting was
in the house of Mrs. Parkhurst, presided over by a prominent
attorney, Henry N. Clement, who formally organized the Association.

The Historian's Book of the P.C.W.P.A. pays Mrs. Eyster the
following tribute: "Mrs. Nellie Blessing Eyster of San Francisco,
president of the P.C.W.P.A. from its organization for two con-
secutive years, was of French-Huguenot extraction on one side and
Anglo-Saxon on the other. Her literary life was subject always to
the higher activities of benevolence and character culture and the
bulk of her writings was devoted to children. . . . She even penetrated China with her books. One on the opium habit was translated into Chinese and widely read. . . . She was an intimate friend
of Oliver Wendell Holmes, who criticised her first book as 'a
charming work, showing great future promise.' *A Chinese Quaker*
was praised by the London *Times*."

The P.C.W.P.A. grew and flourished with the years. Among its notable presidents have been Ina Coolbrith, Mrs. Nelson, Mrs. Thorpe (author of *Curfew Must Not Ring To-Night*), Mrs. Lowenburg, Mrs. Waldraff—and Mrs. Bergstrasser (1944-1946), a lady of many activities. She is fourth vice-president of San Francisco City and County Federation of Women's Clubs; national vice-president of the National Society of Daughters of the American Revolution; on the executive board of the San Francisco Motion Pictures Council; for three years on Junior Membership, including five Western states, Alaska, Panama, Hawaii and China; on the executive board of Women's Chamber of Commerce; in Secret Service while President Truman was in San Francisco at the United Nations Conference; worked as a volunteer with Miss Kathryn A. Sullivan, Director of "Big Sisters." She was also a twelve-time donor to the blood bank, breaking the record of her sex. And she is an honorary member of the Police Department! Her writings have been Indian stories and poetry.

The poet, Marion Mills Brown, will probably succeed her as president of the P.C.W.P.A.

Charlotte Perkins Stetson, widely known in her day as an intellectual and a feminist, was one of the most active members of the Association in its formative years. I was also one of the original members and attended the first meeting, but as I lived abroad for many years and did little newspaper work I soon dropped out.

Many young writers owed their careers to the encouragement and concerted effort of the P.C.W.P.A. Long may it flourish!

Queen's Bench has no affiliation with any of the other clubs, nor does it in any way resemble them. It was founded in 1920 by twenty-one women lawyers. Its purposes are to encourage social activities and contacts among the members, to stimulate an interest in municipal, state and Federal legislation and in the activities of the State Bar of California, to hold discussions relative to the various legal problems of the members and to promote among them a spirit of mutual aid, co-operation and service. Residence in the Bay Area and admission to practice law in the State of California automatically determine eligibility of a woman lawyer to membership in Queen's Bench. The membership in this year of 1946 is 195.

Quite naturally Queen's Bench was vitally interested in the United Nations Conference which assembled in San Francisco in the spring of 1945. They had as guest speakers at one of their luncheons Brigadier General Carlos P. Romulo and two women delegates, Dr. Wu Yi-fang (China) and Mrs. Jessie Street (Australia); at a dinner Ruth Bryan Rohde, special assistant to the U. S. State Department.

Queen's Bench also served as one of the sponsoring organizations in presenting the United Women's Conference, delegates and advisers. The president of that year, Miss Katherine Hanrahan, served on the executive committee—Parliamentary Procedure and Publications.

During the seventh War Loan Drive Queen's Bench received a citation from the United States Treasury Department for selling $140,000 worth of war bonds.

Meetings of Queen's Bench are held twice a month at a luncheon on the first Thursday and at a dinner on the third Wednesday.

I shall have a good deal to say about a number of the members personally in a later chapter.

The oldest and most important literary club in the state is the California Writers' Club in Berkeley. It was founded in 1909 by George Sterling, Jack London, Herman Whittaker and Austin

Lewis, and all California writers of note and promising aspirants as well belong to it—or did until they had a lamentable rift and lost several of their most valuable members. They hold their dinners, with a high table for speakers, at the Claremont Hotel, brilliant affairs to which, upon occasion, guests are invited. Their members number 242.

The greater number of the women's clubs in San Francisco are interested in social service, and those devoted to charity and to educating girls for self-support will ever cherish the memory of Laura McKinstry and Katherine Felton, two women of old San Francisco families who spent the greater part of their lives in social service. The Parent-Teachers' Association is a branch of a national association and is of outstanding importance. The Quota Club, which found jobs for many of Miss Felton's girls, is also a branch, but a very active and notable one. There is also a branch of the Pan-American League (long brilliantly conducted by Mrs. Oliver Remick Grant), and another of the National League of American Penwomen. But the number is endless.

Many of these clubs have no quarters of their own and hold their meetings in a hotel or in the Western Woman's Club, which has a large auditorium, or in the Woman's City Club, an admirable institution, by the way, built by a number of public-spirited women as a residential club for young businesswomen.

As this biography of San Francisco is by no means a feministic chronicle the objection may be raised that I have practically ignored the clubs of the equally important male. My very good reason is that I know little more of the men's clubs than did the Century women of 1888. The Pacific and the Union long since consolidated and the club is familiarly known as the P-U. It is luxuriously housed in the old Flood mansion on Nob Hill. The Bohemian Club took its name from the calling of its members: newspapermen, authors, poets, artists, sculptors and a few professors. It has a beautiful grove of redwoods in Sonoma County where for two weeks in the year it holds its "Jinks," cremates care, witnesses a play by one of its members, has comfortably furnished bungalows and tents, a chef, and enjoys itself characteristically. Its personnel has changed with the years, for many rich men have invaded it. These, however, when they enter that phase of life known as elderly, migrate permanently to the P-U, to which they also belong. The Jewish club, Concordia, absorbed the Argonaut and not only has a handsome building on the corner of Van Ness Avenue and Post Street but a fine golf club on the western rim of the city.

CLIFF HOUSE AND SEAL ROCKS

THE OCEAN BEACH, SAN FRANCISCO

CHAPTER TEN

# *California Labor School*

WE HAVE all been told that once upon a time a lion lay down with a lamb, but who ever heard of two lions of two "local races" going to bed together and snoring in happy unison? Nevertheless it has happened here in San Francisco, that city of contradictions, sweeping divergencies, abrupt and startling changes.

Plans for the Union Labor School were made shortly after Pearl Harbor, and it was opened in August 1943. It was launched by a group—here come the lions—from the AFL and CIO unions "who felt the need for a new type of adult education, geared to the war and adapted to the needs of the many thousands of new union members employed in the jobs of the Bay Area."

The school started with a modest program: twelve classes devoted to unionism, American and world history, citizenship and problems of the war. Much emphasis was put on the "nature of fascism and a need for strengthening democracy against our enemies."

About one hundred students were enrolled for the first term. Teachers were CIO and AFL union officials. The first school was located in a large loft over an automobile salesroom in Turk Street.

From its very inception the school far exceeded the expectations of its founders and rapidly became a new kind of community center for San Francisco. A growing list of unions and union councils became sponsors, giving the school financial support through monthly donations. And this new approach to adult education attracted members of the University of California, Stanford, the State Teachers College of San José, Menlo Junior College—all of whom became teachers at the school within a year. During that same period the number of classes tripled. They were held in the library (such as it was at that time), offices, and even hallways. Local community leaders became interested in the school and actively sponsored it. Forums and conferences on subjects related to the war and to community living were held in the school auditorium.

Certain students attended classes one evening a week for a two-hour period. Many shipyard workers came in their working clothes with tin hats and lunch boxes and went on to the graveyard shift afterward.

Besides war workers, cultural classes were held for housewives, social workers, doctors, lawyers, service men and women, office and professional workers, students from near-by universities and representatives of almost every section of San Francisco life. It was not long before a drama department, arts and crafts department, a Saturday program for children were added to the curriculum.

Conferences on man-power needs, on transportation, the introduction of women into heavy industry, child-care needs, and many other subjects were held at the school, and speakers came from government agencies, from business and industry and from labor unions. The school sponsored a health conference in January 1944, which was held in Larkin Hall in the Civic Auditorium, attended by 280 representatives of labor organizations, public and private health agencies. Out of this conference grew the Northern California Health Committee which is now doing excellent work in this area.

By the beginning of 1944 the school was bursting its seams. Attendance had increased to more than 800 students a term. The men and women who had come to the school for classes in history, unionism and economics now demanded classes in figure drawing, philosophy, psychiatry, architecture and languages.

Because of the increasing interest in and demands on the school new headquarters were necessary, and in June 1944 it was moved to a five-story building at 215 Market Street, but a few steps from the Embarcadero and the Ferry Building. Quite a change from the loft which must have been uncomfortable and crowded, to say the least! In the new quarters the school has a real auditorium, a library of 50,000 volumes, an art gallery, conference rooms and a large number of classrooms. In the autumn of 1944 an East Bay division of the school was established in Oakland. Extension classes are held in many near-by communities.

Attendance has risen to 2,600 students a semester, including those who attend the extension classes and the school in Oakland. Some classes have had as many as 300 students. In 1944 an educational advisory committee was established. On it serve a number of the most notable educators in northern California. (Professor Holland Roberts of Stanford is on the staff as Director of Education.)

Many men and women of high reputation have lectured to classes and forums: the distinguished architect Frank Lloyd Wright, who came from his home in Taliesin, Wisconsin, for the sole object of giving one lecture at the school; Vicente Lombardo, the Latin-American labor leader; the poet Muriel Rukeyser; Adrien Falk, former president of the San Francisco Chamber of Commerce; Attorney General Robert Kenney; Richard Neutra, architect; Orson Welles; and many artists, writers and businessmen, to say nothing of professors.

In 1945 E. Bogosian conducted a three-part course on "Books

That Make up Our Minds"; Isobel Cerney of Bryn Mawr a class on creative writing and on another evening a poetry workshop (whatever that may mean); practical journalism is taught by Gail Hazard on Friday evenings. At the Oakland branch Anthony Boucher, detective-story expert of the San Francisco *Chronicle,* gave a course on writing technique, and William Turner, labor reporter, taught a journalism class.

To quote Joseph Henry Jackson on the Labor School's course, "The Workshop in Public Relations": "The method will be for students to select term projects and follow them through to completion, preparing and using speeches, articles, radio programs, posters, letters, exhibits, press releases, forums and conferences. Along with this practical work will be a series of lectures on what is and what is not news, on current opinion influencing methods and trends, on the recognition and use of propaganda and so on. Newspapermen, advertising experts, economic and public-relations authorities will conduct these lectures and work with students.

"Courses of this kind naturally have their practical value; students can turn to good account what they learn in their jobs sooner or later. But there is another side to it that shouldn't be missed. Learning to handle propaganda of any kind is perhaps the best way to learn how to recognize propaganda. The man or woman who knows the techniques of influencing public opinion and who has put some of these techniques into practice, is prepared to understand and resist propaganda, no matter how cleverly disguised, that is put out for evil ends."

Individual sponsors of the California Labor School include many leaders in state and community activities: editors, civil leaders, businessmen, lawyers, bankers, unions, manufacturers, a judge of the Superior Court, a member of the Daniel B. Koshland-Levi Strauss Company, of the International Center, the International

Labor Bureau, the National Lawyers Guild, one United States senator, one United States representative, one state senator, a bishop and a sheriff. Also Mr. and Mrs. Pierre Monteux.

Today seventy classes are offered each term. Current problems that cry for solution get a great deal of attention in the classes that are a part of the regular curriculum. "Personality in a Changing World" deals with psychological problems and is taught by the city's leading psychiatrists. "Postwar Housing" has an enrollment of 125 students, and its instructors are nationally famous architects and city planners. "Postwar Reconversion" brought together business and labor leaders—one session of the course was taught jointly by Harry Bridges and Adrien Falk, who spoke in complete accord on the necessity of labor-management unity.

The school is financed by regular contributions from unions and industry, registration fees, foundation grants (Columbia and Rosenburg Foundations) and individual contributions: Yehudi Menuhin, William Crocker, Richard Gump and many others.

Unions which contribute to the school provide in this manner for scholarships for all members of their organizations.

Three languages are taught besides English: Russian, French and Spanish. All of these classes are conducted by experienced teachers, many of them university professors.

There are lectures on American history, labor history, public speaking and parliamentary procedure. Nor are the arts neglected: there are a number of class sessions where the aspiring may learn something of writing, painting, sculpture and architecture, as well as crafts and photography.

On Saturday there are cultural classes for children from seven to thirteen: dancing, singing, drama, arts and crafts. There is also a Children's Theater.

Mrs. Yagodka, who has kindly provided me with many of the

details for this chapter, is Publication Director. This is an extremely important office. To quote from one of the school's handsome and artistic bulletins: "The Union Service Department of the School has been established to give assistance to unions and other organizations in the preparation of all written material. This service includes the preparation of leaflets, pamphlets, bulletins, organizational letters, and the editing of union newspapers. The services of a professional writer who has had long experience in the labor movement and is an expert in layout are available through the department. Assistance in editing local union papers is now being given by the Union Service Department, which has also aided in the preparation of several outstanding pamphlets, including 'Made in Berlin' and 'Twelve Thousand Marine Cooks and Stewards.' "

A bookshop has been set up in the library, stacked with current pamphlets and publications required for class study.

To quote again from the bulletin (1942): "STATEMENT OF POLICY: Now in its fourth year, the California Labor School is an integral part of the community it serves. This has been accomplished through a broad program of adult education stressing those subjects which equip men and women to become more effective in strengthening the principles upon which our democracy is based.

"The school's major emphasis, in its classes and other activities, is on fostering a unity of purpose and understanding among all sections of the community. In our classes, forums and conferences, instructors and lecturers represent business, government and labor as well as the cultural and academic fields. And in every instance, planning now for a peacetime world of full employment, of technological and artistic advancement, is the guiding principle of our staff and teachers.

"Thus has been created in the California Labor School a center for unity and concerted action which is hewing a straight path toward a future that promises security and dignity for every man, woman and child in our community. This is our aim and this is the purpose to which the school is dedicated. The sincere support which is given to this program by organized labor, business groups and community organizations, stands as a guarantee of the continued success of the California Labor School in this endeavor."

There are nineteen members of the staff, including the elevator operator and the janitor—verily democratic!

The director who carries this heavy burden is Mr. David Jenkins, an active, genial, highly intelligent and enormously capable young man who looks as if he had not a care in the world.

And now Mr. Eugene Bielawski, formerly with Moholy-Nagy Institute of Design in Chicago, has come to San Francisco to head the revolutionary arts program recently planned by the California Labor School. "We are going to tie up art to industry," he announced. "The program will be arranged so that after the student has obtained a basic understanding of his tools, materials and machinery, he will spend half his day in employment with his chosen profession and the other half in theoretical training at the school."

CHAPTER ELEVEN

# Historic Banks of San Francisco

SOME of these banks have changed their partners and names as often as a Hollywood star. San Francisco might be called the financial Reno.

In 1885 Drexel, Sather and Church became Sather and Church; in 1887 it was the Sather Banking Company, in 1897 the San Francisco National Bank. In 1910 it consolidated with the Bank of California.

Parrott and Company, organized in 1855, merged with the London and San Francisco Bank, Ltd., in 1871, and was purchased by the Bank of California in 1905.

Garrison, Morgan, Fretz and Ralston, founded in 1856, became Fretz, Ralston and Company in 1857; Donohoe, Ralston and Company in 1861; Fretz and Ralston again in 1864. All of which leads up to the Bank of California, which opened its doors on September 6, 1864.

Of the four preceding banks William Chapman Ralston was the presiding genius, and from that mighty but wayward brain sprang, even as Pallas Athena from the anterior of Zeus, a consummation whose destiny it was to become one of the great banking houses of the world.

Sometime in the 1840's my grandfather, Stephen Franklin, then a cotton planter in Louisiana, first met Mr. Ralston, clerk on a steamboat plying between New Orleans and St. Louis, who came to his office in New Orleans, to collect a freight bill. In a manuscript contributed to the Bancroft Library (University of California) he gave his first impression of the man with whom his own life was to be so closely interwoven: "I remember to have been impressed with his appearance at the time as a very bright young man of fine physique and prepossessing manner." Elsewhere in the manuscript he described Ralston as he was in the years of his power and his fame: "Though somewhat brusk and offhand in manner, he was genial, accessible and winning, of fine presence, manly and magnetic, and of boundless hospitality." (He might have added that his eyes were blue, his hair and short beard of the hue generally known as sandy.)

The Bank of California began its career in the rooms of Fretz and Ralston on the southwest corner of Washington and Battery Streets, with a capital of $2,500,000. Ralston had persuaded D. O. Mills, a cold, hard and conservative man with a considerable banking experience, to be president. Ralston himself was treasurer, and Stephen Franklin (whose fortune had been lost owing to the speculations of his partner and who had come to California in the early '50's), was secretary, a position he occupied until his death in 1890.

By July 1, 1866, the capital of the bank had increased to $5,000,-000, and June 27, 1867, it moved to its present site on the corner of California and Sansome. This imposing structure is described in detail by Oscar Lewis in his manuscript history of the bank.

"A two-story structure with arched windows flanked by thirteen-foot stone columns, the whole surmounted by a stone balustrade. The style was described as Venetian-Italian. The material of the exterior walls was a hard stratified stone of a bluish cast, known locally as Angel Island bluestone, after the island in the Bay in which it was quarried. The building covered the entire lot (80 by 67½ feet), being two stories over most of the area, with a one-story extension on the western part of the California Street side. Three doors opened on the street; the main entrance was on California Street, a private door farther west giving entrance to the executive offices in the single-story extension, and a bullion entrance on Sansome Street. In the center of the Sansome Street side was a stairway leading to the second floor, where the bank's attorneys, Barron and Bell, had their office.

"The banking room occupied the entire ground floor of the main building, with nineteen-foot walls rising to an ornamental ceiling, paneled in the Italian style. A counter of San Domingo polished mahogany extended at right angles into the room. Behind the counters the tellers and clerks served the needs of the customers. The counters had no grilles and the banking space beyond was without the wickets and cages familiar today. Gold and silver coin (there was virtually no currency in circulation in California at that time) were stacked beside the receiving and paying tellers. Gas lamps with green shades stood at intervals along the counter and provided illumination on dark days. The private offices of officials: president, treasurer, secretary and land agent, as well as the directors' room, were in the extension to the left of the main entrance. At the rear of the banking room customers could see the front of the main vaults, 'of solid iron and elegant in its design'— the whole surmounted by a handsome clock. Over each of its heavy doors was the head of a watch dog in relief, 'keeping silent and constant vigil over the treasure within.'

"This and the other vaults—there were four in all—aroused particular interest. They were manufactured under Lillie's patent, by Russell, Erwing and Company, in Troy, New York, and were pronounced the best yet made in the United States. Their walls, floor and roof were of chilled iron three inches thick. The doors were also of chilled iron, an inch thicker than the walls, and equipped with combination locks of an improved design. Surrounding the iron walls was an outer wall two feet thick of stone blocks doweled together. The bank was both fire and burglar proof.

"Construction on the new building was started in 1865. It was more than two years building and the cost was approximately $250,000. This removal of the bank to California and Sansome Streets—a site it occupies to this day—had much to do with permanently fixing the city's financial activity in that district. It was at that time that California Street began to be referred to as the 'Wall Street of the West.' "

Zoeth Skinner Eldredge, in his *History of California,* has this to say: "To none but those of the older generation of Californians is it given to know and understand the commanding position held and influence possessed by this great bank. . . . Not only did it at once assume leadership in financial affairs, but in matters social and political it was a power to be reckoned with. . . . The greater mercantile, manufacturing and business houses at once enrolled themselves among its patrons and supporters and it was with pride that men spoke of their connection with the Bank of California. Its board of directors was composed of the heads of the largest houses in San Francisco; the oldest and strongest banker on the coast was its president, and the cashier was considered a marvel of ability, and the ablest financier in California. Throughout the entire establishment the same excellence of appointment was followed. The best of tellers, accountants, exchange experts, and clerks were employed on high salaries. It was an honor to occupy a position in the Bank of California."

On March 25, 1876, the *News Letter,* a caustic weekly, indulged in reminiscence: "When the Bank of California moved to the corner of California and Sansome amongst a parcel of auctioneers, whisky shops and such, even the men who determined the movement had an inadequate perception of its results. When the other banks followed, however, it became to San Francisco what Wall Street was to New York and Lombard Street to London, and perhaps it will remain so."

To quote Oscar Lewis again: "With the entire western third of the nation as its field of operations, the bank promptly made its influence felt in many directions. Enterprises designed to spread the development of this vast territory received its encouragement and support. Thus aid was promptly forthcoming to hasten the spread of agriculture and to foster manufacturing on the Coast. It gave support to the development of trans-Pacific ocean traffic and so laid the foundation for the great Oriental trade that has ever since been a potent factor in the business of Pacific Coast ports. From the beginning the bank extended liberal credit to the Central Pacific Railroad, the western half of the transcontinental line that was, in 1869, to connect the Coast with the Atlantic seaboard. Still another instance of the broad vision of the bank's management was its encouragement of commercial relations with Alaska—a connection that proved a not unimportant factor of the Government's purchase of that rich territory from Russia in 1867, three years after the bank was founded.

"Important as were these connections in extending California's commercial relations with the rest of the world, these were not the bank's only interests during that period. Not the distant Orient nor Alaska but near-by Nevada became the theater of its activity during the first fifteen years of its existence."

In 1863 the Comstock Lode (discovered in 1859) was known as the richest silver-mining district in the world. As Nevada was sparsely settled, the excitement—which rivaled that of the Gold Rush of '49 and the early '50's—was largely confined to California, and by 1864 the major part of the available capital of that state (and hopes as wild as those of '49) was transferred to the Comstock Lode.

*Bonanza!*

Two months after the Bank of California opened for business it established an agency in Virginia City with William Sharon as manager and Ralston's brother James as treasurer. Heaven only knows the amount of capital poured into that bank and two others by the Bank of California (owing to mismanagement the Comstock finances were in a bad way at the time, despite the richness of the lode), but it soon rolled back in a silver flood, many times augmented.

Let it be understood that Ralston was the bank and the bank was Ralston. The president, D. O. Mills, spent much of his time in New York and abroad arranging connections and correspondents for the bank. The public rarely thought of him. It was Ralston who determined the policy of the bank, and it is doubtful if he ever consulted anyone, for it was his habit to come to a decision instanter and act as quickly. It was Ralston who was interviewed by every man of consequence who entered that bank, every man representing one of the growing industries or what not. Although his unique personality overshadowed that of every man with whom he came in contact, no man was so popular, no man so admired, trusted and loved. And probably no man ever had a better time. He loved power, he loved work, he loved excitement and variety, he loved his fellow men, and entertained royally at his beautiful home at Belmont the local friends he favored and such of the world's notables as visited California during his reign.

I recall nothing of the treasurer who succeeded Ralston when D. O. Mills resigned and Ralston became president in name, but I do remember the man who at a later date occupied that office. His name was Thomas Brown, and he was a dour old thing. I believe he was chosen for his sound financial reputation. He dined with us one night and I recall that he hardly uttered a word except "Thanks" or "No, thanks." Our cook had made a delicious dish of escaloped oysters and he said "Thanks" twice to that. His daughter Grace, as pretty and amiable as her father was homely and repellant, was a school friend of mine and I went to her house occasionally but kept out of the old man's way.

As Oscar Lewis quoted what I had written in my autobiography about the secretary of the bank, Stephen Franklin, I will repeat it here: "He lived to the age of eighty, a superb figure of a man, tall, noble, and dignified, who was pointed out to strangers as 'the handsomest of San Francisco's many handsome men.' He was the more conspicuous for being clean-shaven, a novelty for many years." And Lewis continues: "Old-time San Franciscans retain the memory of Franklin as he appeared in the late '80's: a venerable figure who seemed literally to belong to another era. He habitually dressed in the 'old style,' with flaring collar and black silk stock. On the street he wore a black silk hat, and carried an ivory-headed cane. 'His writing,' an associate once recalled, 'was like copperplate, and there is still in existence a Number One minute book of the bank, all in his beautiful script, page after page without blot or blemish.' "

Brilliantly successful and already famous as the bank was it had its tribulations. There were fluctuations in the value of the Comstock shares, in which enormous sums were invested. That unsettled banking conditions generally. And in 1865 there was an issue of United States Government bonds that proved so alluring to investors (it must be remembered that San Franciscans were born gamblers) that large sums were withdrawn from the local banks to reinvest—$400,000 from the Bank of California alone. Of course there was a sharp break in prices. And then came the earthquake of 1868.

San Francisco has had three major earthquakes within recorded history: 1808, 1868, 1906. (There have been many shocks of varying intensity between, although they have decreased since 1906.) After this terrifying visitation in 1868 many depositors liquidated their local investments, packed their trunks and departed never to return.

The money stringency grew more and more severe. The Bank of California faced the most formidable problem of its brief career. It had lent $3,000,000 to the Central Pacific Railroad. Two million dollars had left the state for investment in South America by a group of San Franciscans. "Large shipments of gold had gone to New York, where Jay Gould's cornering of the gold market had increased the premium of the metal and large assignments of gold went east from California. The result was a scarcity of coin so acute that California banks were hard pressed to meet the ordinary demands of their customers. A further complicating feature was that, although the banks had in their vaults gold bullion of a value sufficient for all needs, the San Francisco Mint was shut down and there was no possibility of having the bars minted to meet the dire emergency. True, the local United States Subtreasury contained some $16,000,000 in gold coin, but Treasury Department officials in Washington, and finally President Grant himself, refused appeals of the Western bankers that they be allowed to exchange their gold bars for coin."

But Ralston was ever a man of resource. The love of his life was San Francisco and he was determined to save her. If every bank in the city failed her ruin was inevitable. She might not recover for ten years, if ever. More and more plans for her greatness were taking shape in that fertile brain, and foiled they should not be.

If desperate measures were needed to ensure her safety, taken they must be, and with no loss of time. A run on the banks might occur at any moment, for on every street corner groups of men were muttering, prophesying, all but tearing their hair. And the initial run would be on the Bank of California. If the leading bank west of the Rocky Mountains could meet the demand the other banks would be saved—and San Francisco!

At one o'clock in the morning the downtown district was as barren of life as a necropolis. On the night of the great decision there was no moon and the street lamps were dim and few. Three men, Ralston and two trusted friends, Maurice Dore and Ashbury Harpending, stole out of the Bank of California and walked rapidly to the United States Subtreasury on Montgomery Street between Sacramento and California. The friend whom Ralston loved best remained behind at the door of the bullion entrance on Sansome Street.

A dim light burned within the Subtreasury. There was no watchman at the door, no policeman in sight. Ralston opened the door and closed it behind him. In a few moments he reappeared with several sacks of coin. "Take these to the bank," he said curtly. "The gentleman at the door will give you something to bring back."

The two men shouldered the heavy sacks and covered the short distance quickly. The gentleman-in-waiting tallied the coins and gave the men gold bars in return. Back and forth, back and forth tramped Dore and Harpending until five tons of gold coins had been transferred from the Subtreasury to the bank and five tons of gold bars from the bank to the Subtreasury. As dawn approached they were ready to collapse and their backs must have ached for a month.

The gentleman-in-waiting was the secretary of the bank, Stephen Franklin.

When I read this story many years later—in Julian Dana's *The Man Who Built San Francisco*—I was horrified. My grandfather! That deeply religious man, an elder in a Presbyterian church, superintendent of the Sunday school, leader of the Wednesday-night prayer meeting! And family prayers every night at home that lasted half an hour! (I regret to say that after he had finished a chapter in the Bible and went down on his knees to pray, I sat back on my heels behind him and braided my hair for the night.) But horror passed as my long understanding of him enabled me to follow his mental processes when Ralston asked him to do his part in as illegal an act as ever was perpetrated even in San Francisco. It was not for love of Ralston alone. What right have I, he must have said to himself, to consider my conscience when the whole future of a potentially great city is at stake? There is no one else he can trust. If I fail him the city goes down to ruin. Thousands will be beggared. Half the population will desert the city upon which they are building their own futures. Only the Bank of California can save San Francisco. What is one man's conscience—?

Ralston's timing was perfect. At nine o'clock California Street between Sansome and Montgomery was a solid block of men, their faces drawn and pale, their eyes wild or dim with despair. Someone had started the rumor that the Bank of California was tottering and they had come to salvage what they might. As time passed and the hour approached for those great doors to open some even wept and wrung their hands. As a clock struck ten they held their breath.

The clock sounded its final note—was it the note of doom? But no. The doors were opened as quietly and methodically as ever. The mob rushed in, elbowing, pushing and thrusting, bank-books in hand.

But in a moment they halted, their eyes blinking, their throats emitting queer gurgles or choking. Gold. Gold. Gold. Gold everywhere. Enormous trays heaped with five, ten, twenty-dollar gold pieces three feet high. The famous mahogany counters groaned under their weight. Ali Baba's cave, could it have been evoked, would have looked like a piker beside that dazzling dis-play of mountainettes of gold, gold, gold. There must be at least a million dollars in that great room (there was little less). How had they ever doubted their own Billy Ralston?

What the paying tellers thought as they stood behind those trays may never be known. They looked bland, merely a trifle astonished at this unwonted visitation, but ready to oblige. The mob turned and went out. When a man jumped on a box and shouted the astounding news to the hundreds who had been unable to enter the bank there was a moment of stunned silence, and then a roar went up that must have been heard at the Embarcadero. "Three cheers for Ralston!" "Good old Billy Ralston!" "Our own Billy Ralston, God bless him!"

San Francisco was saved.

(Don't ask me, nor anyone else, how Ralston had his way with the local Subtreasury. That is a secret he took with him into his tomb on Lone Mountain.)

Prosperous years followed for San Francisco. The five silver mines of the Comstock Lode—California, Consolidated Virginia, Crown Point, Belcher, Raymond and Ely—poured forth a seem-ingly inexhaustible flood of silver. The old San Francisco Stock Exchange was no longer able to accommodate the increasing number of brokers and in January 1872 the California Stock Exchange Board was organized and they moved into a larger building.

Daily and hourly until men fell in their tracks from exhaustion, it was a scene of such frenzied excitement that all memory of the Gold Rush was obliterated. A few great fortunes were made. Other millionaires went broke when the speculation microbe had reduced their reason to ashes. But thousands made comfortable fortunes and kept them. In 1872 the market value of the Nevada stocks shot up from $17,000,000 to $84,000,000. Ralston, like others, made many millions.

The excitement of those years added fuel to his creative imagination. As I have said, his passion was San Francisco, his ambition to make her one of the greatest cities in the world. In rapid succession his teeming brain projected and his superhuman energy put through the Mission Woollen Mills, the Kimball Carriage Factory, the West Coast Furniture Factory, the San Francisco Sugar Refinery, the dry dock at Hunter's Point, the Grand Hotel, the reclamation works on Sherman Island, the irrigating works in the San Joaquin Valley, the Rincon Hill Cut, the California Theater— and the Palace Hotel, to be known in its heyday as the finest hotel in the world. No man ever possessed a greater civic imagination. (In addition to these vast outlays, heavy loans were made, by the bank, to ocean and rail transport companies, land and irrigation projects.)

But alas! Gradually, almost imperceptibly at first, the silver mines began to show signs of exhaustion, and later there were devastating floods. Ralston, who had begun these costly enterprises with his own millions, used the bank's reserve to finish them, his unconquerable optimism assuring him that other lodes would be discovered in the Comstock or elsewhere in Nevada, and his own fortune rehabilitated before the bank was inconvenienced. He sold the Palace Hotel to Sharon and borrowed from other banks. But he must have had some dark moments before the end came.

It suited the purpose of one of these banks, intensely jealous of Ralston and of the Bank of California, to watch for the weak moment and call in its loans. Other banks followed suit. On August 27, 1875, California rocked with the news—and vibrations of that earthquake were felt all over the financial world, for Ralston's famous institution was the agent of the Rothschilds—that the Bank of California, long regarded as Gibraltar's twin, had closed its doors.

There was wild excitement in the street, but a grim calm prevailed within. Ralston, after a talk with my grandfather, during which he spoke with determination of his plans for the future, retired to his office and sat alone, awaiting the inevitable decision of the Board of Directors, assembled in the Board room. D. O. Mills, William Sharon, "Lucky" Baldwin and others agreed to rehabilitate the bank out of their personal fortunes. The three mentioned would contribute $1,000,000 each, others sums ranging from $100,000 to $250,000. Ralston's resignation was asked for and received.

Summers in San Francisco are cold with an occasional hot spell. This August day was the hottest of the year. As Ralston left the bank he met his doctor, John Pitman, and informed him that he had shifted a load of care from his shoulders by resigning the presidency of the bank, exclaiming gaily, "I feel like a schoolboy off for his holidays. I'm off for North Beach and my daily swim. Come along with me." The doctor was unable to accept the invitation and begged him to go home and rest. Ralston merely laughed and went off by himself. An hour later the newsboys were shrieking, "Suicide of William C. Ralston! Body washed up on North Beach."

That night Sharon said to my grandfather, "Best thing he could have done." But both Stephen Franklin and Dr. Pitman treated the suicide theory with contempt. Unquestionably he had died from a stroke.

San Francisco gave him the grandest funeral in its history. Half the population followed the hearse to Lone Mountain.

To quote from Eldredge in his *History of California,* when writing of the bank: "The prestige of its name, the romance of its history and the hold it had on the imagination of the people, the character of the men in control, the large amount of its syndicate guaranty as well as the strength and standing of its guarantors, all told in its favor, and proved the perfect success of the rehabilitation—a success more wonderful than was dreamed of by the managers—for, from being the great bank of the state, the Bank of California had become one of the great banks of the nation."

The bank reopened its doors on October 2, 1875. As the clock on the Merchants' Exchange struck ten, flags were run up all over the city, the crowds in California Street and on the roofs of the buildings cheered wildly. An artillery salute was fired on Telegraph Hill. The deposits on that first day of renewed business were $1,020,000.

Times were good again all over the United States. All of Ralston's investments prospered. In 1878 the bank was so firmly established that D. O. Mills, who once more had acted as president, resigned from the office and went to New York to live. William Alvord, long associated with the bank, succeeded him.

In 1869 deposits were $6,000,000, and resources $11,280,000. In 1906 resources had climbed to $40,000,000.

The population of San Francisco increased steadily and the business of the Bank of California with it. And not for this reason only: it had bought out several other banks, the last and most important the London and San Francisco Bank, Ltd., acquired in 1905. The Board agreed that a new and larger building was imperative; both its needs and its proud position as the great bank of the West demanded it.

They purchased adjacent land on both California and Sansome Streets, moved into the building that had housed the London and San Francisco Bank, and wreckage began on the old structure that had sheltered them for nearly forty years. This was in January 1906. At fourteen minutes past five on April eighteenth the third historic earthquake tossed the city about as if it were a featherweight, followed by a fire that reduced San Francisco to a mass of ashes and rubble from the Embarcadero (eastern water front) to Van Ness Avenue.

It was three weeks before it was deemed safe to open the vaults of the Bank of California. To expose the contents before the steel and masonry had cooled might cause the inflammable material within to burst into flame. Meanwhile the wreckage of the old bank was cleared away by the employees. The working class (being fed by the Citizens' Finance Committee, organized by J. Downey Harvey and presided over by another eminent citizen, James D. Phelan, to whom President Theodore Roosevelt had sent personally the $1,500,000 voted by Congress for the relief of the stricken city) was taking it easy on the sand dunes beyond the Western Addition. Nobody blamed them. Wasn't it enough to have been burned out of house and home? Let them take a well-earned rest. That was a time when all men were brothers and what any one of them did was right. "Earthquake love," that amiable cynic, Mr. James D. Phelan, dubbed it. (There were the usual exceptions, of course: the scalawag politicians, thieves, robbers and grafters had gone into hiding.)

But the bank's employees accomplished their task, and in due course the rebuilding began. Meanwhile the bank established headquarters over the ruins of their temporary home. The vaults were opened, the contents found to be intact, and they could accommodate their hard-pressed customers—not only "downtown" but in a building they had rented on the corner of O'Farrell Street and Franklin Street and several months later they moved to 1128 Van Ness Avenue. Other banks, industrial and brokerage houses and retail establishments rented buildings in the same neighborhood and remained there until the devastated area was rebuilt.

In September 1908 the Bank of California moved into its new building. In the darkness of night $54,000,000 in securities and coin were conveyed from where they had sojourned for two eventful years to their permanent home, and on the morning of the eighth the doors were thrown open to a waiting and admiring public. Oscar Lewis gives a description of the new bank with his usual regard for detail: "It was designed by the architects Bliss and Faville and its general outlines are those of a Roman temple. The distinctive feature of its California and Sansome Streets façade is an impressive series of Corinthian columns, their capitals rising to a massive pediment of pure Roman design. The space between the columns is occupied by tall windows of bronze and glass. The exterior material is Raymond granite, quarried in California, over a steel frame, while the interior is finished in Tennessee marble and mahogany. The main banking room was, on its completion, and remains today, one of the handsomest and most spacious in the West. Measuring 112 by 80 feet, it is lighted on three sides by a series of thirty-five-foot windows, while fifty-three feet above is a striking paneled ceiling finished in gilt and pale blue. Partitions of the counting room are of steel, the counters of marble, and the fittings of bronze and brass. Not the least striking feature of the banking room is the ornamental clock facing the entrance. Flanking the dial are two magnificent California lions, carved in a stone of a shade harmonious with the finish of the walls. The group was designed and executed by Arthur Putnam, sculptor of animals.

"The new building was planned with a view of providing the bank with a headquarters of permanence, beauty and convenience, and every detail reflects the care exercised to attain these ends. From the massive vaults in the basement to the intricate ceiling, the big structure ingeniously combines the spacious dignity of classic design with the complex utilitarian functions of the modern banking house. So skillfully was this accomplished that the building has been recognized not only as one of the architectural ornaments of the city but as among the most successful of all adaptations of classical architecture to the special needs of modern business."

"The days of old, the days of gold, the days of forty-nine"— pleasantly exciting days to read about, not so pleasant and far more exciting for the forty-niner who panned a fortune out of the diggings of the Mother Lode, and lived in terror lest he be robbed by less fortunate miners or by highwaymen on his way to the little town of San Francisco for supplies. He packed his gold dust in a wide belt, filled his pockets to bulging, carried the nuggets in a sack which served as a pillow at night, when he slept pistol in hand.

Even in San Francisco there was no one he could trust to take his dust and nuggets on the long sea journey "back East" and deposit them safely, the while he panned out more or dug it out of crevices with a bowie knife.

Two or three banks were started in San Francisco but were unsatisfactory. It was not until 1852 that two young men, Henry Wells and William G. Fargo, with reserves brought from New York and banking experience, met all the requirements of the miners. "Wells, Fargo and Company," they announced, "will transact a general Banking, Exchange and Collecting business. General and special deposits received. Collections and remittances made in all parts of California, Oregon, and the Atlantic states and Europe with promptness and dispatch. Gold dust, gold and silver coin, and bullion, bought and sold. Money advanced on gold dust deposited for transmission and coinage." It was a conservative bank and indulged in none of the crazy speculation that prevailed not only in the rivers of gold flowing down from the Mother Lode but in city land values. In 1855 there were between fifteen and twenty banks in San Francisco and every one of them save Wells, Fargo's crashed in February of that year during a panic caused by the failure of an Eastern bank. Wells, Fargo and Company's deposits doubled during the following month.

But that bank, which had no rival until the Bank of California was founded in 1864, had other and more novel interests. Not only the miners but San Franciscans had long been clamoring for an overland connection with the East. Water-borne mail and treasure were too slow to suit those impatient spirits. Accordingly, in 1858 John Butterfield, an associate of Wells, Fargo, organized the first stage route—a formidable task, for wells had to be dug along the route, frequent stations built and fortified against hostile Indians who delighted to wear bleeding scalps dangling from their belts. Coaches had to be built, honest, fearless and experienced drivers hunted out here and there. Nevertheless, in the autumn of that year the first stages went through in twenty-five days from Tipton, Missouri, across the desert to Los Angeles, thence to San Francisco. When the Civil War broke out the route was forced

farther north—via Salt Lake—and Butterfield had the major part
of his work to do over again. But he was equal to the task, and,
shortly after, the Overland Stage System became a part of Wells,
Fargo and Company's ever-growing business.

It was a day of wild excitement in San Francisco when the first
stage raced down Montgomery Street, the four horses galloping,
the driver shouting as he cracked his whip, the coach bouncing like
a cockleshell in a stormy sea, while the unhappy passengers within
clung to one another and braced themselves as best they could. All
the citizens of San Francisco crowded the sidewalks and cheered
and shouted, then closed in behind the stage and ran with it to the
Post Office. The exhausted passengers were tenderly escorted to
the hotel where they promptly went to bed. The driver was feted
and presented with a sack of gold dust.

After that the stages came regularly, and although excitement
diminished as novelty wore thin, they were always greeted by
cheers and there was always a long line at the Post Office. The
most famous of the drivers were Hank Monk, Mike Tovey, and
that Charles Pankhurst who once routed a gang of highwaymen
single-handed, and who, when he died at the age of sixty-six and
after long years of service, was discovered to be a woman.

But San Franciscans were never satisfied. No sooner had they
obtained an object of desire than they wanted something better.
The stagecoach was an improvement on the long journey either
"round the Horn" or via Panama, but before two years had passed
they were demanding still faster transport. The stage might take
but twenty-five days from Missouri to California, but mail from the
Atlantic states to Missouri consumed more precious time.

And so came into being the most original and whimwham of all mail carriers, the Pony Express, that covered 2,000 miles of wilderness in ten days.

Those young riders must have been men of incredible courage. The stages could be defended by the shotgun messenger who sat beside the driver—Bret Harte served in this capacity at one time—and every passenger carried a gun of his own. The bloodthirsty Indians, whose only weapons were the bow and arrow, after carrying off a number of riddled bodies were no longer encountered by the stages. Even the highway desperadoes, who were after not scalps but the Wells, Fargo treasure chest, were rarely successful even when led by Black Bart—that scholarly patron of Alex Robertson's bookstore at a later date.

But these heroes of the Pony Express rode alone. And not only did Indians pursue them, but they had to combat huge snowdrifts and swollen mountain streams, and they were ever in fear that their relay stations would be isolated by the red men. How any of them escaped is one of the mysteries, but, extraordinary to relate, the greater number made the trip without disaster—and made it in ten days.

The Pony Express, like the stagecoach, was absorbed by Wells, Fargo and Company.

When the transcontinental railroad was built a few years later that was of course the end of both stagecoach and Pony Express.

In 1875 four Bonanza Kings—Flood, Mackay, Fair and O'Brian —founded the Nevada Bank of San Francisco with a capital of $10,000,000. It became a national bank in 1898. In 1905 it consolidated with Wells, Fargo and Company, thus adding to that institution's ever-growing importance. Its capital today is $9,000,-000; surplus, $6,000,000; undivided profits, $3,000,000.

The Wells, Fargo Bank and Union Trust Company after eight

migrations finally settled itself after the fire of 1906 in the eleven-story building it now occupies on the corner of Market and Montgomery Streets. It is proud of being not only the oldest bank in the West, with fifty departments occupied with current business, but it possesses a unique feature: on the ground floor and open to the public is the "History Room" whose contents attracted a great deal of attention at Treasure Island during the International Exposition of 1939-1940, highlighting as they do the history of California between 1849 and 1868—from Gold Rush days to the completion of the transcontinental railroad.

Here are the iron shutters that once protected the Wells, Fargo office at Chinese Camp, pierced by a bullet hole, a pleasant memento of a battle between desperadoes and the faithful agent who lost his life while defending his trust: pick, shovel and pan, examples of those rude makeshifts that "recovered" some $50,-000,000 worth of gold that made many fortunes, a large part of which was lost at the gaming tables in San Francisco, and which cost many lives; a long, formidable-looking bowie knife, the first of the mining implements; the rocker, or miner's cradle, which enabled the placer miner to wash many times as much gold as could be handled in a pan; a Long Tom, or sluice box; paintings and photographs of Lola Montez, Hank Monk, William Cody (Buffalo Bill), Black Bart, Bret Harte, Mike Tovey; one of the old treasure chests; mail saddlebags; firearms; gold slugs that had been stamped by private firms to furnish badly needed currency (smaller transactions were settled with gold dust); a model of a branch office in Columbia (now a ghost town) remembered as having in its possession for a brief time the largest piece of free gold ever found on the American continent, "a giant crab-shaped mass valued at $43,000"; the desk on which Mark Twain wrote *Roughing It*. Here too is a replica of the gold spike—the "Last

Spike"—driven by Governor Stanford into the transcontinental railroad. The original is the property of Stanford University, but reposes in the vaults of Wells, Fargo. It was on exhibition, however, at the San Diego Exposition of 1935 and on Treasure Island during the Golden Gate International Exposition.

There is also a library of some 500 books and manuscripts relating to the period.

Altogether the most interesting bank to visit in San Francisco.

In Spanish countries they have a dish they call *olla podrida*. There is always a large iron pot on the back of the kitchen stove and in this pot are deposited tidbits left over from every meal. These choice particles simmer until they combine into one of the Spaniard's favorite dishes. Many flavors become the one perfect flavor, reminiscent of none. It is not a dish, however, that appears on the table, but is partaken of when, between meals, fancy or hunger dictates.

When I was in Madrid I used to sit at my hotel window and watch the afternoon "promenade" of open carriages that went on for several hours. It was a gay sight. A few of the women wore smart Paris frocks, but by far the greater number draped their head and shoulders in mantillas of black or white Spanish lace, held in place by a high comb or a flaming red flower. I was told that every so often a carriage would leave the procession, drive to the house of its inmates, who entered and refreshed themselves with the national dish, *olla podrida*. This rite over, they returned to their crawling vehicle to take the air, or exhibit themselves, until it was time to dress for dinner.

The memory of that dish returned to me as I read the history of certain San Francisco banks, which, judging by the other banks they have absorbed, must have the digestion of an ostrich.

The Anglo California National Bank of San Francisco is a case in point. In its brilliant career between 1873 and 1946 it has absorbed no less than seventeen other banks (perhaps more) and is still one of the healthiest in the world. Today it has twenty-two bustling offices.

As early as 1868 the eight Seligman brothers, with banks in London, Paris, Frankfurt and New York, played a leading part in the financial history of San Francisco. In that year they were operating a banking office, the outgrowth of an important business established in 1850. In 1873, recognizing the growing importance of California, with its enterprise, its great mineral and agricultural wealth, the Seligman headquarters in London converted the San Francisco banking business of J. and W. Seligman and Company into The Anglo-Californian Bank, Limited, with a capital of $1,500,000. In this year of 1946 the capital funds and reserves are approximately $26,000,000. But that was after many mutations and rebaptisms.

In 1876 the firm of Lazard Frères, an old silk-importing house of New York, London and Paris, opened an agency in San Francisco under the management of Alexander Weill, brother of our old friend Raphael Weill, founder of The White House. Lazard Frères also dealt in foreign exchange and gradually entered the banking business, representing, among other connections, the Government of France on the Pacific Coast. In 1884 it became known as The London, Paris and American Bank, Limited, with a capital of $2,000,000.

These two banks were on extremely good terms.

During the fire of 1906, like many another bank, both the Anglo-Californian and the London, Paris and American were totally destroyed. But not the dynamic soul of Philip Lilienthal, manager of the former, and the restless Sigmund Greenebaum, manager of the latter. Until the debris was carted away and they could erect new buildings they conducted business in their residences in the Western Addition. In 1908, in order to bring the London, Paris and American Bank under the banking laws of the United States, a group of California businessmen secured control of the foreign-held stock and nationalized the bank under the name of The London Paris National Bank. Its total assets were $15,000,000. The Anglo-Californian Bank had assets exceeding $12,000,000 and maintained three branches located on Mission Street, Fillmore Street and Van Ness Avenue, branches that had been established for the convenience of customers during the period of reconstruction after the fire. On April 1, 1909, the two banks were consolidated to form The Anglo & London Paris National Bank of San Francisco, with a capital of $4,000,000 and surplus of $1,500,000. The initial deposits were $18,700,000. Nor was this the end.

At the time of the merger a national bank was not permitted to conduct a trust or savings business. In order to retain and develop the trust and savings business built up by the Anglo-Californian Bank, the organizers of the Anglo & London Paris National Bank in 1909 formed a new bank under a state charter: the Anglo-California Trust Company, with a capital of $500,000, its quarters being the former Mission branch of the Anglo-Californian Bank. This new concern soon absorbed the Central Trust Company of California, and three other banks, and by 1928 had established eight branches. It was aptly called "The City-wide Bank."

Meanwhile the two "Anglos," the Anglo & London Paris National Bank and its offspring, the Anglo-California Trust Company, had experienced a tremendous increase in deposits. Many of the nation's notable business firms from the Atlantic to the Pacific chose the former for their West Coast deposits, while the trust company specialized in trust and saving functions, serving tens of thousands of Californians in every walk of life.

To change the simile once more: the big ostrich took into its nest the littler ostrich and all its offspring. On June 30, 1932, the two banks consolidated under the name of The Anglo-California National Bank of San Francisco, and then proceeded to acquire other banks in the northern part of the state. On December 31, 1945, its resources were $519,462,930 and it served nearly 175,000 depositors.

What next? At the present moment San Francisco is expanding at such a terrific rate of speed that the depositors in time may crowd the sidewalks on either side and the poor tellers die of exhaustion. Well, we shall see. Anything is possible in this most unpredictable of cities.

Odd as it may seem, the Anglo, although bursting with riches, has a strong feeling for beauty, and after several movings has built itself a bank that is an ornament to the city. It is of white granite and the architecture is a pure example of Roman Doric with columns and pilasters. Within, the walls are of Italian travertine, the coffered ceilings of stone, the floors and counters of Italian marble. Its number is One Sansome Street and it is a block long.

This bank has had two personal tragedies in its history. I have related elsewhere the singular death of Philip Lilienthal in 1908. During the 1890's Mr. A. H. Breckenfeld, assistant manager, was unable to endure the loss of his wife. The day following her death, after putting all his affairs in connection with the bank in meticulous order, he lay down beside her and put an end to his own life.

Julian Dana, leading authority on the subject, has written for me this acount of Giannini and the Bank of America:

On May 6, 1870, there was born in San José, California, an American of Italian parentage, Amadeo Peter Giannini. At thirty he was a six-foot-three, two-hundred-pound athlete with a likable

PORTALS OF THE PAST, LLOYD LAKE, GOLDEN GATE PARK

UNION SQUARE

grin and chatter-proof eyes, a retired San Francisco commission merchant with an income of $500 a month and no knowledge of banking. At the close of World War II he was head of the Transamerica Corporation, founder and directing genius of the Bank of America, the world's largest bank, and the most potent financial figure in American life.

The San José farm boy was conditioned like thousands of other Americans. He rose with the sun, loved the land, worked hard because his parents had come to the United States with their future to make, went to school in the proverbial red schoolhouse and developed vast regard for the vegetables and fruits which his rich valley produced. When his family moved to San Francisco he fitted himself into the commission business at twelve, swept ahead with scant formal schooling into a commanding position as one of the city's leading commission men at twenty. Eleven years later he retired with his competency and a supposed urge for leisure.

But the exuberant energy in the Giannini hide refused the new restful days. In no time at all he walked into a small bank as a director, disapproved of the other directors, stormed out with the avowed intention of "organizing a bank for the little fellow." Always the "little man's banker," he made the first swift step that led to a new and expanding era in American banking. For A. P. Giannini was the father of successful American branch banking, the man who visualized what strength and services a branch-banking organization could bring to the average American and his family.

He began in a small way. One bank—named the Bank of Italy for a short period—a few personal friends as directors, an ambition to expand with an expanding state and nation—these were his principal assets in the beginning. Branches began to be added, slowly at first. New ideas popped out of A.P.'s noggin. With the years the Bank of America crept over the state into hundreds of branches, each branch operating with the financial soundness and backing of the entire organization. Never money-hungry—Giannini has rarely been worth more than $200,000 or $300,000 at any period in his life—he had an insatiable eagerness to build what he had in mind.

A man as tempestuously sure of himself as A. P. Giannini is always sure of a good fight in such a building. He had to fight depressions, state political machines, unit bankers, Federal and state banking laws, and all manner of obstacles. At one period of great stress, ill and weak, he left a sickbed to fight borers from within who sought to destroy his beloved bank with Wall Street control. He fought with his back to the wall, and became, with Henry Ford, the only living American to drop an atomic bomb under Wall Street's golden breeches and thrash the tycoons at their own game. That triumphant stand informed Eastern financial figures that the West had produced one tough-fibered giant, who, with his astute son, Lawrence Mario Giannini, at his side, was a very difficult fellow to handle indeed.

A hundred million Americans know him only as A. P. Giannini, who, with J. P. Morgan's passing, became America's Number One banker. To another 10,000,000 Americans he is affectionately known as "A.P.," who "likes the little fellow," runs more than 500 banks to serve him in a thousand different ways, who will fight at the drop of the hat in his interest. Lastly he is known to 10,000 Americans as "that blankety-blank, etc., who runs the Pacific Coast"—provided they are feeling charitable. The last-named handful, usually in the upper-income bracket, hold in their membership men who have fought Amadeo Peter Giannini for forty years and have never heard him cry "Uncle," not even in the case of the most powerful Uncle of them all.

When you walk along a California city street three of every five people you meet are Giannini depositors. Nine of every ten people you pass will, in his lifetime, be served by some Giannini organization in some constructive and friendly way. And every man, woman and child you meet has been the direct beneficiary of Amadeo Peter Giannini's interest in his state and his nation.

Many men see in A.P. a man living out of his age, one who belongs with the Hills, Harrisons and Goulds of a wild and wonderful and wasteful phase of hardfisted American action now considerably out of fashion. They say that the law has caught up with the giants of A.P.'s stature, and they feel they present a well-briefed case. What he has done, they say, can never be done again under the mountain of "must-not" legislation plastered over every inch of every blank wall in America.

But A. P. swears, with an earnestness beyond question, that all he has ever wanted to do was to build his bank as the law specified; that the existing regulatory agencies of government never let him do so; that discriminatory harassment only made him fight harder, think faster, battle longer. "If my opponents hadn't forced me to do it time after time," he rumbles, "there would have been no driving sustained effort to top the field. Unless they had pushed me from behind I would never have pushed ahead."

Giannini's story is as controversial as any of his crisp tart certainties. His life, his friends claim, "is an open book for all to read." Others see the same volume written in a dark code only a Machiavelli could have written.

But whether you love or hate the man is not important. Nothing matters but what such a man has built and how that building has affected the lives of others. A wise man who is strong tries to build so that when Finis is written to his living no inept or malicious hand can destroy the work he has done. A man's supreme attainment is to create the almost imperishable, so that his Age will have learned from him, so that evolution of his art, or strife, or gift of chance, will have taken a forward step that cannot be forgotten or displaced by the march of years.

If there is a master key to Giannini's dream (and no man's life is opened by a single key) it is the hope that he has fashioned the many-edged tool of American branch banking so that it will fit forever neatly into man's hands to run his living by—a many-edged tool that can be sharpened and hafted for every challenge, guided by head and heart to carve out new necessities when change demands.

When will a man like Giannini "retire?" Only when the Fellow with the Scythe gets around to it. As late as May 1945 he made another of his fabulous gestures by handing over the chairmanship of the board. But today he has a $5,000,000,000 bank. In a state of only 9,000,000 people you see him standing feet firm, shoulders wide, head flung high—a smiling Colossus beaming on "the Biggest Bank in America."

We come to the point then that Giannini has done more than he set out to do. He has made his bank around your corner the place where an American can safely put his dollar to work. He has given that bank a thousand arms to render a thousand services, cheaply, efficiently, surely. He has given that bank the strength of a thousand banks. If you claim hotly that no man who comes after him will ever build so big again, then you are perhaps naming him what he really is—the last of the men who dare to build and fight and gain the goal in the ancient and individual American way—the Last of the Giants.

On February 10, 1868, nine Germans, residents of San Francisco, formed the German Savings and Loan Society with the modest capital of $200,000. This sum was increased from time to time until 1890 when the capital was $1,000,000.

The first advertising reads: "Loans made on real estate and other collateral securities at current rates." It was avowedly a bank for the common man, the small depositor, the small homeowner, and was intensely conservative, unspectacular. Its stern honesty was never questioned. It became the most popular and flourishing savings bank in the city, and its patrons were by no means confined to the poor.

In 1918, during World War I, wisdom prevailed over sentiment and its name was changed to the San Francisco Savings and Loan Society, which on June 1, 1925, was abbreviated to the San Francisco Bank. Its president is Parker S. Maddux.

From the day of its founding this bank has pursued its steady course with none of the usual ups and downs. Too conservative, or too conscientious, to speculate, it went through the aftermath of the Civil War, the Comstock crash, the numerous depressions, without a flutter. Today it is the wealthiest savings bank west of Philadelphia. The present resources are $268,829,407.21; deposits, $250,980,816.42; number of depositors, 113,160. And—the present value of a share of the stock is $17,800, the highest price of any bank in the United States, perhaps in the world. The interest on these shares is $600 a year.

The Hibernia Savings and Loan Society (Hibernia Bank) was incorporated in 1864. There is no authorized record of the bank's history. Its main office is located at Market, McAllister and Jones Streets, and it has four branch offices. Richard M. Tobin is president, and Joseph O. Tobin secretary. It has assets totaling $137,-776,348.15, most of which are in United States bonds. It has served 729,477 depositors since its organization, and today the average amount of deposits is $1,627.69. It has paid in dividends to its depositors during its history $142,351,718.51, so its economic contribution to the San Francisco area is in no way inconsiderable. I understand that it is the oldest savings bank in San Francisco.

# CHAPTER TWELVE

# Yes, We Have Slums

THE stranger visiting San Francisco for the first time is impressed with its novel beauty, its solid business precinct, the gorgeous masses of flowers on the street corners of the handsome shopping district—a promenade for well-dressed women—its picturesque Chinatown with its display of Oriental goods, vases and jades, and pretty little children playing on the sidewalks, the towering hills with their magnificent hotels, apartment houses, and cathedrals, Golden Gate Park and the numerous green "squares" scattered throughout the city, the large subdivisions on the outskirts with their great variety of architecture and large gardens, the unique cable cars that slide up and down the steep hills, packed inside and out, men and women standing precariously on the running boards of the "dummies," indifferent to the danger of being swept off or lurched off, the beautiful churches and synagogues, the schoolhouses that look like small palaces, wide Market Street that separates the hills from the valley, lined with shops and hotels from the Embarcadero to Twin Peaks over four miles west, the Presidio with its historic associations, comfortable houses, imposing barracks and menacing guns. True, the downtown streets crowded with streetcars, automobiles and busses, are, with few exceptions, too narrow for comfort, but on the whole the visitor receives an impression of beauty and prosperity. Even the Mission and Potrero districts, where so many of the working class settled themselves after the fire of 1906, have a pleasant homely neatness and good shops.

Nowhere does the visitor see any evidence of poverty. Here at last is a city without a slum, a city with an atmosphere of cheer, well-being, affluence and with a history both romantic and remarkable behind it. Unless he happens to meet the Health Officer or any of the women who devote their lives to social service he is convinced that at last he has seen the one perfect city.

The majority of San Franciscans, even those who had seen certain disreputable streets running south from Market Street, lined mainly with saloons, dingy hotels and bawdy houses, but with no evidence of real poverty, were equally unenlightened until September 1945 when they were horrified by a series of articles in the *News*. Inspired either by the Health Officer, Dr. Geiger, or by mere curiosity, it occurred to a young reporter, James Buckley, to investigate the area adjacent to the Third and Townsend Street Depot in the southern part of the city. He soon realized that he was in a "blighted district" (polite name for slum). He stumbled over broken sidewalks, past dilapidated rooming houses, "hotels," and filthy stores. He choked as he passed trash heaps (i. e., garbage), black with flies and rats, open windows emitting the stench of neglected toilets, musty bedding, bedbugs and boiling cabbage.

Mr. Buckley felt rather sick, but every good reporter has a "nose for news," and here was a story for his paper. He entered one of the tenements, picking his way carefully, for stairs were broken and there was little light. In the halls were garbage cans uncovered and stinking. He passed a leaking toilet almost invisible under a swarm of big green blowflies. Dust, dirt, cobwebs, evidences of gnawing rats everywhere, greasy walls.

He talked with some of the tenants and found them philosophical, but was not surprised to learn that the tuberculosis rate was high, particularly among children. With the multitudinous disease-carrying flies the wonder was that typhoid, typhus, cholera had left anything alive in that blighted area but rats. But the salt Pacific winds have saved the people so far.

A woman who lived in one large room with her family and a rooster, and whose solitary window was closed to keep out the fog, told Mr. Buckley cheerfully that in clear weather she could keep the window open and "when it's good cold weather and a good strong wind is blowing the children and I don't have headaches." She said nothing of the children playing in a courtyard with a leaking sewer, or among the garbage thrown from a window.

Mr. Buckley returned to his desk and pounded out a vivid graphic story for the *News,* to which the startled but gratified editor gave the place of honor on the front page of the next issue of his widely read paper. "Big news!" All the more certain to attract attention now that the killing business was over and news from Europe and the East Pacific somewhat tepid after the daily blood and thunder of the last six years.

But Mr. Buckley's article, or "piece" as they call it in newspaper circles, arresting as it was, paled before the one that followed. Like a thoroughbred bloodhound on the scent he started out at once to find other blighted areas. He found one: this time not far from San Francisco's pride, the magnificent Civic Center. Outwardly it resembled his first discovery with its garbage heap, flies and rats, its unholy smells, but within it was even worse. In a flimsy building of three stories ninety persons were housed in rooms eight feet by eight with cardboard partitions eight feet high. On the first floor there were no windows, and few anywhere.

A pale tired young woman said to Mr. Buckley: "I'm always uneasy when my husband's away at the shipyards, because a man could break down this partition easy. No man's ever tried, but every now and then some of them get drunk and start fighting. That's why so many of the doors have holes punched through them. Of course they didn't mean to do it."

And for this tenement with its ninety inhabitants there are two bathtubs and three toilets in working order. Before each Mr. Buckley saw a line of women awaiting their turn. Conditions in the concentration camps of Germany during the war could not have been much worse.

The manager lived on one of the upper floors where there were windows and the two bathtubs. But even he could not avoid the stenches from toilets and garbage cans. However, he got twenty dollars a month for each of his eight-by-eight rooms, and the nose is an accommodating organ: its sensibilities are quickly blunted.

It is gratifying to know that the Health Department had given its attention to at least one of the shameful buildings in this locality and condemned it. To quote Mr. Buckley: "Want to know the reason? You'll find they cover three typewritten pages nailed on a frame wall from which plaster is peeling. Beneath it are broken steps marked with animal filth and obviously long gnawed by rats.

"Yet this large multi-room two-story structure looks as though it might have been a mansion half a century ago. It has what evidently were servants' rooms. 'First and second floors unfit for human habitation,' says the notice of condemnation in part. 'The place is not rat-proofed, and there is much evidence of rats. The posts supporting the rear porch show signs of decay. The rear porch is weakened and is in a serious condition. The rear stair handrails are missing or loose. The sleeping rooms have gas plates in them. The stove is connected with only a rubber hose, exposing occupants of the house to danger from asphyxiation. The water line in the kitchen sink is open, to the detriment of food. The water-closet bowl is loose and the seat loose and broken. The wooden boxes at the window are used for food storage, although it is plain that the food stored there is accessible to rats.' "

Meanwhile, Mr. Buckley discovered (or perhaps he knew it all along; I am not in his confidence) that plans are being considered for cleaning up these slums, which are a disgrace to San Francisco. City-Planning Engineer L. Deming Tilton, had already made an imaginary reconstruction of twenty blocks of one of the city's worst blighted areas. "He believes it possible," writes Mr. Buckley, "provided the true purposes of the Redevelopment Law are understood by all groups, to turn a dirty disease-breeding area where children can hardly find even trash heaps in which to play, into a clean and beautiful section. There developments would have every modern convenience, with a large park for children and adults and all at a moderate cost. And he foresees providing homes for as many and perhaps even more people than are huddled together miserably under the present system."

To quote Mr. Tilton: "The keynote of the whole redevelopment plan and the conditions of its eventual success, is a clear understanding by everyone—and I mean everyone—that each person in this city is going to benefit by it. The city will benefit directly because the eradication of the underprivileged areas and their attendant breeding places for juvenile delinquency is a direct and substantial saving in municipal expenditures—not even considering the moral side. Cleaning up the bad spots that mar San Francisco's great beauty cuts down the cost of fire ravages and the toll of disease, while the city profits directly by bigger tax revenues. And we, the people of San Francisco, are going to benefit not only by sharing in these savings but because for the first time in decades we are going to get access to some of the potentially finest residential parts of San Francisco from which we have barred ourselves for no better reason than civic laziness."

"This," comments Mr. Buckley, "is how the City-Planning Commission report points the way for reconversion in the next few years—provided court battles do not block the machinery indefinitely. The survey of the twenty square blocks, which remain nameless for the time being to spare the feeling of property owners in the area, shows that those property owners have pre-empted ninety percent of the average block, leaving hardly more than an occasional narrow lane as a back yard for the children of their tenants. . . . By the way, the Commission estimates a given area could be purchased by the city for $6,700,000, the site cleaned and new dwellings erected for $1,500 a unit. The new buildings would be free of rats and rubbish, would be provided with the essential conveniences, ventilation and sanitation, and be protected from termites. Owners who received the average blighted area rental of $25.10 per month, by banding together and selling to the municipal setup under the law, then could repurchase or lease the entirely rejuvenated property, get $47 per month for a three-unit apartment, realize five percent on the investment. Such improvements as a school site and a community center would still require only from thirty to fifty percent of the block area, leaving space for a freeway around the block and park playgrounds in the center. And, by the device of erecting taller buildings on secure concrete foundations, replacing today's wooden structures, the area might accommodate as high as 10,000 people instead of the prewar 7,500."

We shall see. There will be some lively scenes in the courts when men are commanded to sell their houses and gardens in the

Western Addition (their homes) for the benefit of the proletariat. Why not clean up "South of Market Street" instead? It sorely needs it.

It is at least some comfort to know that Michel Weill, the energetic, high-minded young owner of The White House, is president of the City-Planning Commission.

# CHAPTER THIRTEEN

# The Intermediate State

And woman, yea woman, shall be terrible in story,
 The tales too meseemeth shall be other than of yore,
For a fear there is that cometh out of woman and a glory
 And the hard hating voices shall encompass her no more.

THESE lines written by Euripides in the fifth century B.C. may
have been intended to encourage the wives of Athens whose men
spent their days among the marble temples and pillared porticoes
of the agora arguing questions of immediate import, or subjects
dearer to their intellects, their evenings with the gay and often
brilliant hetaerae, and wasted no time on the home. In the dim
and distant past Attica had been a Woman's State and man the
subordinate sex, but it is doubtful if those wives of Athens knew
aught of history, for respectable girls received no education save in
housewifery, the duties of motherhood and a sweet submission to
their overlords.

But they did know that in Egypt women were the dominant
sex and men their creatures. They may also have heard that similar conditions existed in Libya, Lydia, Lycia and in the faraway
land of the Teutons; that in Sparta the women, once dominant,
were now at least the equals of men and wrestled naked with them
in gymnasia.

All this is not a matter of legend but historical fact. One has
only to read Herodotus, Pliny, Tacitus, Diodorus, Strato and Plato,
to say nothing of the great tragic poet Sophocles, who preceded Eu-

ripides and expressed himself with true masculine disgust in his
*Oedipus at Coloneus* as follows:

> . . . Now at all points their lives obey the law of Egypt,
> Where the men keep house and weave, sitting withindoors,
> While the wives abroad provide with ceaseless toil the
>     means of life.

Women in Egypt had been dominant for many years. They
went forth every morning to engage in business, banking, law,
agricultural problems and international relations. Those of a
lower social status tilled the fields, milked the cows, raised the
calves, butchered, tended the vegetable gardens, hauled water
from the Nile, cleaned the temples and public buildings and fed
the sacred cats. The men passed their lives indoors, cooked, kept
house generally, took care of the children and wove the clothes.
Children took the name of the mother and only girls could inherit
property.

In one respect only were women helpless before the stern decree
of Nature. All-powerful as they were it was they who must carry
on the race or it would cease to be. But on the third day after bearing they arose and went about the duties of their sex, while the
husband went to bed with the baby to keep it warm. On some
points history is silent, but one infers that the family cow performed one of the otherwise neglected duties of motherhood.

Centuries of active life in the open had made the women tall
and strong, and their majesty of carriage and authoritative mien
commanded the resentful admiration of men who came in ships to
Egypt to transact business of various kinds with that wealthy and
important state. Nevertheless, they were by no means warlike.
They loved peace, and if attacked hired mercenaries from men's
states to defend them.

At a later date skeletons of Teutonic women seven feet long were discovered. There is no hint that the women of Egypt were giants. Still, they towered above their men, who, spending their lives indoors and living a life of semileisure were of inferior stature, and no doubt buxom. They were on the whole treated kindly by their lordly wives, who often loved them, and as they wished to please, they spent much time in titivating themselves, dyed their hair with henna, and enhanced the brightness of their eyes with kohl. But never for a moment were they permitted to experience a pleasant sense of equality. If they presumed so far as to assert themselves they were soundly cuffed.

But time marches on. It was during the fifth century B.C. that some of the more enterprising of the men sneaked out of the house at night—the women slept heavily after their "unceasing toil"—and talked with those that came in ships. They learned of states where men were dominant, women the subordinate sex, of states too with a tradition of women's dominance in centuries long past. Rebellion, silent and festering, grew and spread. Again the men left the house at night and exercised their muscles, sloughed off fat, "talked big" of the day when they would shatter every restriction imposed by arrogant tyrannical females—rule in Egypt, hold their heads as high as the men of Athens and Sparta, of the great Asiatic states.

It was slow work. It took nearly a century for men to grow tall and strong, defy the astounded and infuriated dominants, give blow for blow when the ladies resorted to fisticuffs. But when Alexander the Great invaded Egypt in 332 B.C., he found the men and women in the intermediate state of equal rights. The Greeks imposed their man's-state ideology. Another century, and women were the subordinate sex.

All of the women's states passed into history. One of Life's cycles was complete. There is no doubt that in times as yet unexplored by historians, men had been dominant, abused their power and awakened the resentment and the energies of the women; that after the period of equality had run its course they were firmly reduced to insignificance—man's place was the home. The women grew more arrogant and oppressive, abused their power and paid the penalty. It was a man's world until the middle of the nineteenth century; then things began to happen. During the passing of the centuries men had grown more enlightened and therefore more lenient. There were schools or governesses for girls, and, when they were old enough, parties where they danced and talked with young men; and, when paterfamilias was not too old-fashioned, they chose their own husbands. Women sat at table when entertaining and listened while men discussed world affairs. They advanced no opinions of their own, but did a good deal of thinking. It was long before even the more intelligent questioned the dogmatism that woman's place was the home, and the God-given superiority of the male. Some were forced by circumstances to become schoolteachers, boardinghouse keepers, even house-to-house dressmakers. (What were the sentiments of the first woman who discovered that she could support herself? Would that she had kept a diary!)

And the time came when men enjoyed the company of intelligent women. Women became silent partners in politics. They even held *salons* where only political and intellectual subjects were discussed. But that, thought the men complacently, was as far as they would ever get; such latitude was permitted because certain women made life more interesting in spots.

But definitely woman's place was the home; she had been created to make life comfortable and pleasant for man, to bear and rear his children, and to companion him when she was wise enough. A few like Madame de Staël, the Brontës and George Sand distinguished themselves, and were regarded with acute disfavor, or condescension, but not as a portent! It never occurred to these all-powerful males that women were entering the outermost suburbs of that intermediate state, sex equality; they were still far from the center.

It was not until the middle of the nineteenth century, therefore, that the men received a terrible jolt. True, they had heard what they regarded as inconsequential babble about the right of women to vote, but told the ladies either playfully or sternly that they were getting beyond themselves; why not ask for the moon and be done with it? American women (the movement started in the United States) were darlings and the brightest in the world, but they never had been and never would be the equals of men. Nature had seen to that. Then began one of the most momentous campaigns in history.

The battle for the enfranchisement of women is too well known to recapitulate here. It was a long hard struggle. Men fought it bitterly—and many women, who feared that sex equality would destroy delicious femininity, with its subtle and precious power, far more important than running to the polls. But on the whole, American women, long drawn out as the struggle was, had an easier time of it than their sisters in Britain, who fought and scratched policemen, went on hunger strikes in jail, besieged the House of Commons, heckled public speakers and were dragged out of halls and beaten.

Suffice it to say they won.

As may be imagined, the girls, with few exceptions, took no interest in this Battle of the Sexes. Questions more personal absorbed them. And they already had certain liberties. They met men on their own level in sport—another portent overlooked by the dominants—they discarded the sidesaddle and the long riding skirt. They even rode bicycles in bloomers!

It was not until World War I that the girls woke up. Tens of thousands of young men had been killed or maimed in what seemed to them a useless and criminal war that settled nothing. They were fired with hatred and contempt for "those old fogies at the top" who had not had the brains to foresee and to prevent that war, to settle differences about a table instead of sending young men out to be slaughtered. When women were strong enough there would be no more wars. Would that they were men! Whether they realized it or not, they began to make themselves look as much like men as possible. They shingled or bobbed their hair, shortened their skirts, drank copiously (during Prohibition), sniffed at sentiment, sneered at religion, treated men as good fellows—and in short became as hard-boiled as the disillusioned men who returned from Europe when the war was over. (As may be imagined, Nature was too strong for them. They fell in love, married, had babies, were good mothers, but, with rare exceptions, retained their independent spirit.)

As time passed more and more women became self-supporting, either through necessity or preference. Fifty or sixty years ago those who were independent of men, besides the ones I have mentioned elsewhere, were authors and other artists, actresses, opera singers, newspaperwomen, a few doctors, government clerks, shopgirls and a limited number of typists. They numbered around 4,000. In 1900 they were competing with men to the tune of 1,000,000 or more, and the figure climbed steadily until in 1940 when it reached 11,278,920, according to the World Almanac. During World War II it increased enormously. And this is exclusive of women in business on their own.

Not for years have women been intent upon financial independence alone. They have become a formidable power in many ways. We have the National League of Women Voters; the National Federation of Women's Clubs; the International Federation of Business and Professional Women's Clubs; besides innumerable social service, education and cultural clubs, all in all numbering many millions in membership. Women have invaded state legislatures and Congress. There is not a small town that has not its women's cultural clubs, forums devoted to the study of politics and governmental questions. Women have become a power in the land and the end is not yet. They are prancing out of the suburbs and advancing toward the center where men will be forced to admit that the intermediate state of the ancients is upon him, that "Equal Rights" has more meaning than one, and to tremble at the prospect of becoming the subordinate sex. Some women today are as tall and powerful as prize fighters, but most of them are admirable in both character and intellect, and the prophecy and warning of Euripides rolling down through the centuries has come to pass in the twentieth.

But to get down to cases.

As this book is the story of San Francisco in its present phase, A.D. twentieth century, I will draw my illustrations from it alone, although it is typical of every state in the Union and many states elsewhere. We have a large number of women in the public eye who are either the equals of men or superior to them. Their struggle has been hard and bitter, but they have conquered. A few are "tough," but the majority have retained their femininity, are soft-spoken and dress as smartly as any women of fashionable society—all of which makes them doubly formidable.

We may as well begin with the lawyers, all of whom are members of Queen's Bench, that club of which I wrote in Chapter Nine.

Of these the most outstanding is the Honorable Thesesa Meikle, Judge of the Superior Court of California, in and for the City and County of San Francisco, and about her I shall quote largely from an enthusiastic member of her own sex and profession.

"Judge Meikle's sphere of public service, even up to this point (1946)—and she is still a young woman—has covered much ground in the fields of law, sociology, psychiatry, and above all, domestic relations and child welfare. . . . The citizens of the city of San Francisco know her well, speak of her with affection, and keep her in her high office because she is courageous and charitable, a genuine woman of the West, and an inheritor of the spirit of adventure and of steadfastness in the principles of the great pioneer women who set the pace which she is keeping.

"Judge Meikle is always available. No appointment is necessary. The word is always given by her associates and court personnel that she may be seen after court. This 'Good Will Hour' of Her Honor has been a source of interested observation to all of us for many years. She is so unstinting of her time and help, moral, mental, physical and financial.

"A sheltered childhood in the home of her brilliant, charming mother, and her father, William Frazer Meikle, a mining engineer of distinction and accomplishment, made the way for her first departure from the family hearth when she taught school for one year. When her family moved to Berkeley she attended the University of California. Her graduation in 1915 was followed by her matriculation in the Boalt Hall School of Law, whence, in possession of her Bachelor of Arts and Bachelor of Laws degrees in 1918, she entered upon the course of jurisprudence, from which she emerged with the degree of Doctor of Jurisprudence in 1919. Then after passing the State Bar examinations and becoming licensed to practice her chosen profession, she began taking the steps that have successively—and so successfully—fitted her for the high calling that is now hers.

"There are scores of quotations that I might refer to in order to let you know her accomplishments as District Attorney's Deputy when the Honorable Matthew Brady appointed her—the first man to recognize a woman's legal abilities—as his assistant. Her next step was into the office of the State Narcotic Division, where as Deputy State Attorney she prosecuted with notable success the narcotic violators.

"Governor C. C. Young appointed her to the office of Judge of the Municipal Court of San Francisco, to which office she was returned by the people at each election through twelve years.

"As Municipal Judge, whether presiding over the General Criminal Department, the Woman's Court, or any other division, Judge Meikle would get down to the Hall of Justice very early in the morning, on occasions, and dispatch the 'worthier' of the inebriates to their paths; at noon, after counseling with her 'Good Will' clients she would go up to visit the visitorless and possibly lawyerless prisoners and bring some human and spiritual consolation and comfort to them.

"In these ministrations and extrajudicial acts of Her Honor throughout the years, she endeared herself to policemen, firemen, court personnel, colleagues and members of the professions. This was proved by their support of her in all elections up to and including the campaign for election to the Superior Court in 1942, with certain notable exceptions! She was elected with a plurality of some 30,000 votes, the first woman to be elected Judge of the Superior Court.

"When Judge Meikle undertook her present assignment as Presiding Judge of the Juvenile Court there came into her already full life of usefulness a realization of a thirty-year dream, namely, to be of service to the children of San Francisco in a direct and practical way; she secured the opportunity for which she is so especially trained and innately fitted, to help by judicial decree, by deed and by personal example the failing of delinquent parents who, in wartime more than in any other, neglected their domestic duties and by their neglect threatened the ruin of their children's lives.

"Judge Meikle's administration of the Juvenile Court, in the handling of its fourteen varied calendars weekly—including the cases of children against adults, felonies and misdemeanors; the delinquent girls; the cases of abandonment and neglect, and all the other cases that come before a Juvenile Court—has been the subject of much gratification to her colleagues on the bench, to the members of the Juvenile Probation Committee, numbering nine distinguished citizens, who, by appointment from her or her predecessor in office, give generously of their time in directing and assisting in this great work, and to the personnel of the court and detention home.

"The organizations may be mentioned with which Her Honor has been actively connected: the San Francisco Chapter of the American Red Cross, of which she has been a director for eighteen years; the Children's Agency of San Francisco, of which she was long a director; the Community Chest; the University of California Alumni Association (she was the speaker at the twenty-fifth anniversary of her graduation); the California Club of California; the Women's City Club; Queen's Bench; the Dolores Branch of the Young Ladies' Institute; the Catholic Daughters of America."

To add a personal impression: Judge Meikle has looks, elegance, charm, wit, humor, gaiety, and is a brilliant conversationalist. Altogether an enviable array of attributes—"no?" as the Spanish say.

Zilfa Estcourt, the bright particular star of the San Francisco *Chronicle's* galaxy of women writers, has this to say of Katherine Hanrahan, President of Queen's Bench for 1945:

"Katherine Hanrahan is a typical career woman. She's good-looking, extremely intelligent, ambitious, and more interested in her work than in anything else. She's a tiny creature, with big brown eyes, soft brown hair and a smile that flashes across the usual seriousness of her face. Like many small women she has tremendous determination and the capacity to carry through whatever she undertakes."

Yes, Miss Hanrahan is all that, but a good deal more besides.

Born in San Francisco, she made up her mind to be a lawyer at the age of six, above all things to argue in court. This ambition persisted through her grammar-school days, but during her years at high school her enthusiasm waned although she was fond of debating. Her academic interest turned toward the teaching field, and at the University of California she took a cultural course of study in the College of Letters and Science, majoring in economics, minoring in political science, history, French and public speaking—all directed toward securing a certificate for high-school teaching at the end of the fifth year. During her undergraduate days her chief extracurricular interest was working two years—Sophomore and Junior—on the managerial staff of the Blue and Gold Year Book.

After receiving her A.B. degree from the University, with Phi Beta Kappa honors, she changed her mind and decided to take a business course. She began work as a legal stenographer in a firm of attorneys engaged in general practice. There her old ambition revived and she took a night course at the San Francisco Law School for four years—four nights a week. There she won a fifty-dollar scholarship in her third year; graduated in 1939 at the head of her class with an LL.B degree, the only girl in a class of nine. And until she passed her Bar examinations her employers knew nothing of that strenuous night life that had not interfered in the least with her daily work.

After being admitted to practice she remained with her old firm for a time as a legal stenographer, in addition doing notary-public work under a recently acquired commission. Then, after a two-month's vacation—high time for a vacation!—she returned to San Francisco in November 1940 and went to work for the Supreme Court of California, carrying on legal research for Associate Justice Jesse W. Curtis. When our time came to enter the war the young men who were in research work for the court were drafted, and women lawyers qualified to fill such positions had their opportunity. Miss Hanrahan continued with Justice Curtis until his retirement in 1944, and is now (1946) with his successor, Associate Justice Homer R. Spence as his chief research attorney engaged in drafting opinions and memoranda for the court.

She has no interest in private practice, in criminal law, or any of the sordid aspects of legal practice. She likes research, the drafting of opinions, and is especially interested in taxation problems, coincident with a natural flair for figures. During the war she served as a member of the Northern California War Work Committee appointed by the Board of Governors of the State Bar of California, assisted in the G. I. Legal Aid radio program, and for two years she worked at the Stage Door Canteen every Saturday night from 7:30 to 9:30, checking white hats and peacoats.

With all this she has found time for some foreign travel, and for such recreation as dancing, ice skating, outdoor life generally. And no one takes a deeper interest in world affairs. She may be small and slender but she must have the constitution of a thoroughbred young race horse.

Lenore D. Underwood, Deputy Attorney General of the State of California and specifically assigned the handling of legal matters connected with the liquidation of the Pacific States Savings and Loan Company, has not only had a distinguished legal career in San Francisco, but has led a full life, notable, say her many admirers, for extraordinary beneficence. "A superb selflessness was the cornerstone of the structure she has built." The net results— public recognition, prominent positions held, and enviable appointments here and there—are less interesting than the many episodes that led her from one activity to another in an ever-progressing scale. Born in the small city of Valoshin, province of Vilna in Russia, she came when a year and a half old to America. Her grandfather was Rabbi Edward, trained in the Valoshin Theological Seminary, which continued to be a recognized institution of learning until 1941 when "Hitler's heretic hordes destroyed the college and desecrated the accumulated records of past centuries."

The family first settled in New Haven, Connecticut, where her father, Harry L. White, an architect, became City Superintendent of Building Construction. He "was almost morbidly determined upon a rounded education for his children." Lenore, next to the eldest and the only girl of the six children, was required after regular school hours to study with a rabbi until she mastered the Bible in pure Hebrew text. This stiff assignment was no cause for joy in a young girl, but there is reason to assume the very intensity of the training was an excellent foundation for future work in whatever might be her chosen field of endeavor. Mr. White had a passion for attending lectures and invariably took Lenore with him. Although she hardly shared his enthusiasm through the long hours which she would have preferred to spend with her friends, she was so impressed by one crusader's talk that she put in part of her next vacation from school in every kind of factory that would employ her—solely to learn firsthand if conditions were as awful as depicted. Untrained, she was put to sewing on buttons at one factory, pressing seams at another, etc.—and she remained just long enough to "investigate," never long enough to draw any pay. In the end she decided that life would not be worth living in such conditions, but she was obliged to wait until she was much older before she found any way to alleviate the woes of the underprivileged.

Whether the urge to do for others was innate or grew out of environment and circumstances would be difficult to determine, but that her response was ever sympathetic is certain. From an understanding mother she had learned how to carry responsibilities with poise, and none too early, for Mr. White died when the youngest boy was two and the mother's cares were assumed by the daughter. "Mastering the multiplying problems became her métier—not just her own—everybody's." She once explained how her inclination for welfare work crystallized. "Such a lot of people in difficulties crossed my path, their bewilderment begging for help! I didn't have much, but I soon learned that a little willingness went a long way. A little genuine interest and common sense applied in the right place would nearly always disclose a way out of the trouble." Of course with a creed like that her future course was inevitable.

The very first job she held in the commercial world was one no one else had the patience to handle; it was deciphering those baffling hieroglyphics that appear at the end of a letter as "signatures." Probably her early bout with Hebrew paid dividends then. Anyway, she was the only person found to whom the illegible was legible.

From then on—with whatever firm she was connected—Lenore simply gravitated to the spot where trouble was, and with calm dexterity would iron out wrinkles, smooth ruffled feathers, or make chaos cosmic. This feature pertained to her first really serious commercial endeavor in San Francisco, with Associated Underwriters (now Crum & Foster). There, to use her own words, she was "demoted" from the more desirable position of secretary to the manager, to the Claim Department which had got into a state of hypertension owing to the amazing facility of a previous clerk to "skip it" and owing also to "the low boiling point of claimants." With Lenore installed high blood pressure was reduced, and the Claim Department ceased to be the firm's madhouse. And with eight hours a day in the business world much of her leisure was spent in social-service work!

In 1923 she married Mr. Henry T. Underwood, a widower with two small sons to whom she became a devoted mother.

Her years have been filled to overflowing, and to tell half of Mrs. Underwood's accomplishments would give the impression that her days each held forty-eight hours instead of the time-honored twenty-four. No one quite knows how she made each fleeting hour do the work of two—or more. We do have her word for it that she was literally driven to the study of law by the needs of the cases which came before her in her work with welfare organizations. Legal angles were always popping up and philanthropic lawyers to handle them were not. Very well! She would learn the law herself and then she'd know what to do for her cherished "wayfarers."

Even during the years at Hastings College of Law she continued her volunteer social-service plans. In 1932 she graduated from the school, passed her Bar examinations and opened her office for practice. Immediately there was more business than Attorney Underwood had anticipated; occasionally there was even someone who expected to pay her, but the greater part of her time was

given to those whose financial status could not meet the require-
ment of lawyers less altruistic.

Although Mrs. Underwood can be positive enough upon occasion she rarely says "No" to any poor soul in trouble, nor to any
of San Francisco's welfare societies, which call upon her constantly, and never in vain. Beginning in 1917 as Local Group
President of B'nai B'rith women, she has since been consecutively
Grand President of District 4—comprising eight Western states—
and National President in 1940. She found time to respond to
Mayor LaGuardia's call to assist with the mobilization of women
in National Defense—which became her war effort after Pearl
Harbor. In behalf of this organizational work alone she flew some
25,000 miles, not to mention numerous trips by land, to aid in
planning for classes in First Aid and Home Nursing.

A staggering record! Show me a man who has crowded as
much—and as varied—work into the span of thirty years.


Edith C. Wilson, Deputy District Attorney of the City and
County of San Francisco, was born in Oakland but has spent
most of her life in the City by the Golden Gate. She attended
grammar school, girls' high school, and the University of California,
receiving the degrees of A.B. and L.L.B. A year later she was appointed Assistant District Attorney, a position she has held with
notable vigor and ability for seventeen years.

And here is the staggering list of her "affiliations":

Charter member of the Yerba Buena Chapter of the Native
Daughters of the Golden West. Legal adviser and honorary member of the San Francisco Women's Chamber of Commerce. Legal
adviser and member of the San Francisco City and County Federation of Women's Clubs. Legal adviser and member of the Cali-

fornia Club. Past President of Queen's Bench. Past President and member of the San Francisco Chapter of the Soroptomist Club.

In practically all of these organizations she has served as president, other officer or member of the board, and is chairman of important committees in many of them—e.g., observer of city government for the Soroptomist.

She is chairman of the following committees for the City and County Federation of Women's Clubs and has been for many years: Child Welfare, Juvenile Court, Youth Co-operative, Women in Industry, Human Relations, State Institutions, Women in Government, Queen's Bench, San Francisco Women's Legislative Council.

Llewellyn T. McMahon, attorney for the San Francisco Office of the California State Chamber of Commerce, ascended to her present eminence by what is known as the hard way. Born in Oakland, she graduated from the grammar school there at the age of eleven, from the "high" at fifteen, from Mills College with an A.B. when she was nineteen. Then she attended the Hastings College of Law, the only girl in her class, graduating in May 1930 at twenty-two with the highest scholastic honors. In October she passed the Bar examinations and was admitted to practice in all California courts and in the Federal District Court and Federal Circuit Court of Appeals. She worked her way through the law school as a secretary in the office of a woman attorney, and no one discovered that she had had no secretarial training but made up her own shorthand system as she went along. She also served on the newspaper staff and the debating team of high school and college.

After admission to the Bar she entered private practice with her cousin Toland C. McGettigan and later with William J. McMahon. This was during the depression and their practice was confined to divorce cases, adoptions, damage suits and an occasional estate matter. Their income was small and fluctuating and it was not until she went to work for the Chamber of Commerce that a steady income met some of the "family responsibilities." Hired originally for three months to organize women's groups throughout the state in support of a campaign for adoption of four initiative measures intended to improve the administration of justice in criminal matters, she was such an astonishing success, with the overwhelming adoption of all four proposals (something never achieved before or since in this state), that she has remained a member of the Chamber's staff ever since.

As the only attorney on the staff she is known as the "legal research department." Her two major fields of activity have been: (1) analysis of proposed state and Federal legislation while it is still pending, instead of after it has become law. Her special field is labor-relations legislation, although she is frequently called upon to help various departments in agriculture, social security, industrial development, taxation, and a variety of other problems; her job being to analyze the legislation and point out what it will mean for good or ill. (2) To try to protect employers generally from that famous legal maxim "Ignorance of the law is no excuse." She has prepared and had distributed throughout the state a number of digests of state and Federal laws. In them the salient points of the statutes with which employers are required to comply are summarized, and information is provided as to the government agencies responsible for enforcement and administration. One of these publications, *A Digest of California Labor Laws,* has had a wide circulation. Not only employers but the government agencies enforcing those laws, and a number of law firms throughout the state, use it constantly. Two more digests, one on California tax laws and one on California licensing statutes are equally in demand. Among various other odd jobs for the Chamber from time to time she supervises its information service.

She is also a member of the legislative staff, attending the regular sessions of the California legislature to observe and report on the progress of legislation which is of vital concern to business, industry and agriculture; and preparing vote records after each of these sessions, listing and describing significant legislation, and indicating the votes of various members on such proposals.

In addition to all this, since 1930 she has been a member of the board of directors of the California League of Women Voters. She originally joined it as an expert on the legal status of women and has continued ever since to demonstrate the thesis, not yet wholly acceptable to the general public, that "women are people." She published a booklet on that subject and has done a good deal of speaking on woman's rights under California law. She has also served as the League's expert on public personnel, working in the various campaigns to improve the merit system for selecting public employees in the state. For the past four years she has served as "election chairman," which does not mean campaigning for individual candidates, but organizing materials and plans for activities throughout the state which will help members of the League and their neighbors in the various communities where "they function, to do an intelligent job as voters."

She has done a great deal of public speaking, endeavoring to explain to laymen in an hour or less the significance of ballot propositions, twenty to thirty in number, including such proposals as "Ham and Eggs" and the "Single Tax," so they may know what each proposal means to them as citizens. She has made some twenty such speeches before each election, all over the state.

For twelve years she has been a member of the board of directors of the San Francisco Y.W.C.A., serving in various capacities.

CITY HALL, SAN FRANCISCO

THE GOLDEN GATE BRIDGE AND STRAIT

She has been chairman of its Public Affairs, making recommendations as to what action it should take on public issues, in order to insure that the point of view of the women and girls in its constituency is fairly represented.

For several years she has been chairman of the Program Planning Committee, responsible for the evaluation of its progress as a Community Chest agency, to see that it is doing the best job possible to meet the needs of women and girls in the community during the war and the reconversion period.

Those are a few of her activities, and one would think they had left her little time for matrimony. Nevertheless in 1940 she married William J. McMahon and makes a delightful home for him in Berkeley.

The Western Pacific Railroad Company, headquarters at San Francisco, employs about ninety women, many of whom occupy clerical positions. Some are secretaries to officials, others are employed at stations along the line throughout California, Nevada and Utah. The highest-ranking of these women is Harriet P. Tyler, counsel in the Law Department.

To Mrs. Tyler fall intricate and important assignments, largely in the realm of finance, involving bond and equipment trust issues, Reconstruction Finance Corporation matters, Interstate Commerce Commission relations, finance dockets and other phases of railroad financing. Her twenty-four years of service with the railroad have given her a varied experience. She has performed at one time or another virtually all the types of work of a railroad law department. She is also secretary of the Alameda Belt line, owned jointly by the Western Pacific and the Santa Fé. She enjoys the distinction—rare for a woman—of being admitted to practice before the United States Supreme Court.

Mrs. Tyler was born in Oakland, California. After high school she attended the San Francisco Law School at night, supporting herself by working during the day as a stenographer in a law office. Immediately after being admitted to the Bar she obtained a position in the office of the clerk of the Supreme Court of California, and in 1931 joined the staff of the Western Pacific Railroad. During World War I she served as chief clerk in the Army's Signal Corps, Western Division.

Mrs. Tyler was one of the founders of Queen's Bench, is a member of San Francisco's Professional and Business Women's Club and has served on its Board of Directors. She is also a past president of the renowned American Federation of Soroptomist Clubs. She is a member of the American Bar Association, of the San Francisco Bar Association, of the National Association of Women Lawyers, of the Western Women's Club, and of the National League for Women's Service.

Married to a distinguished corporation lawyer, Mrs. Tyler's home is at Atherton, and her hobbies, to quote an admirer in the *Baltimore and Ohio Magazine,* are "gardening, the piano, golf, bridge and reading. Hobby No. 1, however, is Mr. Tyler."

Margaret Torreyson passed her early girlhood in an atmosphere of law and music. Her father, a graduate of Yale and later of Hastings College of Law in San Francisco, practiced in the state of Nevada for many years. He was District Attorney of Ormsby County, later Attorney General of the state. He died in 1912 leaving a wife and two small children and little money. Mrs. Torreyson moved to Reno where she gave singing lessons and led the choir in the Episcopal church, while the children out of school hours amused themselves with ice or roller skating according to the season, danced with other youngsters, rode horseback over the mountains and enjoyed themselves generally. After six years of Reno Mrs. Torreyson moved to Berkeley, California, where she obtained a position as bookkeeper in a bank. There Margaret attended the university, but a short time after decided to enter the business college, where she specialized in stenography. When she was eighteen she took a position in a law office in Berkeley, but, not satisfied with earning forty dollars a month, she found a better position in the legal department of the Southern Pacific Company, where she remained for six weeks. It was then she heard there was a vacancy in the law offices of Haven and Athern in San Francisco. She applied for the position and secured it, and there she remained until 1946. She handled all the work for three men, kept four sets of books, and did their reception office work. Rather a difficult assignment for an inexperienced and somewhat diffident girl, but she made good. At the end of two years Mr. Fred Athern—who is now the head of the firm of Athern, Chandler and Farmer, Hoffman and Angell—asked her if she wanted to remain a stenographer all her life. She replied with an emphatic "No," and told him she was thinking of entering a night law school. He encouraged her and she attended the school four nights a week, studying in her spare moments—of which there were not too many, for by that time the office had grown: there were three stenographers of whom she was the head, as well as being office manager. But hours meant nothing to her and many a time she took the midnight boat to Berkeley and returned to San Francisco the next morning on the seven-twenty. And with all this hard work she managed to find hours for play. She rode, swam, hiked, played golf once a week, made an annual trip to Yosemite for winter sports. In 1926 she graduated from the law school and in 1927 passed her Bar examinations. Now her stenographic work was over and she was given the probate work to handle, difficult but far more interesting. And she was also a partner in the firm.

In 1932 the Children's Home Society of California, an agency licensed to place children in homes for adoption, decided that a woman attorney should represent it in the counties of San Francisco, Marin, and San Mateo. Miss Torreyson was recommended for the office and accepted. This adoption work she has found the most interesting and constructive of her career. "One has a feeling of satisfaction," she told me, "in knowing that a child who otherwise would not have a home has been placed with good and fine people who will bring it up as their own, giving it all the advantages of a home."

Because of that work she has been in court a great deal. Other social welfare agencies demanded her services. Aside from the probate and adoption duties she has handled a general law practice, and found another interest in girls who aspire to enter the business world. She often appears before graduating classes in high schools to give vocational talks.

She served for a year as President of Queen's Bench, for two years on the Board of Governors of the San Francisco Bar. In 1934-1935 she was President of the San Francisco Business and Professional Women's Club, and at four different times has been Legislative Chairman of the local club. Because of the legislative work she has gone to Sacramento many times to talk and work with the senators and assemblymen on bills in which the business and professional women were interested. She found that if the women knew what they wanted and put their problem to their representatives in a clear and impersonal manner they would obtain the recognition given to men. She also attended sessions of the legislature when changes in adoption laws were contemplated, and worked either for or against the changes.

During the war she had an interesting assignment when the Army was recruiting the first women for the WACs. She was one of the eight women chosen by the recruiting office of the Army in San Francisco to sit with the examining board and go over the qualifications of those applying for service. When the time came for the girls to appear to display their oral and personal qualifications, Miss Torreyson sat with four boards, each composed of two women and one Army officer. From nine in the morning until five in the afternoon approximately 108 girls were examined by each board. The result was highly satisfactory, for the first group of women going out of San Francisco for training as officers was the finest group at the last training camp. Later she served on boards examining young women for the auxiliary service. More time, more work. When that day's job was over Miss Torreyson and the other women hastened to their offices and completed the work they had to leave undone while doing their duty by the government.

Miss Torreyson's work is well known to all San Franciscans. I wrote and asked her (to satisfy the curiosity of my readers), "Should a woman enter a field where the competition with men must be so formidable?" She replied: "My answer is yes, if she is willing to work hard, take cases she does not particularly like, and work enthusiastically and with no thought that she will not make good. More girls are in law schools than there have been for many years past, and I have great confidence that they will find places in the law. It is not an easy place for women, but many have made good and I have faith in the younger generation. So many women have gone into government agencies and succeeded that much of the feeling of discrimination has been overcome. There should be more women in judgeships, more women legislators. Women have been too hesitant to go ahead in the past, and have been content to take research positions in law offices, rather than go into active practice."

And now, alas, we are to lose her! She is severing her connection with the law firm in which she has been a partner since 1931 and is going south to practice with another woman in Westwood Village, near the University of California at Los Angeles. Not only does the south fascinate her but she feels that the time has come for a letdown after so many years of hard and unremitting work. The reader will probably agree with her!

So much for the women lawyers of San Francisco. There are 175 of them, and more to come.

Miss Mary Ellen Leary has two "firsts" to her credit.

She is political writer and editor on the San Francisco *News,* and the first woman to win the coveted Nieman Fellowship at Harvard University.

A San Francisco resident for over ten years, Miss Leary came to the *News* in 1936 after having received her master's degree from Stanford University. For three years she filed memos and soothed irate subscribers in her capacity as city-desk secretary. Her "break," which represented a rise from city desk to reporterdom came as the result of an accident. A big Mission Street murder broke at a time when no regular reporters were available. After scanning his empty domain the city editor sent Mary Ellen to cover it. She came through in magnificent syle, "scooped" the town, and it was a mere matter of time before she joined the editorial staff.

Like all cub reporters Mary Ellen had her share of murders, fires and conventions to cover, but it was not long before she rose from the ranks of a general-assignment reporter to a feature writer.

Prior to becoming political editor, she covered housing, juvenile delinquency, and education stories.

The Harvard Nieman Fellowship, awarded annually to ten journalistic specialists, provides that the recipient, on the same salary received from his newspaper, shall study for one school year any course bearing on his specialty. Only in 1945 was it opened to women, and Mary Ellen Leary was the fortunate "first." She is now at Harvard studying state government, with particular emphasis on state and local political problems of the postwar period.

Miss Leary has not limited her writing to newspaper work; she has had among other things four by-line articles published in the *Saturday Evening Post.* Two on the OPA, one on airport resorts, the fourth on San Francisco's Mayor Lapham.

Barbara Watson, California manager of the American Mail Line, is a full-fledged shipping executive—the only woman to hold such a position on the Pacific Coast, possibly in the world. It is up to her to "run" the activities of some sixty ships and their crews of the line as they touch in California ports. She is responsible for the last letter-perfect detail which might be necessary on a voyage whose destination may be any part of the globe.

Like any other steamship organization, her staff includes a Port Captain, Port Engineer and Port Steward, but it is the trim, energetic Miss Watson who has the final word and who co-ordinates all departments. It is she who does the hiring and firing. Under her jurisdiction comes many a seasoned sea master.

Following the footsteps of her father, a pioneer railroader, she "lived, slept and ate transportation" almost from her birth in the Indian Territory. Thus it was only natural that some twenty years ago she should turn to it for a livelihood—but never dreaming it would become the consuming interest of her life. After a varying experience with the railroads in the Middle West she associated herself with the steamship industry in San Francisco in 1936.

With the advent of war Miss Watson joined the Division of Emergency Shipping, which was soon absorbed by the War Shipping Administration. There she was assistant to A. R. Lintner, Pacific Coast Director of the War Shipping Administration.

When Mr. Lintner, president of the American Mail Line in Seattle, left San Francisco to return to his duties in that city, he asked Miss Watson to take over and run all California operations of his line. Such a position entails routine handling of a ship, paying off crews, providing new crews and signing them on, storing vessels with foodstuffs for the length of the expected voyage, as well as with deck and engine equipment to keep the ship in shape and repaired at sea—also repairing in port, etc.

Meanwhile, on shore, handling details of cargo has been accomplished before the ship has docked, but there is still a great mass of inbound cargo to be discharged and outbound cargo to be loaded.

During the war, of course, in the rush to keep ships, supplies and men moving to the battle front, everyone in the industry did the job at hand no matter what position he held. It was during one of these hectic times that Miss Watson found herself in Los Angeles harbor waiting to climb from a swaying launch up her first rope ladder. The ship rolled in an alarming fashion, but undaunted she watched a naval officer go up. Following, she copied him movement for movement. With both hands on the rungs he swung back and forth, knocking first one hip and then the other on the side of the vessel. He seemed to know little more about climbing a ship's side than Miss Watson did. She was black and blue for some time after. When it was time for her to descend, a seaman who had watched the performance gave her the advice of an expert and she went down hand over hand in true sailor style, with some control over the ladder. "But for all the old sea dogs, as well as the younger men," she observes, "having a woman boss was an innovation, and it goes without saying that diplomacy had to be exercised." It wasn't only living the job a twenty-four-hour day, it meant giving up all the usual things which spell femininity to the outside world. It's rather difficult to look the clinging vine when you have to go down at 5:00 A.M. on a dock with the wind and rain howling, to set a ship outbound or meet one inbound. It's only in the movies that 'the rain in the hair' type of woman looks pretty."

Being a woman in such a job during wartime with its attending quick trips, often posed hotel problems. The management did not welcome any woman—she could not be put in the dormitories they maintained for men. Consequently, it often meant her sleeping on a ship, in an automobile, or wherever there was space. She regrets, however, that, now the war is over, much of the excitement and fun of improvising and meeting new situations as they arise has gone.

No longer will there be the head-on collision with the military— whose regulations never envisioned a woman running a steamship company, much less boarding a ship on business. "Yet," she says, "with all the scrambles and setbacks I have loved every minute of it, because it is transportation. And transportation to me is synonymous with movement and life."

Miss Watson is engagingly "tough," she has a fascinating personality, is very good-looking, well dressed, and it is a delight to listen to her talk. I can hear Euripides whispering, "What did I tell you?"

Editing a technical magazine has been the somewhat unusual career of Clotilde Grunsky. She is a native of San Francisco, daughter of C. E. Grunsky, "first city engineer of my city." When she was about to enter high school her father was appointed by President Theodore Roosevelt to the Isthmian Canal Commission, and for a number of years she lived in Washington, D. C., and in Montclair, New Jersey. Graduation (as valedictorian) was followed by a year at the Art Students' League in New York and by another of European travel. The family having returned to San Francisco, she spent four years at the University of California, during which she engaged in such extracurricular activities as dramatics, helping to edit the college magazine, writing the Junior farce, and heading the Woman's Honor Society, interests which in no way interfered with her studies. She graduated at the head of her class.

Vocational guidance and pioneer work for college graduates kept her busy for two years after she left college, during which time she conducted a seminar course at the university, taught at summer school, gave a lecture course at Mills College, and wrote occasional articles for woman's magazines. In 1939 she began and carried out a year of research work in vocational opportunity for the University of California. Another piece of research work, more in line with her later interest in engineering, was a study of the relative merits of various types of highway surface, conducted for the Highway Section of the Commonwealth Club of California.

Miss Grunsky is not a graduate engineer, in fact she majored in German and English while at college, but her interest in her father's work and her own liking for science and mathematics led her to include a number of basic subjects in this field among her other studies. It was therefore quite natural that when an assistant was needed by the editor of the *Journal of Electricity,* who was well acquainted with her activities and interests, he should offer her the position. Before long she ranked as associate editor of the paper, having charge of much of the planning and writing of articles. This was new work for a woman, but "nothing that could not be handled by anyone who listened intelligently, and who was willing to take field trips to power plants and to places where electricity was being used industrially." The technical nature of her work entitled her to associate membership in the American Institute of Electrical Engineers.

While still on the editorial staff of the *Journal of Electricity* she became associated with *Electrical Merchandising,* a trade publication of the McGraw-Hill Publishing Company, housed in New York. Later she transferred all her time to this work and became Pacific Coast editor of that magazine. This position she still holds.

She has always been interested in women and their careers, and was one of the early members of the Professional and Business Women's Club of San Francisco. She is a past president of this organization and at the present time (1946) is chairman of its section on International Relations. During the United Nations Conference in San Francisco in 1945, she served first as associate consultant and then as consultant to the American delegation, representing the National Federation of Business and Professional Women's Clubs. She was also one of the originators and served as chairman of publications for the United Women's Conference which was held in San Francisco at this same period. Work for peace and international unity has been a progressive interest since college days, when she started her public speaking career by lectures on peace from the same platform with David Starr Jordan.

She continues her interest in both art and dramatics, and is something of an amateur playwright, having had six or seven plays produced by various club groups. Among other organizations to which she belongs are the American Association of University Women, the Hillside Club of Berkeley, and the Kappa Alpha Theta fraternity.

Hazel Pedlar Faulkner, Executive Director of the San Francisco Center for the Blind, was educated in the public schools and at Stanford University, where she majored in English, with a minor in history. From her grandfather, Judge Belden G. Hurlburt, first Superior Judge of Sutter County and later state senator from Humboldt County, she acquired an interest in world affairs and particularly in the workings of political groups. At college she was always a member of those groups which discussed and studied the responsibilities of citizenship. Graduating into a world in which women were not permitted to vote and so had to make their campaigns and utter their interests through organized women's groups, she renounced her original idea of teaching school and took her first position as a woman's club and society editor on the San Francisco *Examiner,* where she came into contact with women who were working for child-labor laws, pure-food-and-drug acts, engaging in pure-milk crusades as well as propaganda for mental and physical hygiene.

With the granting of suffrage many of the leaders in club groups went into public life as members of state committees and commissions, and thence to the national field. Mrs. Faulkner's faith in the power of women to achieve grew with the realization that ability is not a matter of sex, but is innate, and strengthened by training and experience.

After her marriage, following several years on the *Examiner* staff, while her children were growing up, she was called three times to organize the Republican women of California for as many presidential elections. She served for five years as a member of the

Board of the American Association of University Women, and for two years prior to that as national publicity chairman, during the presidency of Dr. Aurelia Henry Reinhardt, Mills College. Through those years much of the emphasis in the progress of the national A. A. U. W. was placed on the development and organization of international relations and study groups. The A. A. U. W. was the first of the national women's organizations to foresee the need for intelligent understanding of international affairs and to direct the activities of its thousands of members to the study. Part of Mrs. Faulkner's work as a national officer was the completion in this Western area of a $40,000 fund—part of a national $1,000,-000 fellowship fund raised by the A. A. U. W. to provide opportunities for research and study by women scholars who already had made some contribution to the fields of human knowledge. Before Mrs. Faulkner's service on the National Board of the A. A. U. W. she was president of the San Francisco branch and during her two-year term its membership doubled and took possession of permanent headquarters.

Mrs. Faulkner's experience in newspaper and publicity work was responsible for her selection in World War I to handle the magazine feature publicity for the various Liberty Loans in the Twelfth Federal Reserve District—which included eleven Western states as well as Hawaii, Alaska and Guam. In 1917-1918 she was publicity chairman for the Children's Year—proclaimed by the Federal Children's Bureau as part of a wartime conservation program.

In 1937, her children now grown up—she has two sons—she was asked to take the directorship of the activities of the Woman's Board of the Golden Gate International Exposition, a position she held until its close in 1940. That position called for the interesting of women in what the Exposition would have to offer them and arranging for special recognition for women who had achieved.

To accomplish this the Board organized state and county committees in California, with representatives in the eleven Western states, and an advisory committee composed of the heads of state organizations with a national affiliation.

In February 1942 Mrs. Faulkner was recalled to Mills College (where she had organized the publicity work in 1918-1919), and remained there until 1945. During the past six years she has been a member and officer of the National League for Woman's Service, and for five of those years has served as a volunteer in the National Defender's Club, sponsored, maintained and operated by the N. L. W. S. Then, in November 1945, after a four-months' rest, she undertook her present work as Executive Director of the San Francisco Center for the Blind, where she devotes herself to understanding the afflicted who make use of the Center, and at the same time to interest the public in the need for and the possibilities of such an enterprise and the significance and value to the blind of public understanding and support.

A busy woman, Mrs. Faulkner, and a valuable citizen.

One night in the lobby of the opera house between acts I called the attention of a man to a young woman who was talking with great animation to her companions. "Tell me exactly what you think of her," I said. "Size her up—to be elegant."

"Very pretty," he said. "Undoubtedly intelligent. Fashionable. A young woman of leisure who lives to enjoy life and has few responsibilities."

"You are 'way off," I replied. "But this is no place to enlighten you; we should miss the next act if I did."

Elizabeth Banning is an industrial color pioneer. She is a distinguished leader in a modern industrial trend. Believing that a tremendous new concept of color as applied to business, industry and building was on its way, she grounded herself in advanced courses available at Northwestern University and at the Chicago Art Institute. Then she went to Europe, studied with notable color scientists and did practical work with them in paint laboratories. With this solid background Miss Banning at the age of twenty-seven opened her own offices in San Francisco to put this technical knowledge to work for Western business.

That was in 1936. In the ten years that have intervened her success as a color consultant for all types of business, from public utilities to small concerns, has been complete. Big Business, not too hastily but in due course, accepted her interpretation of color as it applied to stores, restaurants, railroad terminals, offices and industrial plants. Her clients now extend from San Francisco to New York, from Hollywood to Canada. She has restyled paint colors for the leading paint manufacturers of the Pacific Coast, developed a unique color plan for multiple units of the principal restaurants and coffee organizations of the West, been retained by one of the large oil companies to develop a color plan for service stations, by a well-known shoe chain and by a nationally recognized sports apparel organization to develop an interior color plan that would attract new customers.

Here are but a few of her clients: Atchison, Topeka & Santa Fé Railroad; Benjamin Franklin Hotel; Gardner Daily, architect; Dohrmann Hotel Supply Company; Fairmont Hotel; W. P. Fuller & Company; Gallenkamp Stores Company; Hotel Bellevue; Jacks and Irvine, Contractors; Joseph Magnin Company, Inc.; Mannings, Inc.; Petroleum Exhibitors; Pig 'n' Whistle; Plantation, Inc.; Roos Bros.; Schwabacher-Frey Company; W. & J. Sloane; Spreckles Sugar Company; Standard Oil of California. She has among her clients a variety of other businesses, including insurance offices, attorneys' offices, medical and dental offices, industrial plants, wholesale merchandising outlets, schools, hospitals and public buildings.

Today Elizabeth Banning forsees the beginning of a new era— "a new approach in the world of peace." She believes the importance of color is greater now than at any previous time. People the world over are feeling the impact of mass grief and mass anxiety as never before in the history of mankind. Color in railroad terminals, restaurants, stores, public buildings—wherever people gather—can inspire moods of enthusiasm, of pleasure, of relaxation, just as the stage designer sets the background for the production or play. "Never before has the careful use of color been so important to so many people—either in their homes or in the vast commercial field."

In private life Elizabeth Banning is Mrs. William C. Morehead and both in her town house and on her Marin County ranch she has interests as intense and varied as the colors with which she works. She loves to cook. She loves to ride her beautiful three-gaited chestnut over the private trails of that Indian Valley ranch— when she's not shooting in the eighties at golf. She collects records—everything from boogie to Beethoven. Fine Palomino horses are her hobby. She attends the symphony concerts. She likes to fly. She is devoted to her pedigreed Dalmatian who is equally devoted to her. She admires people who do things. She loves her husband and her home. And she lives both her career and her private life with equal enthusiasm.

One of San Francisco's most distinguished (and interesting) citizens is Dr. Margaret Chung, physician and surgeon. The fluid in her body may be Chinese but her brain cells are American. Her heart is equally divided between the land of her birth and the age-old country of her ancestors.

Never was there a more notable instance of "from rags to riches," from obscurity to fame. Born in Santa Barbara, California, one of eleven children, with a father who rarely made more than forty-five dollars a week, and a mother whose job was interpreter for one of the local police courts, she probably seldom sat down to a square meal. Only genius and the constitution of a prize fighter can account for the fact that she managed to attend the Southern University of California and then, still undernourished, went to Chicago for further medical training at the College of Physicians and Surgeons. When that phase was over she not only practiced in Chicago but organized that city's first juvenile psychopathic institute for the study of borderland criminal cases, and was appointed by Governor Lowder as criminologist of the State of Illinois.

On her return to Los Angeles, she built up a small practice and managed to save a little money. But her career was to be elsewhere. Two grateful Hollywood patients induced her to go with them to San Francisco, protesting that the time had come for her to take a vacation and have a little fun. And there she discovered Chinatown, fell in love with it, and was convinced that fortune awaited her in that teeming precinct sacred to her own people, moreover, that it was her duty to give them the benefit of her skill in modern surgery and medicine.

For a long month she sat alone in her little office in Chinatown. The inhabitants preferred their herb doctors, and if an operation was necessary there were well-known surgeons in San Francisco. "She was too young, anyhow."

But her chance came. One day she was eating her frugal midday meal in a restaurant when a waitress fell to the floor screaming with pain. Her services were demanded, she diagnosed the case at once, operated as quickly as possible, and saved the woman's life. The "waitress" happened to be the owner of the restaurant and one of the wealthiest women in Chinatown. From that time on Dr. Chung's office was crowded, her fame spread and she received large fees from American patients. She furnished her offices attractively, drove about in a handsome limousine, and was able to indulge freely in her favorite dish, corned beef and cabbage.

But other duties, another fame, awaited her. In 1931 she became acquainted with seven young men, former students of the University of California, who had taken a year's training in aviation with the Navy. But the Navy had no use for them and they asked Dr. Chung to secure commissions for them in the Chinese Army. This Dr. Chung was unable to do, but she befriended them—they were unable to find jobs of any kind—took them to her house for dinner, sewed on buttons, patched, sewed up their cuts when they drank too much and got into fights, and if they landed in jail bailed them out. Their numbers increased, and naturally they all adored her. They insisted on calling her Mom and when she protested that as she had no husband they would all be illegitimate, they replied they were quite willing to be known as "the fair-haired bastards of Mom Chung." In some respects she was a stern mother. She told them that her standards were high and no man could remain a son of hers who drank himself into jail or misbehaved in any way. Each man must "make the world a better place because he lives!"

When war came "Mom's boys" numbered 780. She gave each of them a little jade Buddha, which seems to have acted as a talisman, for although they fought with Army, Navy and Marines only two of them lost their lives. And all of them sent her scraps of planes they had shot down, a collection that fills one of her offices in Chinatown. Mom's boys became known as Hellcats,

Rippers and Flying Tigers. Upon her was conferred the honor of selecting the first two hundred American aviators to China. During the earlier years of the war between China and Japan, the United States Government had refused her a permit to go to the country of her ancestors and establish there modern well-equipped hospitals and dispensaries, but it was to her they turned when they were in immediate need of aviators.

Not long after Dr. Chung achieved another triumph, and this time a quick one. To quote Shirley Radke in the *Christian Science Monitor* (October 3, 1942): "One day last February, Dr. Chung walked into an office of the Navy Department in Washington, D. C., and discussed with one of its officials the immediate importance of establishing a Woman's Auxiliary in the United States Naval Reserve. She outlined the possibilities in her customary concise manner, and before she left that office, the bill had been prepared for introduction into the House. She made her own contacts in Congress and saw the bill passed by the House in the amazing time of 10 minutes, before she boarded a plane for home. That bill was passed by the Senate later, signed by the President, and now is actively attracting young women into the organization popularly designated as the WAVES."

Truly a remarkable achievement in the City of Red Tape!

Until the end of the war Dr. Chung talked on the radio and lectured all over the country on the necessity of a more active understanding and appreciation among the United States, China and the other Allied Nations. Many of those eloquent broadcasts went not only over national networks but by short wave to Europe and Asia.

As may be surmised, all of Mom's boys who passed through San Francisco lost no time in calling on her and expressing their

undying gratitude and affection. She entertained them royally, at
elaborate dinners and at receptions where many of the town's celebrities were asked to meet them.

I think it was in 1938 that I had the pleasure of meeting Dr.
Chung at a cocktail party given by my friend Richard Halliburton
in the Blue Lagoon, a restaurant in Maiden Lane, on the day before
his last farewell to San Francisco. She is a handsome woman and
looked less authoritative than amiable and charming. It was impossible to have more than a word with her, for she was surrounded
by admirers, but I gathered that she was very fond and proud of
Dick, who wore one of her little jade Buddhas. Alas, that he
should be one of the two for whom the magic talisman failed! Nor
did an unkind Fate permit him to die in action, an end to his brilliant life that he would have infinitely preferred.

Among Mom's Fair-haired Bastards (a club recognized by the
United States Government as the Phi Beta Kappa of Aviation) are
Admiral William F. Halsey, Jr., General James Doolittle, Eddie
Rickenbacker and many others little less distinguished.

During the war Dr. Chung also founded "The Golden Dolphin," composed exclusively of the crews of United States sub-
marines. Each submarine of "Mom's boys" in this organization sank
over 150,000 tons of enemy shipping, many of them 200,000 or
more. There were 200 members, and one of them was Admiral
Chester Nimitz, who is Golden Dolphin 100.

Dr. Chung has the distinction of being the only woman ever
decorated by the Chinese Government.

This American-Chinese lady, feminine as she looks, has what
was called not so long ago a "man's mind." One hears that
would-be compliment applied less and less in these days. One also
is reminded that in ancient Egypt there was a time when ambitious

young men preened themselves when assured that they possessed a "woman's mind."

Margaret V. Girdner, Director of the Bureau of Texts and Libraries of the San Francisco Public Schools, is the administrative officer in charge of the selection, purchase and distribution of the materials of instruction used in all the city's schools from kindergarten through senior high. This includes not only the purchase of text and library books but also the visual aids used in instruction, such as maps, charts, globes, slides and classroom films. Each of the twenty-one high schools, junior and senior, of the school system has a library under the direction of one or two professional librarians, and the administration of these libraries, in addition to the service of the excellent Teachers Professional Library housed in the Administration Building (Civic Center), is under the supervision of Miss Girdner.

She is a native Californian of pioneer ancestry. She graduated from Stanford University in 1915, after majoring in California history and the history of Latin America. Following a year and a half of graduate work in history and education she entered the California State Library School for training in her chosen field. After two years' experience in exploring various types of library service as assistant in charge of school work in the Siskiyou County Free Library, reference assistant in Palo Alto Public Library, assistant in charge of circulation in the State Library in Sacramento, she was further convinced that teaching and school librarianship were her main interest, and it is in these fields that she has pioneered. She was the first librarian in the Palo Alto High School and in the Pasadena Junior College, and came north in 1925 to organize the first school library in San Francisco at the High School of Commerce. Upon completion of the organization of this library she was transferred to our Galileo High School, where she served as senior librarian until appointed in 1938 to the position of the Supervisor of the Texts and Libraries. She was given the title of Director in June, 1946.

Her interests are with books and young people and the training of teachers and librarians in presenting books to children.

Miss Girdner has been a member of the faculty of the San José State College and the College of the Pacific, teaching the various subjects of library administration and children's literature. In addition to her other duties she is an instructor in the University of California Extension Division.

Her particular enthusiasm is the critical reviewing of children's books and for seven years she edited the Children's Book Week issue of the San Francisco *Chronicle* for Joseph Henry Jackson.

Miss Girdner has been active in many organizations, professional or concerned with community service. Her memberships include Phi Beta Kappa, Kappa Delta Pi, honor society in education; Alpha Phi; the American Association of University Women; the American Library Association; the California Library Association; the School Library Association of California; the California Teachers Association; the National Education Association. For seven years she has served on the board of the San Francisco Y. W. C. A., and is now on the Executive Board of the Camp Fire Girls of San Francisco. During 1944-1946 she has been chairman of the San Francisco regional committee to recommend entries for the annual George Foster Peabody Radio Awards.

To four great teachers Miss Girdner gives credit for training in her profession: David Starr Jordan, President of Stanford University (respect for scholarship); Dr. Edward P. Cubberly, Dean of the School of Education of Stanford University (respect for the ideals of American education) ; James L. Gillis, librarian of the California State Library (respect for the public library as a service institution) ; Joseph P. Nourse, principal of Galileo High School and Superintendent of the San Francisco Public Schools (respect for the democracy of the American high school).

Miss Girdner's personality must have played no little part in the great success she has made of her life. Tall, handsome, always beautifully dressed, she is amiable, cordial, brilliant, dignified and altogether charming.

One who is pre-eminent in the club life of San Francisco is Mrs. Oliver Remick Grant. In her particular line she is unsurpassed. She is also "different" in other ways. Every drop of blood in her veins is Italian. Her father, Louis Ferratoli, was sent from Italy to New York City at the age of fourteen, to live with relatives while attending school. He was a thorough American by the time he attained his majority and lost no time in becoming a citizen of the United States. At school he had specialized in food chemistry and before long he had a biscuit factory of his own. Her mother, Rosina Sanguinetti, was born in New York. Shortly after Louis' graduation they married and went to San Francisco for the honeymoon, and so fascinated were they by that colorful city they remained there for several years. Two children were born there and when Laura was not quite a year old they returned to New York.

She grew up the one girl among four sons, and in her home life participated in all their sports, seeing nothing of other girls save at school. She was a hard-working student, first at Mount Saint Ursula Academy and then at the famous Hunter College, where she specialized in modeling, drawing and painting. She graduated from that cultural institution at the age of eighteen and taught for a time. But it was not long before she, like less intellectual and accomplished girls, fell in love and married.

Oliver Remick Grant, a native of Maine, was one of the ninth generation to be born in the old homestead at Kittery on ground given to his family under a grant from King George III. Both the Remick and the Grant families came to New England from Old England about 1628. Oliver received his early education in Europe. Later he attended Columbia University, graduating from the School of Mines, and he is a member of the Tau Beta Pi honorary fraternity in Engineering, and the Sons of the American Revolution.

Mrs. Grant continued her studies. She took postgraduate courses at Columbia and Harvard in literature, journalism and art. Her major interests were music and portraits in oil. She and her husband found time to travel in Europe where Mrs. Grant spent most of the time visiting art galleries and literary shrines. During World War I when the teacher shortage became acute she offered her services to the City of New York and taught again "for the duration." Later, after a competitive examination, she joined the faculty of Hunter College, as critic instructor in its Model School, holding that position until 1930 when Mr. Grant was sent by the General Cable Corporation to fill the position of District Engineer for the Western States, with headquarters in San Francisco.

Mrs. Grant had visited California on a lecture tour and had a natural affection for the city of her birth. Nevertheless, after her activities in New York she found mere household duties and social pastimes too tame for endurance. In 1931 she formed a club of young people from modest homes who were either going to college or working and who were longing for wholesome companionship and clean entertainment, which were difficult to find in that degraded era of Prohibition. That fine group of women who belonged to the Sorosis Club took an interest in her project and willingly leased their clubhouse for the weekly Friday night dances and entertainment program for her eager young group. The Laurel Club was launched. Her orchestra was composed of four boys from the Menlo Park School who welcomed the extra money needed for their tuition. The fifteen-minute intermission programs, when many well-known artists gave their services, were not only enjoyable but instructive. Mrs. Grant carried on that club for three years and then turned it over to the young people to manage, and only the advent of World War II caused its dissolution. She preserves letters from Chief of Police Quinn, Mayor Rossi and other city officials, highly commending her venture.

And so began Mrs. Grant's career as a clubwoman in San Francisco. In 1931 she had been invited to join the San Francisco branch of the National League of American Pen Women as an active member, on the credentials of her professional lectures, art work, sale of short stories, feature articles and poems. In 1934 she was elected to the Executive Board and she was editor of *Pen Gram* from 1935 to 1937. In 1936 she was elected president and served for two years. During that time she presented at the regular monthly programs many notable authors, poets, artists and speakers. One of her "discoveries" was the San Francisco child prodigy, Leon Fleisher, who gave his first public piano recital at one of these monthly meetings, not only before the Pen Women but a number of invited guests likely to be interested. One of them was Albert Bender, whose purse was always at the disposal of talent, and he and other public-spirited citizens who heard the child on that day sent him, accompanied by his mother, to Lake Como to study under Artur Schnabel. Hitler's war sent them back to New York, where he continued his studies. When he was seventeen he played before the San Francisco Symphony, winning great acclaim, and 1945-1946 he made his first transcontinental tour and gave two recitals in Carnegie Hall, New York.

In 1938 Mrs. Grant, finishing her presidency of the local Pen Women, became National Western Regional Director. For two years she worked tirelessly to bring the 1939 Mid-Administration Pen Women Conference to San Francisco, and despite rivalry and counterclaims succeeded. (I went to their dinner in the Fairmont Hotel. There were several hundred of them and the speeches began with the soup!)

For four years, 1940-1944, Mrs. Grant was National Lecture Chairman, and during this time contributed monthly articles on various aspects of lecturing, as well as other feature articles to the *National Bulletin*. And as if this were not enough she undertook another heavy responsibility.

It was in 1930 that the Pan-American League International was founded at Miami, Florida, with adult and student branches and representatives throughout the United States and Latin America, its purpose being the permanent solidarity of the twenty-one American republics.

During Mrs. Grant's presidency the granting of scholarships was begun by the local branch in conjunction with National Headquarters and in close co-operation with the Pan-American Union in Washington, D. C., and the State Department. Then followed, through her contacts, establishment of branches in Salt Lake City, Guatemala City and Mexico City. It was a strenuous period and upon completion of her presidency, far from taking a rest, she filled the office of first vice-president, in order to carry out further the broadening program. In 1941 the National Board elected her to her present position, director for California, with the specific work of establishing adult and student branches in California and suggesting branches in other cities where she may have the proper contacts. California now has seven adult branches. Two of these she founded, Sacramento and San Mateo and another, a student branch at the San Francisco State College. Still others are in the process of formation.

All adult California Branches are now giving scholarships, either as individual branches or jointly with other branches, and each year the number of scholarships increases. The recipients have been students from various Latin-American republics and from various professions. These have been sent to Mills College, Casa Pan-Americana, the University of California, the University of Southern California, Claremont and Pomona Colleges and the Massachusetts Institute of Technology.

In 1944, in recognition of Mrs. Grant's outstanding work, the National Board awarded her a life membership and its highest honor, a citation and enrollment in the "Order of Adventures in Friendship."

In the spring of 1945 Mrs. Grant was appointed by the Founder President International, Mrs. Clark Stearns, to represent her at the United Nations Conference on International Organization at San Francisco and this appointment was recognized by the State Department.

Recently she was awarded an additional citation by the National Board for the excellent manner in which she carried out, with the co-operation of many prominent San Francisco hostesses, the elaborate entertainment of the delegations of the twenty-one American republics to the Conference for the Pan-American League. She has also received official letters from the then Secretary of State, Edward R. Stettinius, Jr., the Assistant Secretary of State, Nelson Rockefeller, and the Director General of the Pan-American Union, Dr. Leo S. Rowe, in appreciation of her services to the Latin-

American delegates, and many letters from the chairmen of the various Latin-American delegations.

Mrs. Grant has indulged in purely personal work, too, that has brought her notable awards for short stories, poems, painting. She has made an intensive study of Jack London and lectured on him all over the country. How she finds time and energy for such a crowded career no one but herself (and her husband whom she never neglects) can ever guess. In this blighted era she is doing her own cooking, housework, marketing. Fortunately she lives in an apartment, not a house.

One thing that has struck me forcibly while writing this chapter is the good looks, the smart appearance and the freshness of these women who work like navvies. Mrs. Grant is no exception, and she is quite capable of filling even higher and more exacting offices. Personally, I should like to see her Mayor of San Francisco. Aside from her other abilities she is a born executive and has a will of tempered steel. How she would make those politicians that infest the City Hall take a back seat and humbly do as they were told!

Now we come to San Francisco's illustrious businesswoman— and in a field hitherto man's sacrosanct preserve. Another "First."

Hazel Louise Zimmerman is the only woman investment broker in the United States. Yearly she averages over $1,000,000 in sales. Two and a half million is her highest annual record. She serves more than 400 women clients, here and in Southern California. "Women like to work with women," Miss Zimmerman maintains, "if they can feel sure the woman knows her business." She writes a financial column which appears weekly in the Los Angeles *Times,* and journeys southward regularly to lecture on investments to women's groups at the Town House in Los Angeles.

Miss Zimmerman was born in Michigan and came to California in 1932. To quote B. K. Gallatin in *San Francisco Life:* "Before she was thirty she was sales manager in the San Francisco offices of an Eastern investment house, with twenty salesmen under her charge. Ten years ago (in 1936) she realized what had been a constant aspiration and established her own business, an investment house for women. . . . Personality, Miss Zimmerman contends, is vastly overrated. Success in business, she believes, lies in the ability to submerge one's individuality in that of the customer. Regardless of this mobility of character, however, Miss Zimmerman can hardly be considered a nonentity!

"Rather generously proportioned, she is naturally expansive in her gestures and her laugh is ready and full. Her hair is gray, simply coifed. Her eyes are her best feature. Alert and bright they echo every intonation of speech. Poet and business woman, she is a blend of the fundamental traits of both. She wears dramatic hats and jewels, sensible shoes and clothes that are simple in color and subdued in design. Not infrequently she dots a stream of statistics with a striking collection of adjectives and adverbs. The effect is unusual. Her poetry on the other hand shows conciseness of expression and an almost mathematical purity of form.

"Her record as a poet is impressive. Her first book of sonnets, *Green Grows the Laurel,* published in 1936, won the national award of the Eugene Field Society for 'its outstanding contribution to contemporary literature.' In 1944 *The Wind Returns,* another collection of sonnets, won the Mark Twain Award. . . . Her work is frequently sad. Love, the major theme of her sonnets, is treated with poignancy and restraint. Heartbreak and desolation creep in quite often. Particularly interesting are the 'message' poems. The mood of these is very different. Addressing the fearful hearts of today, Miss Zimmerman challenges, coaxes, shames and pleads.

Much of her own determination and strength of character are revealed.

"Hazel Zimmerman is a traditional poet and an exemplary businesswoman. If achievement is a true measure of success she unquestionably merits recognition. Her pre-eminence in the difficult world of finance has long been established. In the realm of literature her future is more than promising."

Show me a male financial genius who is also a poet!

Dr. Aurelia Henry Reinhardt (born in San Francisco, April 1, 1877), after receiving degrees from the University of California and Yale University, and having initial experience in university teaching at the University of Idaho, married Dr. George Frederick Reinhardt of the faculty of the University of California, and made her home in Berkeley, in 1909. Two sons were born before the death of Dr. George in 1914.

Invited at once to teach in the university, Dr. Aurelia by 1916 had assumed the presidency of Mills College, an institution modeled after the New England academies in the 1850's and for decades doing a worthy service in the education of the daughters of the pioneers in California.

With a knowledge which wide study had given her and an energy which the task demanded, Dr. Aurelia set about transforming an institution of manifold traditions into one of the most notable colleges for women in the United States.

The contributions of Mills to contemporary curriculum and method of American colleges is recognized in the honorary degrees bestowed upon its president in Laws, and in Literature. Among the institutions which have so shown their approval are Mount Holyoke, Williams, and Oberlin College, as well as the Colorado College, and the Universities of California and of

Southern California. The 700 students at Mills are by no means all Californians. Girls come to it from Central and South America, Mexico and even from Europe. Needless to relate, its faculty is surpassed by none. Men and women who have risen to eminence in literature, science, any of the arts and professions, are as proud to receive a degree from Mills College as from the University of California.

Donations poured in, many from wealthy alumnae. Albert Bender, one of the trustees, presented it with an extensive library, not only of books but of manuscripts he wheedled out of authors.

In December 1925 the *Christian Science Monitor* commented on the proudest of the many expansions: "The newly dedicated Mills College Art Gallery is a distinct addition to California equipment for art entertainment. Built as a unit in a design which contemplates a large future building, it provides well for the future. The gallery, as it now is, is as nearly perfect for the display of paintings as any gallery built with museum intent. Mills College has a fine collection of gift paintings from artists and patrons with which the gallery was opened. The more than 200 canvases of superior standard include a group of California artists."

Today that "museum" contains not only notable pictures, but the finest specimens of pottery, hand-woven textiles, oriental art, sculpture, etchings and Indian art of the Northwest. Mrs. M. C. Sloss, of whom I have written elsewhere, contributed her collection, "Mother and Child in the Graphic Arts."

There is a summer session for lectures, music and dramatic performances, invariably attended by many San Franciscans.

The time came when college statutes regarding retirement applied to the president herself. So Dr. Reinhardt closed her years of administrative service, but she left her inspiration behind her. There is no doubt that Mills will go on expanding, increasing in reputation. She is well, busy with lecturing and writing, and the dynamo within her will probably explode. Perhaps she is writing her memoirs; they would be lively reading.

"Lady Aurelia" is a striking exponent of woman in the intermediate state; very tall, handsome and dashing. Her personality is so stimulating that at times it is almost overpowering. Nature certainly equipped her for success.

And here is the record of another woman's achievement unsurpassed by her thirty-two male rivals in the same field.

Fernande Romer, a Californian of French parentage, was born in Alameda, across the Bay from San Francisco. In 1898 she married Georges de Latour, and two years later they purchased 115 acres in Napa Valley and planted a vineyard. Mrs. de Latour, charmed by the natural beauty of the property, situated at the foot of the blue hills with Mount St. Helena in the near distance, named it Beaulieu (Beautiful Site). Success did not come easily at the start. It took faith, pioneer courage and perseverance to plant "shy-bearing" vines, to continue in their belief that California could produce wines as fine as any in the France of their ancestors.

I shall quote freely from a brochure written in 1945 by Jerome Landfield with an introduction by Paul Verdier, as they know a lot more of the subject than I do. "Beaulieu wines are probably the most widely and favorably known of all the California wines. They are produced by the Beaulieu vineyards and winery at Rutherford in the heart of the beautiful Napa Valley, which has often been compared with the Bordeaux region in France.

"Beaulieu was founded by Georges de Latour, scion of one of France's oldest families of vintners, who came to California in 1883, and thereafter devoted much time to a careful study of soil

Courtesy of Californians Inc.

THE TOP OF THE MARK

THE PALACE OF FINE ARTS

and climate and experimentation in the search for the location best suited to the production of fine wines. . . . After selecting Rutherford he began importing from his native France cuttings of the choicest grape varieties and kept adding to his acreage until at the present time it comprises some 500 acres unsurpassed in the quality of its carefully selected grape varieties.

"Next he erected and equipped a winery in which were employed the best methods and practice of French wine making, a field in which he was an expert. Beaulieu wines, properly matured, were placed on the market, and their remarkable quality received immediate recognition. Gradually the winery was enlarged and improved until now it has a production of 250,000 gallons a year and storage capacity of 1,500,000 gallons. . . . The Beaulieu winery has a bin capacity capable of storing 500,000 bottles.

"During the Prohibition era Beaulieu held a government permit for the making of wines for sacramental and governmental purposes and was highly commended by the church authorities for their excellence. This made possible the continued operation of the winery, the upkeep of its vast cooperage, and the cultivation of the vineyards. . . . The excellence of Beaulieu wines has been attested by a number of the highest awards at the California State Fairs, and at various Expositions. Among these may be mentioned the Grand Prize and three gold medals at the Golden Gate International Exposition in 1939."

Until Mr. de Latour's death in 1940—he was many years older than his wife—Fernande had worked with him and knew as much of the business, every detail of it, as he did. She was well equipped to carry on the business, and, refusing offers of between $5,000,000 and $6,000,000 for the Beaulieu Wineries, became the head of the firm in March of that year. Her policy remained that of her late husband: to produce wines of the finest quality. She devotes every day to the business; every operation at the vineyard, such as planting, grafting, pruning, etc., is decided upon in accordance with the experience acquired during her long association with her husband. All wines are tested periodically before and after any blending is performed. Mrs. de Latour's palate is keen and trained. A new wing has been added to the winery to increase the facility to age and bin wines according to the orthodox manner. Distribution of Beaulieu wines has been established throughout the United States, and they are increasingly famous for their fine quality.

But let no one think that Beaulieu absorbs all her energies. She entertains lavishly both in her country house and in San Francisco, and no hostess is more popular, more charming, more gracious, more sought after. Two other diversions are music and charities.

She has two children, Richard and Hélène (Marquise de Pins), who are as interested in the business as she is, and were equally indifferent to the appetent millions that would have deprived them of their beloved Beaulieu with its graceful mansion and sunken gardens, its background of redwoods and mountain, the broad acres of grapevines in one of the loveliest of California valleys.

Verily, the jealous gods have succumbed to this remarkable woman and showered largess instead of curses upon her.

Is there anything more to say? Could there be anything more? Merely this—Fernande de Latour is the most beautiful woman in San Francisco.

The San Francisco Women's Chamber of Commerce, an admirable institution long needed in the city, was incorporated under the laws of the State of California in July 1937. The purposes for which it was formed are to advance the commercial, industrial and civic interests of the city and county of San Francisco and to foster and generally to perform those things which may result in constructive service to the community at large. "The object in general is to afford women the opportunity to participate in civic activities such as community welfare, civic improvement, business service, hospitality, and the attraction of investments and conventions—and to place emphasis on women's importance in the community."

Among its accomplishments so far are: Women's Day at the Port—bringing their attention to the city's greatest asset, the Harbor; lighted house numbers—a campaign directed towards the lighting of house numbers in every residential section of the city; co-operation in cleanup drives; safety campaigns; War Bond drives; the March of Dimes, Red Cross drives, to mention but a few.

Then there has been the hospitality program: during the 1939-1940 Exposition, taking visitors on tours of the city; hospitality to service men and women during the war; information and hospitality to visitors during the United Nations Conference.

In 1941 the women began to turn their attention to something quite as important as civic betterment. By the middle of that year thousands of young men were in Army and Navy training centers. The women adopted the San Francisco League for Service Men as their medium for performing every kind of service for the men in uniform. They entertained them in their houses, collected recreation material, and assisted in many ways to make the young men's stay in San Francisco and near-by establishments pleasant. It was during the war years that they recognized the serious problems of youth and delinquency that have manifested themselves in every great city. The Chamber keeps in close touch with the situation in San Francisco through its honorary member, Mrs. Kathlyn Sullivan, Director of the Big Sister Bureau of the Police Department.

From its executive offices in the Monadnock Building letters and other communications of the Women's Chamber of Commerce are sent out by the able and energetic executive secretary, Mrs. Cecil L. Cooley—whose other duties are equally numerous and exacting. Mrs. Eugene Bowles was elected the first president, but because of illness was unable to serve, and in November 1937 Mrs. William J. O'Donnell, first vice-president, took her place and served as president until 1941, when an invalid husband and her own ill health deprived the Chamber of her valuable initiative and enthusiasm. Mrs. Henry Dippel was then elected president and fills that high office to the satisfaction of all concerned. She was re-elected in 1945.

The Women's Chamber of Commerce is continuing its national and community welfare activities, the many problems of the immediate postwar period, and its original program for civic betterment: a better and a cleaner city, provision for refuse disposals, improved transportation, adequate parking facilities, increased "Stop" and "Go" signals, better street signs, additional playgrounds, return of the neighborhood mailbox, improved street lighting facilities, better housing, city-wide courtesy, harmony between labor and business management. An interorganization educational program which would lend assistance to the merchants and general public has been consistently developed.

The Chamber holds an annual luncheon to which representatives of the principal social, civic and improvement clubs are invited, and where momentous questions are discussed and decisions made. Altogether the Women's Chamber of Commerce is an indispensable part of the city's structure.

I have mentioned a few of the women in San Francisco who are the equals of men in ability, enterprise and success. There are many more in this city alone and thousands more in cities large and small in the United States and elsewhere. Year by year they multiply.

We are now in the "Intermediate State," although still far from the center. Women beware! There is no human happiness possible save in sex equality. When women were dominant they despised men, secretly or otherwise. Dominant man today, no matter how polite, considerate or generous, cherishes a pleasant sense of superiority to the subordinate sex. And women know it, are resentful, rebellious, either longing for or determined upon full equality, according to their mental caliber. The time will come when the efforts of the most energetic and determined will be realized and it will be for them to hold the scales even—permanently even, to achieve a happiness that has eluded both men and women since the world began. Today complete and permanent happiness has been achieved only by priests and nuns.

# CHAPTER FOURTEEN

# San Francisco Builds Her Future

1

"Serene, indifferent of Fate,
Thou sittest at the Western Gate."

OH, IS she? And was she ever? When Bret Harte wrote those lines San Francisco was just about the most tumultuous little city the Union had ever possessed. Perhaps he was dreaming of the future, of a great and stately city at "Continent's End," calmly prosperous, with ample time for all the pleasures of life, not too ambitious, and, yes, serenely confident of its future.

It is true that she has had intervals of holy calm, almost of stagnation, but they have been brief. There have been insane periods of speculation when fortunes were made and lost and suicides were many; others when San Francisco was called "the wickedest city on earth," and vigilance committees were formed and malefactors hanged. And oh, Bret Harte, if you are floating around in the ether, look down upon us now!

In 1940 the population of San Francisco was 634,536. In this year of 1946 it is 800,000, the new Gold Rush having begun in December 1942 after we were deftly pitchforked into World War II. Thousands poured into this part of the state lured by the high wages of the "essential industries" that sprang up in the Bay Area—men, women, whole families. New "towns" were hastily thrown together to accommodate them, but thousands found quar-

294

ters here and there in San Francisco. Moreover, the hotels were
so crowded by Army men on leave, or naval officers and sailors
from ships in the harbor, that no mere citizen could obtain a
room for more than five days. The night clubs, the restaurants had
waiting lines a block long.

San Franciscans held their breath. This war must end in due
course and their beautiful city would no longer be pandemonium.

But alas! Thousands of newcomers fell in love with San Francisco and settled there for life. The narrow downtown streets are
so whamjammed that no parking is allowed save by special permit, and the public garages in such heavy demand that it takes
longer to get out than to get in. The sidewalks are so crowded
that one crawls rather than walks, and until the shops were sold
out it took an hour to buy a pair of gloves. And as for the markets, butchers and grocery stores, it is a wonder that the desperate
housewives have not been tenderly escorted into one of our many
asylums for the insane.

Thousands of new dwellings are needed, but owing to the
shortage of labor and man power there is little building. In time,
of course, San Francisco will grow down the peninsula; there is
plenty of land. But meanwhile men and women, many of them
able to pay a high price, are ringing doorbells in the residence
districts begging for a room. The new British Consul General,
Cyril Cane, has been living first in one house and then in another
lent to him by friends whom he made when he was here before.
Sir Godfrey and Lady Fisher, his predecessors, lived in the Fairmont Hotel, but the Canes have children.

Well, it is a phase and will pass as others have passed, and
although San Francisco may never be as big as Los Angeles—
whose population in the city proper is 1,504,277—she is firm in
the belief that she is the City of Destiny, the Gateway of the

Pacific, if only on account of her magnificent harbor, one that has few rivals in the entire world.

And in 1945 did she not have the honor of being the headquarters of the United Nations Conference International Organization? There were delegates of fifty nations, representing 1,800,000,000 people, more than eighty percent of the world's population. Including their staffs and the Conference secretariat—to say nothing of newspapermen from every nation represented—there were 3,500 of them, and even the (hitherto) all-powerful Army and Navy had to pack bags and get out of the hotels. Two large buildings in the Civic Center, the Veterans' and the Opera House, were taken over for the central activities of the Conference and in them were installed some sixty trunk telephone lines for communication with the outer world; in addition fifty-nine special "tie lines" were laid for communication between Conference and delegate headquarters in the city itself. The average number of telephone calls each day was approximately 12,000, and one day reached a peak of 20,000. Special operators had to be employed and, of the thirty-eight recruited for the purpose, twenty were employed for their knowledge of foreign languages. For transportation to and from the hotels there was a fleet of 215 sedan cars, forty-eight privately owned limousines, twenty-five Army jeeps and fifty Navy busses. From the 2,500 persons representing press, radio and newsreels an average of more than 150,000 words were sent out each day via telegraph and cable. Radio commentators were constantly on the air giving accounts and interpretations of latest developments, and about 160,000 feet of film were taken by the newsreel operators and thousands of pictures were made.

Each individual delegate paid his own personal and official expenses, but the general expenses of the Conference, estimated at little less than $2,000,000, were met by the United States as the host government.

That was a hectic time socially for San Francisco. Daily, nightly, the delegates were entertained at luncheons, cocktail parties, dinners and balls. The picturesque Arabs with their white flowing garments were the favorites, although the women were swooning over Anthony Eden. The lobbies of the hotels swarmed with autograph hunters, many of them children. The auditorium of the Opera House was crowded with those fortunate enough to obtain tickets. Lady Fisher gave an afternoon party at the Francisca Club at which I had a long talk with Cranborne, one of the most interesting men I ever met. Lord Halifax was the guest of honor. Anthony Eden had departed—probably he had fled in self-defense. But it was one of the gayest parties of that lively season. Champagne flowed and the "spread" was equally enticing. In fact it is doubtful if those delegates had ever in all their lives eaten so many, so various and so delectable dishes as they ate during their stay in San Francisco—in private houses and in the famous restaurants, Italian, French, Greek, Russian, Spanish, Mexican and Chinese.

When the Conference was over the members were enthusiastic in their praise of San Francisco, its hospitality and its beauty. Even the climate behaved and there were few fogs and winds.

There were fourteen parties given for the Latin Americans alone by San Francisco hostesses at the request of Mrs. Oliver Grant, representative of the San Francisco branch of the Pan-American League. But the most notable and no doubt the most enjoyable was given elsewhere.

Feeling that one large party should be given honoring the Latin-American republics, Mrs. Grant suggested to the State Department an all-day Sunday outing, including a visit to a winery and climaxed by a barbecue luncheon at the Jack London ranch in the Valley of the Moon. The suggestion was met with enthusiastic approval, permission was given at once to take the delegates out of town for a day, and the Sonoma Chamber of Commerce, the Sebastiani Winery and Mrs. London eagerly co-operated.

At 9:30 in the morning of the twenty-seventh of May, the party of 350 delegates and their wives and twenty-five newspapermen left San Francisco in state limousines and Navy busses, preceded by jeeps and highway patrol. The weather was fine and the beautiful scenery of Marin County gave a fitting introduction to the most enjoyable day of the entire Conference.

In the old plaza at Sonoma, beneath the Bear Flag Monument, the visitors were greeted by the mayor, the president of the Chamber of Commerce and the Board of Supervisors, a Boy-Scout band and a group of Campfire Girls. After a brief program the guests were escorted to the Sebastiani Winery, where a gaily appointed table was set in the winery garden. Here, as guests of Mr. Sebastiani, canapés and rare California wines were served, unlimited cigars given the men, and lovely corsages to the ladies. In small groups the entire party was taken through the winery and presented with especially labeled bottles of the finest sauterne and Burgundy.

Then came the drive of six miles through vineyards and orchard country, to the Jack London ranch. At the entrance to this famous property invitations were courteously but firmly requested by M.P.'s and the attendant secret-service men. (It may be mentioned in passing that on the day before jeeps with antiaircraft guns had been stationed at various spots on the hillside surrounding the ranch.)

At the handsome stone ranch house the guests were welcomed by Mr. Irving Shepard, nephew of Jack London, and Mrs. Shepard, in the unavoidable absence of Mrs. London. Shortly after, a big gong sounded, the same gong that had always summoned Jack's guests to the table, and all passed through an arch which gave entrance to the compound, enclosed by an old twelve-foot stone wall, covered with crimson roses and carpeted with a well-kept lawn, on which the tables were set. Against the brilliant California sky flew the flags of the twenty-one American republics.

The tables were decorated with a profusion of roses, and the bright frocks of the pretty young volunteer waitresses gave an added note of color. The American Women's Voluntary Service, of which Mrs. Grant had long been a member, had lent her the silver from the Memorial Opera House Conference canteen, the women of Sonoma had sent their choicest linen, and the Sonoma Chamber of Commerce had furnished the cooks and the food, built the tables and the huge barbecue pit. The luncheon consisted of a fruit cup, barbecued chicken, vegetables, salads, ice cream, coffee, milk, red and white wines and beer.

After this sumptuous repast was over, the guests were shown Jack London's workroom with its original manuscripts and other treasures. Many visited his grave, while others wandered about the lake, rested in hammocks or on the grass. Absolute informality prevailed, a welcome change from the arduous duties of the Conference. At four-thirty they departed, full of good will for the U.S.A.

2

I began this chapter with a rather dark picture of San Francisco, but that applied only to the resentful majority of its citizens whose comfort and pleasures were woefully upset. As early as 1944 certain enterprising men foresaw the possibilities of a future for the city hitherto undreamed. And that majority, smug for too many years, is gradually being enlightened by the daily column of Robert C. Elliott in the San Francisco *News*.

Mr. Elliott, industrial editor of the *News* for thirteen years, has given close attention to every type of business, not only in San Francisco but from Canada to Mexico, from the Rockies to the Golden Gate, and is beyond question the leading authority on the subject. He has visited every type of industry and is the confidant of bankers, businessmen, civic leaders, and the nation's biggest industries. And as no one on this planet knows less of business than I do, I shall quote him freely.

"The San Francisco Bay Area, repeatedly and authoritatively, is being ranked as America's Number One region of expansion and opportunity. Why? High lights of industrialization taking place around the Bay include important new strides in the steel, electrical equipment, food processing, petroleum and chemical industries, construction, and bigger markets for retailers and foreign traders.

"The spotlight can be turned on these Bay Area developments: Three hundred national manufacturers are surveying the possible location of new plants in California and many are already under way in the Bay Area. Scores of long established highly diversified plants around San Francisco Bay are entering mass markets with consumer goods they never made before; they are investing millions in expansion and creation of more jobs. Thirty million dollars a year are being invested in postwar expansion of Northern California gas and light facilities. The Ford Motor Company at Richmond is back in production. General Electric is engineering a new plant in San Francisco Bay Area expected to employ 2,000 when in full production of heavy electrical equipment. Westinghouse predicts three times its prewar employment. A new $25,-

000,000 steel rolling mill for strip, sheets, and tin plate heads the Bay Area's growth in the steel industry, which finds strong companies making Diesel engines, food machinery, and a sizable list of products. The chemical and petroleum industries are breaking new industrial frontiers around the Bay. Agriculture and food production are stronger than ever. Retailing is prepared for unprecedented pent-up peacetime business. Merchants are on the threshold of completely lifting the face of downtown San Francisco with new store buildings. The Bay Area is going to exploit foreign trade and the tourist industry with redoubled vigor.

"Construction is preparing to go all out trying to fill California's program for vast building by private industry and business construction of 625,000 homes much needed in the next five years, and city, county and state public works of which $500,000,000 worth already are in sight. And not to be overlooked—globe-circling heavy construction and engineering will be done by the Bay Area miracle firms. The West is rolling in the billions of liquid assets with which to make good on continuing as the nation's Number One area of economic expansion. It has the management, know-how, and labor skills. . . .

"Here are some of the manufacturers who have already announced Bay Area expansion: Western Crown Cork and Seal Corporation plans a $3,000,000 layout on thirty-three acres on Bayshore Boulevard, San Francisco, to employ 1,500 on Pepsi-Cola projects and a $500,000 bottling works in Oakland.

"International Mineral and Chemical Company has twenty-five acres at San José for an amazing California product—monosodium giutamate concentrate, made from waste beet sugar pulp into a powder with which you can 'boil up' chicken or vegetable soup that tastes like the real thing.

"H. J. Heinz Company, with Pacific Coast main plant at Berkeley, is completing a $150,000 cannery at Tracy, forecast to provide 500 year-round jobs.

"Bercut-Richards Canning Company is building a $600,000 cold-storage plant at Sacramento to employ 3,000 at its peak.

"Reynolds Metals Company plans a San Francisco aluminum-foil, packaging and label plant to employ several hundred.

"Fifty major manufacturers purchased unimproved industrial property during 1945 in Oakland, Emeryville, Albany, southern Richmond, and the fast developing factory region around San Leandro and Hayward. Twelve million dollars are in prospect for buildings alone, not counting machinery. The factories will run the gamut from consumer goods, steel, a million-dollar gypsum wallboard plant, machinery, die casting and glass products."

There are dozens more, but these will suffice, with four exceptions. Also it may be noted here, the Peace (sic) has not diminished the energies of Henry Kaiser.

"The Western Merchandise Mart, which attracts 60,000 buyer-visits a year to San Francisco will invest $1,800,000, spreading out its great building the full Market Street block between 9th and 10th streets and running 225 feet down 9th. Frank K. Runyon, president of the Mart, says this nine-story center of Western whole-saling—already representing a $3,000,000 investment—will be made half again as large. Already home-goods manufacturers, distributors, and wholesale firms throughout the nation have reserved the office and showroom space when the building is completed on January 1, 1947.

"One thousand factories are represented in the Merchandise Mart. They supply a half billion dollars' worth of home goods annually to merchants in the Western and Pacific area. Two thousand families, about nine thousand individuals, draw a good livelihood in direct pay checks from this ever-expanding Bay Area

institution. Their incomes total six million dollars a year. . . .
Out-of-town buyers in normal times frequent the Mart regularly,
with peak attendance at the semiannual markets in February and
August. The prosperous retail store executives and buyers of home
goods from the eleven Western states are customers of the San
Francisco hotels, restaurants, night clubs, banks and transportation companies. So with the postwar lifting of travel restrictions,
businessmen will hang out the welcome sign for the visitors to the
nation's third largest industry. . . . Not only do the exhibitors and
factory representatives furnish the home in eleven Western states
with everything from paring knives to love seats and perambula-
tors, but cottages in Canada, huts in Alaska, haciendas in Mexico;
and those little grass shacks in Hawaii are perked up with electric
washers, radios and art goods, purchased in this Market Street
center. 'Six markets in one' are provided, embracing the entire
home furnishing field, furniture, mattresses and springs, floor cov-
erings, domestic textiles, draperies, etc."

Innumerable jobs for war-worn veterans.

The most interesting and creative industrial project is Apparel
City, a $5,000,000 investment for the entire garment manufacturing
industry, furniture and household goods. When finished it will
be a collection of light-flooded modernistic buildings, with courts,
a canteen, auditorium for exhibits, parkways and a swimming pool.
It will cover thirty-two acres in the Potrero district in southeast
San Francisco.

For several years the garment industry, with extensive plants,
and headquarters in the business area, has done a roaring business.
"In making California a world style center, the state already has
the outstanding place in sportswear, and department store buyers
come from all over the country, ever increasing as the industry
grows by leaps and bounds to the clip of $350,000,000 a year

trade. When Apparel City is finished it will recall Treasure Island at fair time—dramatizing styles!"

"Expansions totaling $3,500,000 are announced for the Shell Development Company research laboratory at Emeryville. Twelve hundred persons, including a brain pool of scientists of international standing, will pioneer at the Bay Area plant into untapped wonders of petroleum and industrial chemistry. They will continue the scientific hunts leading to new plastic products, better synthetic rubbers, new uses for water gases, improvements in petroleum manufacturing, and uses for all products. . . . Shell calls its Emeryville operation 'the West's largest research organization,' and its expansion will further stack it high with DuPont, Eastman, Dow, Bell Telephone and other corporations that are making the greatest investment in research to pierce new frontiers of industry."

And another new group of modernistic buildings.

Another vast project is also under active consideration. "The World Trade Center, a thirty-five-million-dollar sort of Rockefeller Center for all foreign trade, consulate, shipping and associate industries is a stirring creative project for lower downtown. Its feasibility has been established, and efforts are being made to get the state to buy and lease the site. The shift to the Pacific is on, and scores of industries have tangible prospects of selling to mass markets abroad. . . . The West Coast will be served by the biggest merchant marine in history, as well as airlines fanning out to all parts of its trade territory, the nation, and the world. . . . Once again 'Westward the course of empire takes its way'; the orbit of the world affairs is beginning to shift from a shattered decadent Europe; Americans are pressing westward for new frontiers of opportunity and freer living. . . . The potential one billion customers of the Far East are the reasons why once again Americans pursue the ancient myth of a great Orient trade, reaching out for the world's densest markets in Asia." (It should not be forgotten that Ralston was the first to establish trade with the Orient.)

This immense and imposing group of buildings will rise just west of the Embarcadero, facing the southern arm of the Bay.

Here are some of the "face liftings" in view for the shopping district: "The famed New York department store of R. H. Macy and Company has bought O'Connor, Moffatt and Company and will expand on three streets. Hale Brothers will invest six million dollars for a new building and store property at Market and Fourth Streets. I. Magnin Company, affiliated with Bullock's, will rebuild the Butler Building into a white marble and black granite department store. Woolworth Company will raze the Flood Building and erect a Market Street five and dime store. Crystal Palace Market is improving at a cost of $1,250,000." There will be a $2,000,000 Kohler & Chase building, eight stories and penthouse, and $1,000,000 legitimate theater, seating 2,000.

"The list could go on and on to a total of tens of millions. . . . Many investments will be made to cater to tourists, expected in unprecedented numbers, for even prewar travelers spent more than thirty-three million dollars a year in the Bay Area. . . . About one hundred firms have building plans. Sears, Roebuck is the latest— a four to five-million-dollar new store here. . . . Surveys for a new Bay Bridge are already underway. . . . A state official reports that California will build 125,000 homes a year for five years. Metropolitan San Francisco has 48,832 lots on which postwar houses are planned in nine counties." That looks as if we would absorb all the towns between South San Francisco and San José, sixty miles down the peninsula.

And two new hotel skyscrapers are to go up on Nob Hill. But

another project on that fashionable eminence is enough to make our guardian angel fly down to the top of Twin Peaks, shake her fists at the vandals and utter loud lamentations. The Fairmont Hotel, as beautiful, as symmetrical a structure as any in ancient Greece, is to build a tower before its entrance some thirty stories high. Well! San Francisco is the city of destiny. She is marching on toward grandeur and ever-increasing importance and must expect to have a few blots on her scutcheon.

Five years from now if all those grandiose plans are triumphant realities, if San Francisco is the rival of New York in size and importance, if it becomes a debatable question which is the greatest city in the United States, will she have lost forever her old and unique personality; be just another money-mad city, talking in billions, where a mere million is as negligible a fortune as the contemptible hundred thousand the Big Man of the small town has slowly and painfully accumulated?

I for one do not believe it. San Francisco has a soul, an ego, preserved through many mutations, that are indestructible, and her love of beauty is innate, stemming from those far-off days when she was called Yerba Buena and its proud inhabitants *knew* they had laid the foundations of a great and beautiful city.

Moreover, she is a city of hills; there is no monotony in her landscape. Her Golden Gate Park is the most beautiful in the world. Those subdivisions of which I have written elsewhere are like something out of Grimms' fairy tales. Nor will she ever consent to the overrunning of Chinatown with its gorgeous window displays of jades, crystal, china, figurines and lovely brocades to decorate the walls of those who have taste as well as wealth; nor of Little Italy with its splendid church dedicated to Saint Peter and Saint Paul, facing a small park with trees that look like weeping willows but are not, its innumerable gay restaurants and shops, its lively and almost segregated dark-skinned people, as busy as ants and as methodical. Artists will never be driven from Russian Hill and Telegraph Hill, where they ever draw inspiration from the superb view of the Bay with its islands (all but Alcatraz, and one of these days those prisoners will be removed to a more appropriate locale in the desert, and its barren slopes forgotten under villas surrounded by trees and gardens, as lovely to look at as Belvedere), Mount Tamalpais that looms above the Golden Gate, the simulation of a sleeping woman on its crest, the curving sweep of Marin hills beyond, green in late winter and early spring, golden in summer; lofty Mount Diablo (named by the Indians, who believed that a devil dwelt within) in the east towering above the cities of the Bay Area.

The old swanlike ferryboats have gone, but yachts skim those waters sometimes blue, sometimes green, and the Italian fishing boats swarm through the Golden Gate with the morning's catch— and anyone may run down from his height and buy a crab boiling in a pot on the sidewalks of Fisherman's Wharf.

And at night! If one is weary of crowds and bustle and the constant talk of money, money, money, let him go to the "Top of the Mark" cocktail lounge, order a drink whether he wants it or not (he would be invited to leave if he did not), and from that lofty eminence on the summit of Nob Hill revel in one of the loveliest pictures this world has to offer.

The lounge is almost dark. The walls are of glass. On every side one may see San Francisco and the cities across the Bay in a perfect beauty that only night can give them. Not a hint of commerce, business big and little, crime, hatreds, despair, greed, magnificence or poverty. From Twin Peaks to Mount Diablo, from North Beach to the southernmost rim of the city, broken only by the Bay, one looks down upon a multiplicity of glittering lights—no, not quite unbroken, for that sea of glorified fireflies is diversified by a skyscraper here and there that looks like a huge Christmas tree illuminated from base to crown, and the Bay Bridge, the Golden Gate Bridge are two necklaces of lights as round and as brilliant as the lamps of Aladdin. And there are scattered lights on Tamalpais, among the redwoods at its base, on the islands of the Bay.

And even the city lights do not blend into a monotonous whole. Each is pricked out with a life of its own, yet with not a reminder of the buildings unsightly or handsome from which they emanate.

Time passes. The lights grow dim, twinkle out. Where all was beauty naught is left but a memory. The clock strikes twelve. The guests depart. But if one is unsatisfied, if one craves more beauty, even of another sort, and if one is so fortunate as to have a friend on the floor just below the lounge, and he is away, and the key is in one's purse, one leaves the lift at the eighteenth floor and takes possession.

The windows face north and east, and one takes a chair hopefully. The south and the west have nothing more to offer, but the tule lands of the north, the vast Pacific—who knows? They too have a beauty all their own to give—but will they? Aha! Yes! Here it comes!

Tall white spirals at first, just beyond the Gate, spirals that waver and mingle in fantastic shapes. Heralds of a fog bank born far out in the Pacific. You picture the Farallones, that barren group of islands thirty-three miles away, its lighthouse and coast guards already submerged, its foghorns blaring their warning to ships of war homeward bound.

The spirals blend, thicken. The row of lights on the Bridge disappear. The great fog bank rolls in. It is a low fog, but it covers the Bay, the islands, the eastern shore, the city. One looks now down upon a soft white ocean, lighted only by a full moon and a canopy of glittering stars. One asks in startled wonder, Is there really a city—life—beneath that lovely imponderable white; is anyone awake, breathing, on those islands, in those towns across the Bay? Do they lie forever buried, obliterated as completely as if atomic bombs had descended from on high? Is one alone in a dead world, with not even the sound of a fire siren to break that awful silence, nothing but the low moaning of the foghorns in the Bay? One hardly knows whether to be elated or terrified.

And there is no movement in that white mass. It is as immobile as the dead, as white as sea foam, but far more nebulous. Will it never lift again, never return whence it came? Has that ominous white intruder imposed the sleep of eternity?

Another hour passes. Another. A high mist has floated in and obliterated the moon and the stars. One feels suspended in space, alone, terribly alone. If one's brain could function one would feel a dread certainty that the end of the world had come.

Ah, but one's mind *has* been torpid! One's eyes are drawn as by a magnet to the east. There is a faint glow above Mount Diablo. It rises, deepens. Slowly, but as inevitable as birth and death, a large round body as red as the blood in healthy veins mounts higher and higher. That white sea below turns a rosy pink, then as red as the orb itself. It moves, sways, gives an angry shake, then rushes out through the Golden Gate. The Bay sparkles. Lights appear on the islands, in the cities. The sun is blazing along his routine journey and all is well.

THE END

INDEX

# INDEX

Abernethy, Saskatchewan, 133
Adam, 112
Adams, Ella, 37, 182
Adams, John, 62
Adams, Maude, 42
Adams family, 37, 181
*Adventure*, the, 112, 144
"Aeolia Heights," 138
Aeschylus, 98
AFL, 193
Africa, 134
Agar, Herbert, 36
Aiken, Ednah, 46, 149
Alameda, Calif., 288
Alameda Belt Line, 257
Alaska, 97, 103, 139, 140, 153, 154, 189, 204, 269, 303
Alaska Commercial Company, 153
Albany, Calif., 302
Albert, Prince of Belgium, 42
Alcatraz, 307
Aldan, 23
Alemany, Bishop, 66
Alexander I, 15, 18
Alexander the Great, 240
*Alien Corn*, Howard, 95
All Alaska Sweepstakes, 138
Allan, A. A., 138
Alpha Phi Fraternity, 81, 278
Alps, 157
Alsace-Lorraine, 50
*Altar of the Legion, The*, Brodeur, 144
Altrocchi, Julia Cooley, 108-110
Altrocchi, Rudolph, 109
Alvord, William, 213
Alvord family, 181
American Academy of Arts and Letters, 135
American Academy of Pediatrics, 142
American Association of University Women, 268, 269, 278
American Bar Association, 258
American Embassy, 86
American Government, 51

American Historical Association, 111
American Institute of Electrical Engineers, 267
American Law Institute, 155
American Library Association, 278
American Mail Line, 263, 264
American Medical Association, 142
*American Mercury*, 128
American Publishing Company, 82
American Red Cross, 171, 178, 247
American River Electric Company, 172
*American-Scandinavian Review*, 144
American Women's Voluntary Service, 299
Ames, Pelham, 31
Ames Book Shop, 83
Amundsen, Roald, 140
*Anatomy of Melancholy, The*, Burton, 133
Anderson, Sherwood, 79
*Anger of the Bells*, Rath, 143
Anglo & London Paris National Bank, 223
Anglo-California Bank, 161, 162, 165, 223
Anglo-California National Bank, 172, 222, 223
Anglo-California National Bank of San Francisco, The, 224
Anglo-California Trust Company, 172, 223
Anglo-Californian Bank, Ltd., 222
Anglo, Paris and National Bank, 172
Antiquarian Booksellers, London, 70
*Anybody's Gold*, Jackson, 131
*Anza's California Expeditions*, Bolton, 111
*Ape, the Idiot and Other People, The*, Morrow, 101
Apparel City, 303-304
Arctic Ocean, 138
Argentina, 144
*Argonaut*, 44
Argonaut Club, 180, 192

313